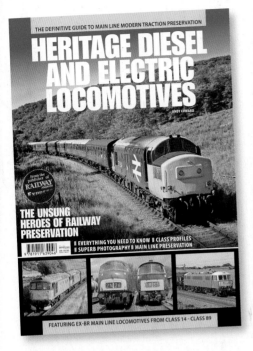

Basking in the West Yorkshire sunshine, Class 31 D5830 and 37075 stand outside the locomotive shed at Haworth on the Keighley & Worth Valley Railway on June 8, 2014. The golden-ochre Class 31 was visiting the line from the Great Central Railway, while 37075 is a KWVR-based locomotive. ANDREW SEWELL

COVER PICTURE: Large Logo liveried 37264 passes through Spring Wood on the North Yorkshire Moors Railway, while working a service between Pickering and Grosmont on August 7, 2014. TOM MCATEE

COVER INSET LOWER LEFT: Both painted in matching Civil Engineers grey, 33109 *Captain Bill Smith RNR* and 33103 *Swordfish* approach Horncliffe on the East Lancashire Railway during the summer diesel event on July 7, 2018. TERRY EYRES

COVER INSET LOWER CENTRE: Class 42 'Warship' D821 *Greyhound* and D1062 *Western Courier* await their next duties at Bridgnorth on the Severn Valley Railway on May 20, 2011. Both locomotives have now been in preservation for far longer than they were in service with British Rail and D821 was the first main line diesel locomotive to be bought privately for preservation by the late Colin Massingham. MARTIN HART

COVER INSET LOWER RIGHT: One of the hardest-working preserved main line locomotives is Class 86 locomotive, E3137/86259 *Les Ross/Peter Pan*, which is owned by former West Midlands Radio DJ Les Ross. The immaculate electric blue locomotive approaches Winwick Junction at speed, while working a Steam Dreams return 'Cathedrals Express' service from Preston to London Euston on May 22, 2018. TERRY EYRES

CONTENTS

EDITOR:
Andy Coward

PRODUCTION EDITOR:
Pauline Hawkins

DESIGN:
Craig Lamb
Kriele Ltd
design_lamb@btinternet.com

COVER DESIGN:
Michael Baumber

PUBLISHER:
Steve O'Hara

PUBLISHING DIRECTOR:
Dan Savage

COMMERCIAL DIRECTOR:
Nigel Hole

ADVERTISING MANAGER:
Sue Keily

ADVERTISING EXECUTIVE:
Craig Amess

MARKETING MANAGER:
Charlotte Park

ISBN:
978-1-911639-04-6

PUBLISHED BY:
Mortons Media Group Ltd,
Media Centre, Morton Way,
Horncastle,
Lincolnshire,
LN9 6JR.
Tel: 01507 529529

PRINTED BY:
William Gibbons and Sons,
Wolverhampton

COPYRIGHT:
©2019 Mortons Media Group Ltd.
All rights reserved.

MORTONS
MEDIA GROUP LTD

No part of this publication may be produced or transmitted in any form or by any means, electronic or mechanical, including photocopying, recording, or any information storage retrieval system without prior permission in writing from the publisher.

All pictures marked * are published under a Creative Commons licence. Full details may be obtained at http://creativecommons.org/licences

INTRODUCTION

The origins of diesel and electric locomotive preservation date back to the early 1970s. At the time, railway preservation was growing in popularity with a number of heritage lines being established across the country.

Meanwhile, at Barry in South Wales, a steady stream of derelict former British Railways steam locomotives were being rescued from Dai Woodham's scrapyard for restoration to working order. These locomotives would eventually find use hauling trains on heritage railways and many of the

locomotives rescued from Barry went on to become the mainstay of the many heritage lines now established across the country.

However, thoughts of preserving what was still considered to be 'modern traction' were often far from the minds of the railway preservation pioneers, who saw steam as being the main attraction for visitors travelling on heritage railways, even though the interest in diesel and electric traction was growing now that steam had been eradicated from the BR network.

All that changed in 1973 when Colin Massingham and some friends purchased Class 42 'Warship' diesel-hydraulic locomotive D821 *Greyhound* from BR. The purchase of the 'Warship' came after an earlier attempt to preserve North British Type 2 locomotive, D6319, had failed due to that locomotive being scrapped in error. However, the preservation of D821 started a movement that has gone on to become a major part of the heritage railway movement.

Since the preservation of D821, hundreds of diesel locomotives and a number of electric locomotives have gone on to enjoy a more leisurely retirement hauling services on heritage lines and, in more recent times, a few have been re-registered for operating on the national rail network following the relaxation of British Rail's ban on the operation of privately owned locomotives on BR's lines during the mid-1990s.

After a few other diesel locomotives had entered preservation during the late 1970s, primarily diesel-hydraulic

HERITAGE DIESEL AND ELECTRIC LOCOMOTIVES

This publication aims to list all the diesel and electric locomotives that have been secured for preservation in the heritage railway sector. Each class of former BR main line diesel and electric locomotives that is represented by the preservation sector is included. Each section features a brief potted history of the locomotive design, a description of the preserved locomotives, as well as information about locomotives returned to main line use and any other locomotives from a preserved class which are still in commercial use in the UK.

locomotives, BR began offering a small number of diesel locomotives for sale to preservation through its tendering process. This saw a steady flow of locomotives secured for preservation.

By the 1990s, the modern traction preservation movement was growing rapidly and as various locomotive designs were being withdrawn, more and more locomotives were being purchased and we now have some types, such as Classes 20, 25, 31, 37, 47 and 50, which are very well represented in preservation.

Such is the nature of the sector that a number of previously preserved locomotives can no longer be classed as preserved. These locomotives may have been scrapped, sold back to a main line operating company for further use, or sold on for industrial use. This has been the case particularly with Class 20s, 37s, 56s and 73s, where a number of previously preserved locomotives have been sold on for further use away from the heritage movement.

It is often said that buying the locomotive is the easy part and the most successful groups and owners have understood the need to ensure that they have a large stock of spares and funds available to ensure the long-term survival of their locomotives. There are now many well-established and respected diesel and electric owning groups, who work wonders by keeping these now historic locomotives operating, often with the support of only small numbers of active volunteers. Anyone interested in the preservation of modern traction should consider joining one of the established groups and lending a hand if possible to ensure that future generations can also enjoy them in years to come.

In recent years, the flow of diesel and electric locomotives entering preservation has slowed considerably from the peak of the late 1990s and early 2000s, but there are still occasional announcements to say that another heritage locomotive has found salvation.

The most recent former main line locomotive to enter preservation is the first production High Speed Train Class 43 locomotive, 43002 *Sir Kenneth Grange*, which has been preserved as part of the National Collection and is due to move to the Railway Museum at York during the summer of 2019.

The first production HST power car is sure to be followed in the future by other locomotives, but it's a constantly changing scene and those early pioneers couldn't have envisaged just how popular modern traction preservation would become. From acorns to oak trees.

Andy Coward
Editor

The most recent addition to the ranks of preserved diesel locomotives is the first production HST power car 43002 *Sir Kenneth Grange*. On July 17, 2019, the locomotive is posed on a low loader outside the STEAM Museum in Swindon, as it makes its way towards Ely for storage prior to moving to the Railway Museum in York. JACK BOSKETT

GALLERY

All across the country, countless teams of volunteers have worked hard to restore hundreds of heritage diesel locomotives for us to enjoy on our various heritage lines. While many railways still see steam traction as their main focus, in recent years there has been a growing appreciation of more modern traction and this has seen many heritage railways establishing large fleets of diesel locomotives that have become an attraction in themselves. Heritage Diesel and Electric Locomotives aims to showcase the work and achievements of everyone who has been connected in the restoration, maintenance and operation of these historic locomotives for the enjoyment of enthusiasts and future generations.

The wonderfully restored station at Llangollen on the Llangollen Railway is a great location for photographic charters, with the station lending itself to many suitable cameos. Representing the BR blue era with a posed DMU 'drag' 25313 stands in the station during an East Midlands Railway Photographic Society evening photographic charter on January 19, 2008. 25313 is now based on the Wensleydale Railway where it is undergoing an overhaul. TERRY EYRES

LEFT: On July 20, 2008, Class 47 D1524 and 33109 *Captain Bill Smith RNR* stand at Embsay station on the Embsay & Bolton Abbey Railway during a diesel weekend on the line. 33109 was visiting from the nearby East Lancashire Railway, while D1524 is a resident on Embsay, but the Class 47 has now been stored out of use for several years and its future is currently unknown. NIGEL VALENTINE

RIGHT: The ever-reliable 31271 *Stratford 1840 – 2001* heads a short train through Burrs on the East Lancashire Railway on July 6, 2014, during a working visit to the line. This locomotive is owned by A1A Locomotives and nominally based at the Midland Railway Butterley, but is currently on a two-year loan to the Llangollen Railway. TOM MCATEE

In a scene that could almost be from the 1960s, Class 40 D335, Class 47 D1501 and Class 14 D9531 stand outside the East Lancashire Railway Carriage & Wagon Department shed at Buckley Wells on June 15, 2012. The ELR boasts one of the largest fleets of heritage diesel locomotives on a UK heritage railway and diesel locomotives are regularly rostered on the line. NIGEL VALENTINE

RIGHT: The Epping Ongar Railway is one of the more recent heritage railways to be established and its location close to London gives it a huge potential for growth. The EOR is another pro-diesel heritage railway and one of the resident locomotives on the line is 31438. During an East Midlands Railway Photographic Society evening photographic charter on September 27, 2014, the BR blue Class 31 stands in Ongar station with a short train of wagons. TERRY EYRES

It's hard to believe that the relatively recent InterCity livery is now being applied to preserved diesel locomotives and is now regarded as a heritage livery in its own right. On May 20, 2017, D05 Preservation Ltd's 47828 stands alongside the Class 50 Alliance's 50031 *Hood* at Kidderminster, with both carrying InterCity livery. The Class 50 never carried InterCity during its working life, but it suits the design well. TOM MCATEE

Oozing atmosphere as its BR blue livery shines in the sun on May 16, 2019, Class 25 D7535 stands in the yard at Bewdley on the Severn Valley Railway awaiting its next duties. The locomotive was attending the railway's annual diesel event, where it was one of the visitors. For many years D7535 has been based on the Paignton & Dartmouth Steam Railway, but it has recently changed owners and is now owned by the South Devon Railway-based South Devon Diesel Traction. CHRIS OWEN

LEFT: Class 46 'Peak' locomotive D182 in experimental blue livery departs from Bury Bolton Street station, passing Class 42 D832 *Onslaught*, with a service for Rawtenstall on July 10, 2016, during the East Lancashire Railway's summer diesel event. KEVIN DELANEY

BELOW: At the 2017 Old Oak Common open weekend, diesel locomotives which all played a part in operating services on the Western Region of British Railways are lined up with 50035 *Ark Royal*, D1015 *Western Champion* and D821 *Greyhound* posing for the cameras on September 2, 2017. KEVIN DELANEY

Two of the most recent additions to the ranks of preserved diesel locomotives are 31105 and 31233, which are now based on the Mangapps Railway Museum in Essex. The pair are pictured at Mangapps on November 6, 2018, shortly after their delivery from Network Rail, which had employed the locomotives during their final years of main line service. JOHN JOLLY

Photographed during an organised evening photographic charter in connection with the 50th anniversary celebrations of the introduction into service of the Class 50s, 50044 *Exeter* and 50007 *Hercules*, disguised as scrapped 50006 *Neptune*, outside Kidderminster Depot on the Severn Valley Railway on October 3, 2018. TERRY EYRES

Class 20 D8137 and 47367 *Freightliner 1995* stand outside the diesel shed at Toddington on the Gloucestershire Warwickshire Railway on October 8, 2017. KEVIN DELANEY

BELOW: A pair of Sulzer Type 2s, 26038 *Tom Clift* and D7628 *Sybilla*, stand at Goathland on the North Yorkshire Moors Railway on July 14, 2018. ANDREW SEWELL

The passage of 20214 and Class 26 D5301 doesn't bother the sheep in the neighbouring fields as the locomotives head a service from Lakeside to Haverthwaite during a mixed-traffic event on the Lakeside & Haverthwaite Railway on April 10, 2005. The Class 20 is still based on the railway, while D5301 has since moved to the Caledonian Railway. NIGEL VALENTINE

CLASS 14

Withdrawn by British Railways after an indecently short working life, it is surprising that so many Class 14s still survive in preservation, but this is thanks to many of them finding a second working career in industrial use.

The Class 14 was designed to be a versatile Type One diesel-hydraulic locomotive that could be used for light freight work, trip workings and yard shunting across the Western Region of British Railways. They were designed to be functional locomotives, with a single cab towards the centre and narrow bonnets on either side. They were fitted with a Paxman 6YJX engine located in the larger section and access to the engine and other components was through doors which ran along the bodyside.

The order for 56 locomotives was placed by the British Transport Commission in 1963. Numbered D9500-D9555, they were built at Swindon Works and deliveries of the locomotives began in July 1964, with the final example completed in October 1965.

The final locomotive, D9555, was also the last locomotive to be built at Swindon Works, bringing to an end a long and proud tradition of locomotive building in the town.

The locomotives were painted in dark Brunswick green and the cabs were finished in a light green, complete with white numbers and a BR coach emblem on the cabsides. The front of the locomotives featured yellow and black 'wasp stripes' in a style that had become popular with BR's shunting locomotives. The fronts also featured headcode boxes and a yellow buffer beam.

The class was concentrated on the South Wales area, although it had originally been planned that they would operate on most routes of the WR. However, by the time they were being delivered the impact of Dr Richard Beeching's The Reshaping of British Railways report was starting to hit the railway network and many of the routes and freight yards

which the locomotives had been built to operate on were being closed.

A number of the virtually new locomotives were stored by BR and some were transferred through to the North Eastern Region in 1966, allocated to Hull for use on trip workings, although this move was also short-lived.

In December 1967, D9522 and D9531 became the first to be withdrawn, with D9531 having spent less than three years in service, and it went on to survive in preservation.

Over the next 18 months the remainder of the fleet was withdrawn, with the final examples succumbing in April 1969, less than five years after D9500 had been delivered to the Western Region.

The locomotives did not survive in service long enough to gain TOPS numbering.

With the exception of eight Class 14s which were scrapped, the remainder found employment in private ownership, with 46 bought by the British Steel Corporation (BSC) and the National Coal Board (NCB). The remaining two were purchased by Earles Cement at Hope in Derbyshire.

Five of the locomotives were subsequently exported, including the two Earles locomotives in 1976 and three that had previously worked for BSC five years later.

It is believed that all five exported locomotives have since been scrapped.

Their second working lives came to an end during the 1980s when they were taken out of service by BSC and the NCB. The decline of the coal mining industry during the mid-1980s spelt the end for the NCB examples, while the BSC locomotives were also stored at a similar time. Many were still in relatively good condition and as a useful Type One design it was inevitable that a number would go on to find a more leisurely retirement working as preserved locomotives on heritage railways across the country.

The fleet pioneer, D9500, is now owned by Andrew Briddon and is located at his base at Darley Dale on Peak Rail. While the locomotive has been cosmetically restored to BR two-tone green, it has yet to haul a train in preservation and requires a complete overhaul before it can return to use. MARTIN HART

The ultimate Class 14 train, with nine locomotives hauling a special evening train on the East Lancashire Railway during the railway's 14s@50 event, which celebrated the 50th anniversary of the introduction of the type into BR service. A tenth '14', D9523, also took part in the event, but had suffered an engine fault earlier in the event. The powerful combo, headed by ELR-based D9531, heads through Burrs on July 26, 2014. TOM MCATEE

CLASS 14

BUILT:	BR Swindon 1964-1965
ENGINE:	Paxman 6YJXL
NO. BUILT:	56
NO. PRESERVED:	19
OTHER SURVIVORS:	0

THE PRESERVED CLASS 14s

Nineteen Class 14s have been preserved, with 16 having been returned to active service. The locomotives are versatile and well suited to hauling both passenger and works trains. Most of the preserved examples are restored to original BR two-tone green livery, but a number of other colour schemes have been adopted on some locomotives which, although most of these liveries are attractive, are unauthentic to the design. D9513 on the Embsay & Bolton Abbey Railway is the only current member of the fleet to be painted

into NCB blue livery, retaining its NCB 38 identity.

While no Class 14 is registered for operating under its own power on Network Rail metals and the prospect of such a move is very unlikely, perhaps the nearest one to have come to this is D9504, which is now based on the Kent & East Sussex Railway. D9504 spent a period of time on hire to the company responsible for the construction of High Speed One, where it was used to haul works trains along the then-new railway line along with a fleet of Class 20s.

Of all the operational Class 14s, it is somewhat surprising that just one example is painted in National Coal Board blue livery. NCB No. 38 (D9513) is usually based on the Embsay & Bolton Abbey Railway, but is pictured at Bury Bolton Street station during the East Lancashire Railway's 14s@50 event on July 26, 2014. MARTIN HART

Following its return to service in 2014, D9537 was outshopped in a desert sand livery, inspired by the colours carried by D1000 *Western Enterprise* when it was new. The locomotive has since been repainted into black livery with small yellow warning panels and is now based on the Ecclesbourne Valley Railway. NIGEL VALENTINE

A matching pair of Class 14s are captured at the Dean Forest Railway on September 5, 2015, as D9555 and D9521 run around their train. D9555 was the final locomotive built for BR at Swindon Works. MARTIN HART

D9523 and D9539 stand at Leyburn on the Wensleydale Railway on August 3, 2013. Maroon-liveried D9523 is a resident member of the Wensleydale fleet, while D9539 was visiting from the Ribble Steam Railway. ANDREW SEWELL

Andrew Briddon owns two Class 14s, D9500 and 14901 (D9524), which are both located at his Darley Dale base on Peak Rail. Fleet pioneer D9500 has yet to haul a train in preservation, but has been cosmetically restored and its owner intends to restore it to working order at some stage in the future, although it requires a complete mechanical and electrical overhaul before it can work again.

Mr Briddon's other locomotive, 14901, was originally preserved on the Bo'ness and Kinneil Railway and unlike the other preserved Class 14s, this particular locomotive is fitted with a Rolls-Royce DV8TCE power unit. It has spent a number of years hired out to various heritage lines, but returned to Darley Dale in spring 2019 for an overhaul.

The East Lancashire Railway (ELR) is the current home of two Class 14s, with D9502 and D9531 based on the line.

D9531 was bought from NCB Ashington and returned to service by the Bury Hydraulic Group in 1988. It saw active use on the ELR for a number of years before being withdrawn in 1997 for a complete rebuild, which took 15 years to complete. It has since settled down to be a popular member of the fleet.

D9502 was purchased by a group of ELR volunteers in 2014 from its previous home with the Heritage Shunters Trust on Peak Rail. This is another locomotive which has never run during its time in preservation, but prior to the start of its overhaul in 2014, it was famous for still carrying the (rather worn) original BR two-tone green livery that had been applied by BR when it first entered service 50 years earlier.

The same ELR-based group has also restored D9537 following purchase from its previous owner. D9537 returned to service in 2014 after an 18-month

restoration and it was painted into fictitious desert sand livery (the same colour scheme was carried by diesel-hydraulic Class 52 pioneer D1000 *Western Enterprise*). It has since been repainted into a black livery and after visiting a number of heritage railways it was announced in mid-2019 that D9537 would be based at the Ecclesbourne Valley Railway for the foreseeable future.

The third Class 14 which has never yet hauled a train in preservation is D9518, which is now based on the West Somerset Railway (WSR) after spending many years in store at the Rutland Railway Centre and the Nene Valley Railway (NVR). A long-term restoration is now being carried out on the locomotive at Williton under the auspices of the Diesel & Electric Preservation Group (DEPG). The DEPG also operates D9526 on the WSR.

The NVR is another line which has

14901 is displayed in the yard during the Old Oak Common open day on September 2, 2017 carrying its blue and yellow livery. Unlike the other survivors of the Class 14 fleet, this locomotive has been re-engined and is now fitted with a Rolls-Royce DV8TCE engine. This locomotive was originally D9524. KEVIN DELANEY

The Class 14s have had a long relationship with the Nene Valley Railway, which has been home to a number of the surviving locomotives over the past three decades. One of the locomotives to remain based at the NVR is BR blue 9529, which is seen awaiting departure from Wansford with a train of continental coaches on April 11, 2015. MARTIN HART

The attractive golden ochre livery carried by D9551 is shown to good effect in this photo of the locomotive at Bridgnorth on May 18, 2017. The livery was inspired by the colour scheme once carried by Class 52 'Western' diesel-hydraulic, D1015 *Western Champion*. MARTIN HART

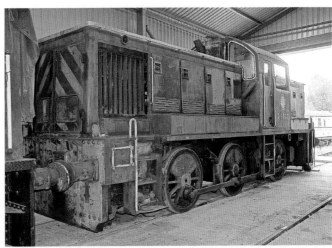

Although clearly suffering from rust and corrosion, the original BR green paintwork, applied by BR at Swindon Works in 1964, is still clearly identifiable on D9502 while it was in store at Rowsley South on Peak Rail. This locomotive has since been moved to the East Lancashire Railway, where it is now undergoing a complete overhaul to return it to service. MARTIN HART

had a close affinity with the Class 14s. The line is currently home to D9520 and BR blue 9529, while it was previously also the home of D9516, D9518 and D9523. Both D9520 and 9529 see regular use on NVR services.

D9516 and D9523 were formerly owned by the late Gerald Boden and spent many years on the NVR. Following his death in 2011 both locomotives were subsequently sold, with D9516 moving to Didcot Railway Centre, while maroon-liveried D9523 moved initially to the Derwent Valley Railway, before relocating to the Wensleydale Railway where it remains.

Dean Forest Railway-based D9521 is another well-travelled Class 14,

which has spent time on several preserved lines around the country. The locomotive is now painted in BR blue livery, but retains its D9521 identity.

D9525 is probably the most powerful locomotive in the care of the Heritage Shunters Trust at the trust's Rowsley South base on Peak Rail. The locomotive has spent a number of years out of service undergoing an overhaul which is due for completion during 2019. It is named *Ian's* in memory of former owner, Ian Goddard, who passed away before the work was completed.

D9539 is based at the Ribble Steam Railway and is often used to haul trains around their line at Preston Docks.

Another Class 14 to return to service

in recent times after several years out of use has been D9551 on the Severn Valley Railway. The locomotive is another to be painted in an unauthentic livery, carrying the same golden ochre colours that were once carried by D1015 *Western Champion*.

D9553 is currently stored out of use on the Gloucestershire & Warwickshire Railway (GWR) at Toddington and although it has seen some use on the GWR, it has not worked a train for a number of years.

The last-built Class 14, D9555, was also the final locomotive to be built for British Railways at Swindon Works and is now preserved on the Dean Forest Railway where it is regularly in use.

LOCO	NAME	PREVIOUS IDENTITIES	OWNER	LOCATION
D9500		D9500	ABL	PKD
D9502	*Kerys*	D9502	Private	ELR
D9504		D9504	Private	KESR
NCB 38		D9513	Private	EBAR
D9516		D9516	Private	DRC
D9518		D9518	DEPG	WSR
D9520/45		D9520	Private	NVR
9521		D9521	D9521LG	DFR
D9523		D9523	Private	WR
14901		D9524	ABL	PKD
D9525	*Ian's*	D9525	HST	PKR
D9526		D9526	DEPG	WSR
9529		D9529	Private	NVR
D9531	*Ernest*	D9531	BHG	ELR
D9537	*Eric*	D9537	Private	EVR
D9539		D9539	Private	RSR
D9551	*Angus*	D9551	SVRC14CL	SVR
D9553/54		D9553	Private	Private
D9555		D9555	Private	DFR

OWNERS KEY: ABL – Andrew Briddon Locomotives, BHG – Bury Hydraulic Group, D9521LG – D9521 Locomotive Group, DEPG – Diesel & Electric Preservation Group, HST – Heritage Shunters Trust, SVRC14CL – Severn Valley Railway Class 14 Company Ltd

LOCATION KEY: DFR – Dean Forest Railway, DRC – Didcot Railway Centre, EBAR – Embsay & Bolton Abbey Railway, ELR – East Lancashire Railway, EVR – Ecclesbourne Valley Railway, KESR – Kent & East Sussex Railway, NVR – Nene Valley Railway, PKR – Peak Rail Rowsley South, PKD – Peak Rail Darley Dale, RSR – Ribble Steam Railway, SVR – Severn Valley Railway, WR – Wensleydale Railway, WSR – West Somerset Railway

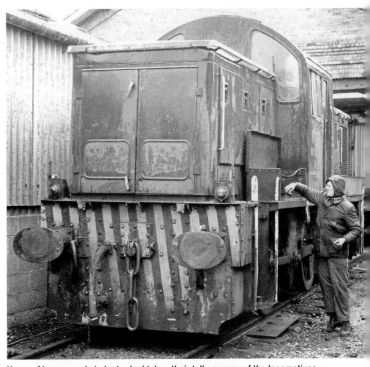

Years of heavy use in industry had taken their toll on many of the locomotives when they entered preservation. A rather grimy D9500 is inspected shortly after it had been delivered to the Llangollen Railway. STEVE KEMP

CLASS 15

Under the British Railways Modernisation Plan, a total of 10 Type-One pilot scheme locomotives were ordered from British-Thompson-Houston (BTH) for light freight and empty coaching stock duties. The Yorkshire Engine Company in Sheffield was subcontracted to build the locomotives, with the first one handed over in October 1957.

A follow-on order for a further 34 locomotives was placed with BTH, although this time the locomotive building was contracted to Clayton, with these locomotives completed between 1959 and 1961.

The locomotives were fitted with a Paxman 16YHXL power unit and when delivered they were painted in dark green, with lighter green applied on the cab fronts around the windows. They featured a single cab towards the centre of the locomotive.

They had been designed to haul trains around the Eastern Region around Anglia, but a downturn in traffic and the impact of the Beeching Report meant that the locomotives were largely rendered redundant, allowing the rundown of the fleet to get under way, as BR couldn't find an alternative use for them.

Under the TOPS numbering scheme, the locomotives were classified as Class 15, although none of them survived in traffic long enough to receive TOPS five-figure numbers.

The life of the Class 15 fleet was relatively short-lived and

The sole-surviving Class 15, D8233, goes up in the world as it is lifted off its bogies for the first time since the 1970s at the East Lancashire Railway Locomotive Works on March 24, 2018. RORY LUSHMAN

the first locomotive, D8217, was withdrawn in March 1968. Over the next three years the entire fleet had been stood down from service, with the final examples withdrawn in March 1971.

Following withdrawal, four Class 15s were taken on by BR's Departmental Division for carriage heating duties and after the removal of non-essential equipment they saw use on these duties for a further 10 years before they were taken out of use. While last-built D8243 managed to survive until 1991, its disposal left D8233 as the only surviving Class 15 locomotive.

THE PRESERVED CLASS 15

D8233 was originally preserved in 1984 on the South Yorkshire Railway, moving to the East Lancashire Railway in 1986. In 1988 it was on the move again to Mangapps Railway Museum, but in 1993 it was acquired by Pete Waterman and moved to Crewe, where he planned to restore it to operational condition.

Although the locomotive looked presentable, it was in poor mechanical condition and would require an extensive overhaul before it could haul a train again. For various reasons, little restoration work was carried out on the locomotive and in 2005 agreement was reached between the Waterman Heritage

Trust and the Class 15 Preservation Society for the C15PS to take on the locomotive and restore it.

In 2006 the locomotive moved to the East Lancashire Railway, returning to the railway that had briefly been its home in the mid-1980s. Since arriving on the railway the locomotive has

CLASS 15

BUILT: British-Thompson-Houston, 1957-1961	
ENGINE: Paxman 16YHXL	
NO. BUILT: 44	
NO. PRESERVED: 1	
OTHER SURVIVORS: 0	

undergone much restoration work and a replacement engine was purchased for D8233, which was started intermittently during an ELR diesel weekend, to give visitors a foretaste of what's to come when the restoration is completed.

Work is currently focused on overhauling the locomotive's bogies and while the restoration is progressing well, there is no date set for completion of the restoration. As the only surviving Class 15, there is much anticipation about the return to service of D8233 and it is bound to be a popular attraction when its restoration is completed and it takes to the ELR rails once more.

On July 6, 2013, D8233 stands part-restored on Platform 1 at Bury Bolton Street station on the East Lancashire Railway. The locomotive was displaying its newly installed Paxman 16YHXL power unit, which was periodically started throughout the weekend for visitors to witness. MARTIN HART

On July 9, 2019, D8233 is stored in the East Lancashire Railway Locomotive Works where its restoration is rapidly advancing. The Class 15 Preservation Society volunteers are working on the restoration of D8233 and also the sole-surviving Class 28, D5705. ANDY COWARD

LOCO	PREVIOUS IDENTITIES	OWNER	LOCATION
D8233	D8233, ADB968001	C15PS	ELR

CLASS 17

The sole-surviving Class 17, D8568, departs from Highley station on the Severn Valley Railway during a visit to the line on May 20, 2017. The owning Diesel Traction Group has most of its locomotives based on the SVR, although D8568 is usually based on the Chinnor & Princes Risborough Railway. KEVIN DELANEY

British Railways ordered 117 Type One locomotives from the Clayton Equipment Company, with the locomotive construction carried out by Clayton at its Derbyshire plant for locomotives D8500-D8587. Beyer, Peacock in Gorton, Manchester was subcontracted to build D8588-D8616.

The locomotives featured a central cab, with the two outer ends of the locomotives used for housing a Paxman 6ZHXL engine. Delivery of the locomotives began in September 1962 and the final locomotive was completed in April 1965.

When they were built the locomotives were painted in two-tone green, with the cab fronts and window surrounds painted in a light green and the engine and the rest of the bodywork painted in dark green.

Under TOPS the locomotives were allocated Class 17, but none of them survived in traffic long enough to gain TOPS five-figure identification. The locomotives were allocated mainly to the Scottish and Eastern Regions of British Railways, although some were also found on the London Midland Region. They were used on freight traffic.

BR suffered many problems with the reliability of the engines installed inside the Class 17s and even after much work to try and address the problems, they still suffered from reliability issues and were not deemed to have been a very successful design, leading to their premature withdrawal from service.

The Class 17s were another design which was decimated during the late 1960s and early 1970s and following the

withdrawal of the first locomotive, D8537, in July 1968, it would only be just over three years later before the final examples were stood down in December 1971.

The early withdrawal of the relatively large fleet is one of the main reasons why only one example has survived into preservation, as modern traction preservation was unheard of at the time they were taken out of service. The survival of D8568 is thanks to it being taken into industrial service, with it moving to a cement factory in Harpenden in Hertfordshire during 1972. Five years later in June 1977 the locomotive was sold again to Ribble Cement in Clitheroe, Lancashire, where it saw use for around five years before being put up for sale.

THE PRESERVED CLASS 17

D8568 was purchased for preservation in 1983 by the Diesel Traction Group and it moved to the North Yorkshire Moors Railway, where it made its debut in April 1983, still resplendent in its Ribble Cement livery.

In 1985 the locomotive was taken out of service for an overhaul, with the locomotive's engine seeing much attention from DTG volunteers.

It was repainted into original BR green livery in 1989 and returned to service in April 1989. D8568 then ran on

the NYMR for a further two years before it was relocated nearer to where most of the active DTG members were based.

In 1992 D8568 was moved to the Chinnor & Princes Risborough Railway,

CLASS 17	
BUILT:	Clayton Equipment Company, 1962-1965
ENGINE:	Two Paxman 6ZHXL Power Units
NO. BUILT:	117
NO. PRESERVED:	1
OTHER SURVIVORS:	0

which remains its home railway to the present day, although it has also visited the Severn Valley Railway for working visits, where the other DTG locomotives, D821 *Greyhound*, D1015 *Western Champion* and D7029 are based.

There is no intention for the Class 17 to ever return to main line use and it is destined to remain working on heritage railways. D8568 remains a popular locomotive whenever it is in use and, as with other sole-surviving types, it is an important part of our railway heritage.

Hauling a matching rake of chocolate and cream-liveried Mark 1 coaches, D8568 makes its way along the Chinnor & Princes Risborough Railway on April 6, 2019. KEVIN DELANEY

LEFT: Looking slightly weatherworn, but sporting full yellow ends, Class 17 D8568 hauls a train along the Chinnor & Princes Risborough Railway on April 6, 2019. The locomotive has been based at Chinnor since 1992. KEVIN DELANEY

LOCO	BR IDENTITIES	OWNER	LOCATION
D8568	D8568	DTG	CPRR

OWNER KEY: DTG – Diesel Traction Group

LOCATION KEY: CPRR – Chinnor & Princes Risborough Railway

CLASS 20

The locomotive which went on to become the Class 20 was another design to come as a result of the 1955 British Railways Modernisation Plan. Under the pilot scheme, 10 Type One locomotives were ordered from English Electric and these would be powered using the English Electric 8SVT engine. The new locomotives would be numbered D8000-D8009 and were built at EE's Vulcan Foundry Works.

The design of the locomotive featured a single cab at one end of the locomotive, although the cab featured two driving positions for whichever direction it was moving in. While visibility from the cab end was very good, the view looking forward along the long bonnet of the locomotive could be quite restrictive and eventually BR tended to operate the locomotives as coupled-pairs to help address the visibility issues.

Follow-up orders saw the overall number of locomotives increased to 228, with the locomotives numbered D8000-D8199 and D8300-D8327. When delivered, most of the locomotives were painted into BR dark green with a light grey roof, while a number of the later-built examples were delivered in the then-new rail blue livery, while still carrying pre-TOPS numbers.

The locomotives could operate at a maximum of 75mph and quickly gained a reputation for being reliable workhorses and it was arguably the most successful Type One design to come out of the Modernisation Plan, particularly when they were operated in pairs.

Under TOPS the English Electric Type One locomotives became Class 20. There were a number of various sub-classes and also various cosmetic differences between the locomotives, such as the addition of headcode boxes to later-built examples.

As essentially a freight locomotive, they were used extensively around the BR network, but it was not unknown for pairs of Class 20s to work passenger services and the locomotives gained a popular following among railway enthusiasts.

The first withdrawal from the Class 20 fleet came in January 1976 when 20074 was condemned and a handful of other locomotives followed shortly afterwards. However, the fleet still remained in healthy numbers until the early 1990s when the number of withdrawals accelerated.

However, while most of the fleet had been withdrawn by the mid-1990s, the emergence of the privatised railway saw a number of the locomotives given a second lease of life under operators such as Direct Rail Services, which overhauled a fleet of 15 Class 20s for use on nuclear flask trains operating in Cumbria, with these becoming Class 20/3 and renumbered 20301-20315. Spot hire operators hiring locomotives for use on Network Rail metals and industry have also benefited from the use of Class 20s.

A small fleet of six Class 20s was purchased by Hunslet Barclay and these were given a classification of Class 20/9 and were used for weed-killing duties. All but one of these locomotives remain but they are now owned by Harry Needle Railroad Company.

A number of Class 20s were used during the early 1990s by the company responsible for the construction of the Channel Tunnel. At the end of the hire period some of these locomotives entered preservation, while others were scrapped.

Four locomotives were also exported to France during the 1990s for French operator CFD and the locomotives were modified for their new role prior to export, as well as being repainted into a distinctive orange, white and blue livery. All four were subsequently repatriated to the UK following their disposal by CFD and two of these are now in preservation, while the other two have been scrapped.

With the train highlighted by the setting sun, the Scottish Railway Preservation Society Diesel Group's 20020 arrives at Bo'ness with a train from Manuel on July 22, 2016. TOM MCATEE

20031 is preserved on the Keighley & Worth Valley Railway and is painted in triple grey livery, with small coal sector decals. During the railway's diesel gala, the locomotive stands at Oxenhope awaiting departure on May 4, 2019, coupled to Virgin Trains-liveried coaches that were visiting the line along with the 125 Group's Class 41 HST locomotive. KEVIN DELANEY

CLASS 20

BUILT: Vulcan Foundry, Newton-le-Willows & Robert Stephenson and Hawthorn, 1957-1968

ENGINE: English Electric 8SVT power unit

NO. BUILT: 228

NO. PRESERVED: 17

OTHER SURVIVORS: 32

THE PRESERVED CLASS 20s

There are currently 17 Class 20s officially preserved, with almost twice as many in commercial ownership, so it is possible that the number of preserved locomotives could increase in the future.

The pioneer Class 20, D8000, is part of the National Collection and can be found on display at the Railway Museum in York. Although it has not worked a train for several years, it has previously visited several heritage railway diesel events, but in recent times it has been undergoing repairs. However, a new policy by the museum means that D8000

and several other diesel locomotives in their collection are now to be displayed as static exhibits and, therefore, it is unlikely that D8000 will operate under its own power for the foreseeable future.

The Midland Railway Butterley is probably the heritage railway most closely associated with the preserved Class 20s, with the Class 20 Locomotive Society based on the railway, along with the Midland Class 20 Association's 20048 and the Somerset & Dorset Locomotive Company's D8059 and D8188 all based on the railway.

While maintained in immaculate condition, 20214 on the Lakeside & Haverthwaite Railway is rarely used in passenger traffic on the line, so is a popular choice with enthusiasts when it does work on the three-mile heritage line. On April 10, 2005, 20214 and Class 26, D5301, run around their train at Haverthwaite during a diesel operating day on the line. The Class 26 has since left the railway and moved to the Caledonian Railway. NIGEL VALENTINE

The Type 1 Locomotive Company's fleet of locomotives are all based on the Great Central Railway, with D8098 being a regular performer on the line, having been based on the GCR since the early 1990s. On September 8, 2012, D8098 shines in the sun at Leicester North, freshly repainted in a new coat of original BR green, while running round its train before returning its train to Loughborough. ANDREW SEWELL

The Somerset & Dorset Locomotive Company owns two Class 20s, D8059 and D8188, both of which are immaculately painted into BR green livery and regularly work together. The pair have recently moved to a new home on the Midland Railway Butterley, but have spent several years working on the Severn Valley Railway. On June 17, 2017, during a previous visit to the MRB, D8059 leads D8188 into Butterley station, contrasting somewhat with the InterCity-liveried coaching stock. ANDREW SEWELL

Class 20, D8137, represents the English Electric Type One on the Gloucestershire & Warwickshire Railway and is captured in full song as it makes its way along the line on October 8, 2017. KEVIN DELANEY

The Class 20 Locomotive Society owns 8001, 20205 and 20227, but all of the society's locomotives are generally away from their home base at the moment, with 8001 currently on extended loan to the Epping Ongar Railway, 20205 on main line hire to 20189 Ltd and 20227 currently outbased at the North Norfolk Railway.

Representing the Class 20 in Scotland is 20020 on the Bo'ness & Kinneil Railway. The locomotive is owned by the Scottish Railway Preservation Society Diesel Group and has been another well-travelled locomotive, heading out on several occasions to visit other heritage railway diesel events along with other Bo'ness-based locomotives.

20031 is preserved on the Keighley & Worth Valley Railway, where it has been based since purchase in 1991. It ran for many years in BR green livery, but in 2007 it was repainted into Trainload Freight triple grey branding with small coal sector decals. It has retained this livery ever since and the Class 37 also based on the railway, 37075, has been painted into matching colours, although the '37' is unbranded and doesn't carry any sector markings.

Another consistent performer since the early 1990s is D8098 on the Great Central Railway at Loughborough. Owned by the Type One Locomotive Company, the Class 20 was the first locomotive bought by the group, which now also owns fellow GCR residents Class 31, D5830, and Class 47, 1705 *Sparrowhawk*. D8154 is based on the neighbouring Great Central Railway (Nottingham) where it is restored in BR blue livery, but carrying its pre-TOPS numbers. Another Class 20, 20007, was previously based on the GCRN, but this locomotive has since been sold to 20189 Ltd and returned to main line use away from the heritage railway scene.

20228 on the Barry Tourist Railway was one of the four Class 20s to be returned to the UK following their use with CFD in France. Of the four locomotives, two have since been dispatched for scrap, while CFD 2002 is being restored on the Battlefield Railway, but in the case of CFD 2004, its owners have decided to return it to its original UK specification and it is now repainted into BR blue livery and most of the modifications carried out for its use in France have been reversed.

There are three Class 20s which have yet to be restored to working order on their respective railways. D8057 moved to the Churnet Valley Railway in 2017 after being sold by its previous owner. The locomotive is painted in BR green livery, but its restoration to working order has not been completed and work on its rebuilding has continued since it moved to Cheddleton.

Former CFD locomotive, 2002 (the former 20063) is being restored to

On a misty February 24, 2019, D8154 stands at Ruddington Fields on the Great Central Railway (Nottingham). On this day D8154 was working alongside the sole-surviving Class 41 HST locomotive, which is also based on the GCRN. KEVIN DELANEY

Another Class 20 that is based on the Midland Railway Butterley is 20048, which is owned by the Midland Class 20 Association. In 2019 the locomotive is nearing the end of an extensive overhaul by its owning group, but on September 14, 2014, 20048 runs around its train at Hammersmith on its home railway. ANDREW SEWELL

20031 in its triple grey livery provides a contrast between its train of BR maroon coaches as it approaches Mytholmes Tunnel between Haworth and Oakworth on June 8, 2014. KEVIN DELANEY

20205 is owned by the Class 20 Locomotive Society, but is usually on hire to 20189 Ltd for main line use, alongside that company's fleet of main line registered Class 20s, 20007, 20142 and 20189. On June 15, 2019, 20205 and 20189 stand at Butterley on the Midland Railway Butterley awaiting their next duties during a diesel event on the line. When not in main line use, 20205 is based at the MRB. KEVIN DELANEY

working order on the Battlefield Line, while D8169 is now located at the Wensleydale Railway awaiting a return to service, having originally been preserved on the Stainmore Railway at Kirkby Stephen.

One Class 20 that has recently left preservation has been former CFD locomotive, 2001, which was formerly 20035. The locomotive has been based at Toddington on the Gloucestershire & Warwickshire Railway for a number of years, where it has been slowly stripped of spare parts to benefit GWR-based D8137, which is fully operational on the railway. The heavily stripped Class 20 left the GWR for scrapping in July 2019.

OTHER CLASS 20s

By far the largest owner of the surviving Class 20s is Harry Needle Railroad Company, although several of his locomotives are stored at various sites and are not operational. Those locomotives that are serviceable are used on both the UK main line network and also in industrial use at various sites.

Several HNRC Class 20s were previously preserved, but have been sold on and some of these are still located at heritage lines, where operational examples are occasionally used on passenger services, such as 20166 on the Wensleydale Railway.

Direct Rail Services had a fleet of 15 Class 20s overhauled during the 1990s for main line use and these were classified as Class 20/3. In recent years the locomotives have mainly been ousted in favour of other more modern locomotives, but some of their remaining eight locomotives are usually revived in the autumn for use on railhead treatment trains. The DRS Class 20s are usually stored at Barrow Hill and it is likely that most or all of these locomotives will be disposed of by the company in due course.

20189 Ltd operates three Class 20s of its own, 20007, 20142 and 20189, and these are supplemented by use of the Class 20 Locomotive Society's 20205 and 20227 when required.

LOCO	NAME	PREVIOUS IDENTITIES	OWNER	LOCATION
D8000		D8000, 20050	NRM	RMY
8001		D8001, 20001	C20LS	EOR
20020		D8020, 20020	SRPSDG	BKR
20031		D8031, 20031	Private	KWVR
20048		D8048, 20048	MC20A	MRB
D8057		D8057, 20057	Private	CVR
D8059		D8059, 20059, 20302	S&DLC	MRB
2002		D8063, 20063, CFD2002	Private	BFL
D8098		D8098, 20098	T1LC	GCR
D8137		D8137, 20137	Private	GWR
D8154		D8154, 20154	Private	GCRN
D8169		D8169, 20169	Private	WR
D8188		D8188, 20188	S&DLC	MRB
20205		D8305, 20205	C20LS	On Hire
20214		D8314, 20214	LHR	LHR
20227	*Sherlock Holmes*	D8327, 20227	C20LS	NNR
20228		D8128, 20228, CFD2004	Private	BTR

OWNER KEY: C20LS – Class 20 Locomotive Society, LHR – Lakeside & Haverthwaite Railway, MC20A – Midland Class 20 Association, NRM – National Railway Museum, S&DLC – Somerset & Dorset Locomotive Company, SRPSDG – Scottish Railway Preservation Society Diesel Group, T1LC – Type One Locomotive Company

LOCATION KEY: BFL – Battlefield Railway, BKR – Bo'ness & Kinneil Railway, BTR – Barry Tourist Railway, CVR – Churnet Valley Railway, EOR – Epping Ongar Railway, GCR – Great Central Railway, GCRN – Great Central Railway (Nottingham), GWR – Gloucestershire & Warwickshire Railway, KWVR – Keighley & Worth Valley Railway, LHR – Lakeside & Haverthwaite Railway, MRB – Midland Railway Butterley, NNR – North Norfolk Railway, RMY – Railway Museum York, WR – Wensleydale Railway

NON-PRESERVED SURVIVING CLASS 20s

DIRECT RAIL SERVICES: 20301, 20302, 20303, 20304, 20305, 20308, 20309, 20312

HARRY NEEDLE RAILROAD COMPANY: 20016, 20056, 20066, 20069, 20081, 20087, 20088, 20096, 20107, 20110, 20121, 20132, 20166, 20168, 20311, 20314, 20901, 20903, 20904, 20905, 20906

20189 LTD: 20007, 20142, 20189

• Please note that some of these locomotives are operational, while others are stored or being used as spares donor locomotives.

MAIN LINE PRESERVED CLASS 20s

There are currently two main line registered preserved Class 20s in the UK, with the Class 20 Locomotive Society's 20205 and 20227 both seeing use on the main line, although London Transport-liveried 20227 has not seen any main line action for a couple of years and is currently based on the North Norfolk Railway. 20205 is on hire to 20189 Ltd and is used on main line contracts alongside 20189 Ltd's own three main line registered Class 20s, these being 20007, 20142 and 20189.

While 20205 and 20227 are currently the only preserved Class 20s to be main line registered, a number of previously preserved Class 20s have been purchased by commercial operators and returned to use on the main line network.

MAIN LINE REGISTERED PRESERVED CLASS 20s

Loco	Owner	National Network Certification Status
20205	Class 20 Locomotive Society	Main Line Certified
20227	Class 20 Locomotive Society	Main Line Certified

CLASS 23

The Class 23 locomotives were designed by English Electric and 10 locomotives, to be numbered D5900-D5909, were built at Vulcan Foundry in Newton-le-Willows and were delivered to British Railways in 1959. The locomotives were fitted with a Napier Deltic T9-29 power unit, which was a smaller version of the engines that were later fitted into what would become the Class 55 'Deltics'.

The 10 locomotives had been intended to work in the London area and they were all allocated to Hornsey Depot, before moving to Finsbury Park. However the locomotives were not deemed to be a success and numerous problems with reliability and performance were experienced with the fleet, with the power units prone to cylinder liner problems, which required the engines to be changed.

Such was the extent of the problems that BR took the decision to store many of the locomotives while it sought a solution to the problems that had been experienced.

To address the problems that had been experienced with reliability, the decision was taken to refurbish the 10 locomotives and they underwent a programme of modifications and overhaul. The project was deemed to have been successful and the locomotives settled down to become much more reliable than they had previously been.

Following their modifications the locomotives were all released back into service painted in a mainly dark green livery, with small yellow warning panels on the cab fronts and a lighter green band running around the base of the locomotives at solebar level. The livery choice was similar to that applied to the 'Deltics' that operated on the East Coast Main Line and which were also powered by Napier Deltic power units. Under TOPS, the locomotives would become the Class 23, but they would not survive in traffic long enough to receive five-figure BR identities. Only one locomotive, D5905, received the new rail blue livery, with all the others being withdrawn before they gained the new corporate identity.

With such a small fleet it was inevitable that BR would eventually seek to get rid of the Class 23, as they were considered to be non-standard and other locomotives could be used to replace them, despite BR having spent a lot of money trying to address their problems. The first locomotive to be taken out of service was D5906 in September 1968, with the final example withdrawn, D5909, in March 1971. Following its withdrawal from normal service, D5901 was used by the Railway Technical Centre at Derby for a number of years but after its use by the RTC came to an end, it became the final member of the class to be cut up for scrap in February 1977.

THE PRESERVED CLASS 23

With the final example of the Class 23 fleet being scrapped in February 1977, the Class 23 story was thought to have been brought to a close. However, one of the Napier Deltic T9-29 power unit and generator sets was claimed by the National Railway Museum and stored for many years out of sight and seemingly forgotten at York.

However, the engine was rediscovered in 2001 and was subsequently sold by the NRM to a group which was closely linked to the Deltic Preservation Society at Barrow Hill. The engine and generator set were moved to Barrow Hill and remained in store for six years before work began on overhauling the engine to return it to a serviceable condition.

Over an 18-month period, the volunteer group successfully returned the engine to working order and it ran for the first time in preservation in October 2008. However, despite the fact the engine was now operable, there was no way of properly demonstrating its

capabilities as it had no locomotive to operate in.

In 2009, a scrap Class 37, 37372, was purchased to house the engine and it moved to Barrow Hill, where after suitable modifications the engine was installed. However, it was then decided that the Baby Deltic Project (BDP) would carry out the considerable alterations to the Class 37 to turn it into the same profile as one of the long-scrapped Class 23s. The BDP aims to create its locomotive as authentically as possible and this has seen the Class 37 nose ends shortened to match the profile of the original Class 23s and the body has also been shortened. The locomotive

will eventually be fitted with a set of Class 20 bogies.

The project to convert 37372 into a 'Baby Deltic' is now rapidly advancing and the donor locomotive has undergone considerable alterations to give it the same appearance as a 'Baby Deltic'. However, there is still a lot of work to be done before the locomotive is finished and it is sure to be a popular addition to the ranks of preserved diesel locomotives working in the UK. Once completed, the locomotive will carry the number D5910, assuming the next fleet number from the original series, had more than 10 locomotives been built for BR.

While there are several proposed diesel locomotive rebuilds being promoted to recreate some of the lost types, the project to recreate a 'Baby Deltic' is certainly one that now seems destined to become a reality, as the team behind it has worked hard to bring back a locomotive design that many had considered was consigned to the history books.

CLASS 23

BUILT:	Vulcan Foundry, Newton-le-Willows, 1959
ENGINE:	Napier Deltic T9-29 Power Unit
NO. BUILT:	10
NO. PRESERVED:	0
NEWLY BUILT:	1

LEFT: With bodywork alterations to the donor Class 37 largely complete, the new D5910 now has the distinctive appearance of the Class 23 Baby Deltic. The project to recreate this lost locomotive has been progressing with the donor locomotive for the past decade, but is now making tremendous progress. The locomotive is pictured inside Barrow Hill Roundhouse on August 26, 2018.
PAUL HADFIELD

LOCO	BR IDENTITIES	OWNER	LOCATION
D5910	Bodyshell from 37372	BDP	BHR

OWNER KEY: BDG - Baby Deltic Project

LOCATION KEY: BHR – Barrow Hill Roundhouse

On May 9, 2013, a suitably weathered D5061 stands at Grosmont on the North Yorkshire Moors Railway. The locomotive, the final Class 24 to be owned by BR while it was part of the Departmental Sector, has been based on the NYMR since the mid-1990s and has seen extensive use on the railway since it entered service there, although it is currently out of use awaiting an overhaul. ANDREW SEWELL

CLASS 24

The Class 24 was another locomotive devised as a result of the British Railways Modernisation Plan. Twenty pilot scheme Type Two locomotives were ordered, powered by a Sulzer 6LDA28 engine, capable of a maximum speed of 75mph. Construction of the fleet was split between Derby, Crewe and Darlington Works and they were built in stages between 1958 and 1961. The locomotives were delivered in dark green, with a grey roof and a thin white band at solebar height. Yellow warning panels were added to the cab fronts during the early 1960s. A few were painted in two-tone green in a style similar to that which had been applied to brand new Class 47s when they were built.

The first 50 locomotives, numbered D5000-D5049, were classified as Class 24/0 and these included the 20 prototype examples and the first 30 production locomotives. There were various differences in the build of various batches, which were done as the locomotive design and weight were evaluated. The initial 20 had weighed in at 79 tonnes, which was heavy for a Type Two design and efforts were made in subsequent builds to try and reduce the weight.

The final 101 locomotives were modified to reduce their weight to 73 tonnes thanks to smaller fuel tanks and the removal of some components that had been fitted to the '24/0s'. This batch became classified as Class 24/1.

The locomotives were mainly used in the London Midland and Eastern Regions of BR upon their introduction, but their use became more widespread and they could be found at almost any part of the BR network on a variety of passenger and freight workings.

Under the TOPS numbering scheme the numbering of the locomotives was kept as simple as possible with all D5XXX numbers becoming 24XXX, i.e. D5096 became 24096. The exception to this rule was pioneer D5000 which became 24005 under the TOPS scheme, due to the original D5005 having been withdrawn in December 1969. There were gaps in the 24XXX series where various locomotives had been withdrawn prior to

Resplendent in BR blue livery, Class 24 5081, normally based on the Gloucestershire Warwickshire Railway, hauls a demonstration freight train through Pilsworth, between Bury and Heywood, on the East Lancashire Railway during an East Midlands Railway Photographic Society charter on September 11, 2012. TOM MCATEE

LOCO	NAME	PREVIOUS IDENTITIES	OWNER	LOCATION
D5032	*Helen Turner*	D5032, 24032	NYMR	NYMR
D5054	*Phil Southern*	D5054, 24054, ADB968008	BT2G	ELR
D5061		D5061, 24061,		
		RDB968007, 97201	24061PG	NYMR
5081		D5081, 24081	Private	GWR

OWNERS KEY: 24061PG – 24061 Preservation Group, BT2G – Bury Type Two Group, NYMR – North Yorkshire Moors Railway

LOCATION KEY: ELR – East Lancashire Railway, GWR – Gloucestershire Warwickshire Railway, NYMR – North Yorkshire Moors Railway

the introduction of the TOPS numbering scheme.

As a relatively large class of locomotives, the withdrawal and rundown of the fleet was gradual, although there were several early casualties due to fires and collisions. The first example was withdrawn following fire damage in 1967 and over the next 13 years the fleet was progressively run down until the withdrawal of 24081.

After the type had been withdrawn from BR service, three former '24s' were retained for use as departmental locomotives, being used as carriage heaters in the case of 24054 and 24142, while 24061 was transferred to Derby where it was used by BR's Research Department.

An undated view of D5032 *Helen Turner* while it was in service on the North Yorkshire Moors Railway. The locomotive is now midway through a major overhaul after spending more than 40 years based on the NYMR, having initially come to the railway on hire from scrap merchant TJ Thomson & Son to haul services in 1976 during a steam ban on the line due to a heatwave. The NYMR purchased the locomotive outright in late 2016. STEVE KEMP

D5054 *Phil Southern* and 33109 *Captain Bill Smith RNR* arrive at Bury Bolton Street station on February 16, 2019, with a service to Heywood during the East Lancashire Railway's diesel weekend. The locomotive had just returned to service, having been out of service for a number of years undergoing a major overhaul. NIGEL VALENTINE

THE PRESERVED CLASS 24s

Out of the original order of 151 locomotives, four Class 24s have survived into preservation, with two currently operational and the other two undergoing overhaul.

The long hot summer of 1976 saw the North Yorkshire Moors Railway (NYMR) agree to a one-year-long hire of an operational Class 24 locomotive, 24032 (D5032), from scrap dealers TJ Thomson & Son, who had bought it from BR for scrapping following withdrawal. The locomotive was required as the railway had been forced to ban steam services due to the greater risk of lineside fires and it was used extensively on the railway while the steam ban was in place. The following year the loan of the locomotive was extended and it was repainted into two-tone green livery.

The locomotive was named *Helen Turner* in 1982 after the daughter of TJ Thomson's managing director and was repainted into a more authentic BR green livery. It was taken out of service for a major overhaul in 2001.

In the autumn of 2016, the NYMR bought D5032 from TJ Thomson & Son and the locomotive will now remain on the railway and it should return to use when its protracted overhaul is completed.

5081 (24081) was saved for preservation in 1980, having been the final Class 24 in regular service on BR. It was originally based at the now-defunct Steamport Museum at Southport before moving for a period to

the Llangollen Railway, but is now based at the Gloucestershire Warwickshire Railway, where it has recently returned to use following an overhaul. Unlike the other three '24s' in preservation, 5081 has spent all of its time in preservation painted in BR blue livery.

Following withdrawal from regular BR service in 1976, 24054 (D5054) was used as a carriage heating unit, being renumbered ADB968008, before being acquired for preservation by the Bury Type Two Group and moved to the embryonic East Lancashire Railway in Bury, Lancashire. The locomotive was used on a number of works trains as the line between Bury and Ramsbottom was being restored.

In July 2007 the locomotive was named *Phil Southern*, in memory of one of the founding members of the Bury Type Two Group and a former ELR director, who had passed away a couple of years previously. Prior to its naming D5054 had received a new coat of BR green livery, with small yellow warning panels on the cab front. A major overhaul of the locomotive and a further repaint into BR green livery was completed in early 2019 and D5054 has returned to regular use, along with the extensive collection of preserved diesel locomotives in use on the ELR.

The final Class 24 to enter preservation was D5061, which is now also located on the NYMR. It was preserved in 1989 following many years in use as part of BR's Research Department, with it being renumbered 97205 and named *Experiment* during its time based at Derby, outlasting other Class 24s on the BR network by several years.

Initially moved to the Midland Railway Butterley (then known as the Midland Railway Centre), it was originally painted into an unauthentic

D5054 *Phil Southern* stands at Ramsbottom station on the East Lancashire Railway with an evening service for Bury Bolton Street on January 12, 2008. STEVE KEMP

With its steam heating boiler in use, D5061 departs from Goathland on the North Yorkshire Moors Railway on March 22, 2014, with its workworn paintwork and uniform rake of maroon coaches helping to create a scene that would easily fit into the 1960s railway network. ANDREW SEWELL

maroon livery, retaining its *Experiment* name. In the mid-1990s it was moved to the NYMR, where it was returned to original BR green livery and it has remained at the NYMR ever since. D5061 is currently out of service awaiting an overhaul.

None of the preserved Class 24s are approved for main line running on Network Rail, although it is possible that the NYMR could at some stage in the future register D5032 or D5061 for use on their services through to Whitby, as they have done with Class 25, D7628.

CLASS 24

BUILT: BR Crewe, Derby and Darlington Works, 1958-1961

ENGINE: Sulzer 6LDA28

NO. BUILT: 151

NO. PRESERVED: 4 (1 Class 24/0, 3 Class 24/1)

OTHER SURVIVORS: 0

CLASS 25

The Sulzer Type Two locomotives that went on to become the Class 25 were a development of the earlier pilot scheme locomotives (Class 24) and went on to number 327 locomotives when the order was completed. They were fitted with a Sulzer 6LDA28B power unit and could operate at speeds of up to 90mph, which was higher than the maximum speed of 75mph attained by the earlier design.

They were built between 1961 and 1967, with the numbering sequence of D5151-D5299 and D7500-D7677.

Construction took place at the BR Works at Crewe, Derby and Darlington, while some were also built by Beyer, Peacock in Gorton, Manchester. With such a large order of locomotives, there were a number of cosmetic differences between certain batches of locomotives. Beyer, Peacock was subsequently unable to complete its batch of locomotives, with D7659 being the final locomotive to be assembled at Gorton Works and the remainder of the company's order had to be completed by Derby Works.

Some locomotives were delivered in dark green livery, with a thin white band around the base of the locomotive's bodywork, while the later-built examples (from what would become the Class 25/2 variant) were delivered in two-tone green livery, in a style similar to that carried on the Sulzer Type Four fleet (Class 47).

The go-anywhere nature of the locomotives led to them becoming known as 'Rats' and they were popular on freight services in particular, although it was not unknown for them to also work on passenger turns.

As with other classes with a large number of locomotives, there were a number of sub-classes created. Under TOPS they became the Class 25 and all but two locomotives went on to receive five-figure TOPS 25XXX identities.

The first 25 locomotives were classified Class 25/0 and these featured a newer engine to that fitted inside the Class 24s and they also featured modified generator and traction motors. These were numbered D5151-D5175. The Class 25/1 featured different traction motors to the Class 25/0s and some of the locomotives were fitted with steam heat boilers while other examples weren't fitted with boilers, as they would mainly work on freight services.

The Class 25/2 were built with a different body style to the earlier builds and these featured the larger central cab window for the first time. There were also several differences between batches of locomotives in the Class 25/2 sub-class. The Class 25/3 featured electronic control systems and later builds of this batch also featured dual-braking.

The final sub-class was created by BR in the mid-1980s, when 12 Class 25s were classified as Class 25/9 for use on a contract that subsequently did not materialise. While it had been envisaged that this work would extend the working lives of these locomotives, in reality they succumbed earlier than had originally been expected.

The first Class 25s to be withdrawn were both a result of collisions, with D5278 condemned in May 1971 and D7605 in March 1972, but the first 25 locomotives from the Class 25/0 sub-class were withdrawn first between 1975 and 1980. Withdrawals of the remaining locomotives took place throughout the 1980s, with the final service examples being stood down in March 1987.

One locomotive, 25912, was retained for special duties and charters and for its final months in traffic it was repainted into two-tone green and named *Tamworth Castle*. It was finally withdrawn in September 1991, bringing an end to the Class 25 story on British Rail.

Following purchase from BR, 25313 was owned by the Llangollen Diesel Group on the Llangollen Railway. However, the locomotive was subsequently sold by the LDG and moved to the Wensleydale Railway, where its restoration has been under way for a number of years and it has now been purchased by Harry Needle. During an evening photographic charter, 25313 stands at Llangollen station with a demonstration goods train on January 19, 2008. TERRY EYRES

The North Yorkshire Moors Railway is home to D7628 *Sybilla*, which is also certified for main line running on NYMR services over Network Rail metals to Whitby. The locomotive is probably the hardest-working example of the preserved Class 25s. It is pictured heading a train into Levisham station on May 26, 2013. ANDREW SEWELL

CLASS 25

BUILT: BR Crewe Works, Darlington Works, Derby Works and Beyer, Peacock Gorton Works, 1961-1967

ENGINE: Sulzer 6LDA28B

NO. BUILT: 327

NO. PRESERVED: 20

OTHER SURVIVORS: 0

THE PRESERVED CLASS 25s

The Class 25s were the first type of British Rail locomotives to be preserved in a relatively large number, with some 20 examples secured for preservation. The survivors have certainly enjoyed differing fortunes over the past three decades, but with several examples coming back into use after being out of service for a number of years, the future is looking bright for most of the preserved Class 25s.

Currently operational are D5185 on the Great Central Railway, 25059 on the Keighley & Worth Valley Railway, D7612 and D7535 on the South Devon Railway, D7628 on the North Yorkshire Moors Railway and D7629 on the East Lancashire Railway, with D7659 on Peak Rail due to join the operational examples in the near future. The remainder are either stored out of use or undergoing overhauls.

Derby Industrial Museum purchased 25321 from BR and the locomotive has been loaned to the Midland Railway Butterley ever since. It is currently out of service awaiting repairs and a repaint into BR green, but is expected to return to service soon.

Another Class 25 undergoing repairs is 25235 on the Bo'ness & Kinneil Railway. Having been used on the railway and other heritage lines, it is now having an overhaul carried out at the excellent diesel depot facility at Bo'ness.

Railway engineer Harry Needle is no stranger to Class 25s and he purchased 25901 from BR and moved it to the East Lancashire Railway (ELR) in 1991, where it was subsequently restored to original two-tone green livery as

25059 has spent its life in preservation based on the Keighley & Worth Valley Railway and regularly sees use on the line. Now resplendent in BR blue and sporting LED headlights, 25059 stands at Keighley station awaiting departure with a train to Oxenhope on June 24, 2017. ANDREW SEWELL

Now owned by South Devon Diesel Traction following many years based on the Paignton & Dartmouth Steam Railway, D7535 has spent the 2019 season visiting a number of other railway diesel events. On May 11, 2019, D7535 nears Harmans Cross while visiting the Swanage Railway. PAUL HADFIELD

Immaculately restored to BR green is D5185 on the Great Central Railway. Owned by the Northampton Type Two Group, the locomotive is pictured at Swanage station during a working visit to the annual Swanage Railway diesel event on May 10, 2015. MARTIN HART

25322 *Tamworth Castle* was the final Class 25 to be withdrawn by BR and then moved to preservation on the Churnet Valley Railway. The locomotive has now been out of service for nearly 20 years awaiting an overhaul. On April 19, 2018, 25322 is posed on a rake of engineering wagons at Cheddleton station during a photographic charter. TERRY EYRES

D7612. The locomotive was later sold to South Devon Diesel Traction (SDDT) and moved to the South Devon Railway (SDR), where it remains in operational condition.

In recent years Mr Needle has purchased former Llangollen Railway resident 25313 from its previous owner on the Wensleydale Railway, 25057 from the North Norfolk Railway and D7633 from the Dean Forest Railway. While most of Mr Needle's locomotives are regarded as commercial assets of his company, he has stated his intention to keep his Class 25s as preserved locomotives and he intends to restore them to service, although his railway engineering business activities will take priority ahead of their return.

Also owned by SDDT are D7535 and D7541. D7535 spent many years based on the Paignton & Dartmouth Steam Railway and saw occasional passenger use on the predominantly-steam railway.

However, in 2018 agreement was reached between SDDT and the PDSR for D7535 to be exchanged for SDDT's 37275, with the Class 37 moving to the PDSR and the Class 25 joining its two classmates at the SDR. Since arriving at Buckfastleigh, the Class 25 has gained full yellow ends and has spent much of the 2019 season visiting other heritage line diesel events, where it has proved to be a popular attraction.

D7541 last saw use on the North Yorkshire Moors Railway (NYMR) in 2000, before being stored out of use awaiting a major overhaul. The locomotive has been undergoing a complete rebuild at Buckfastleigh for the past decade, with extensive bodywork and mechanical attention carried out.

Another Class 25 which has been out of service for many years is Pete Waterman's D7659, the last locomotive to be built at Beyer, Peacock's Gorton Works. Originally preserved on the

ELR in 1988, the locomotive remained at Bury for a number of years and was restored to BR two-tone green livery. It then moved to Crewe, before relocating to Bo'ness in 2004 for overhaul.

A few years later it moved to West Coast Railway Company's depot at Carnforth, where one of the company's senior engineers was intending to return it to use. However, this work was never completed and after relocating again to Washwood Heath, it finally moved to Peak Rail at Rowsley South along with several of Mr Waterman's other diesel and steam locomotives, where over the past two years it has been undergoing restoration to serviceable condition.

Now resplendent in original green livery, it is expected to enter service on Peak Rail before the end of 2019.

The two Class 25s at the Caledonian Railway are both undergoing prolonged restoration work, with neither having worked for many years. It is unknown

D7523 is currently undergoing an overhaul at Shackerstone on the Battlefield Railway on behalf of its owner on the Epping Ongar Railway. On April 30, 2012, D7523 stands at North Weald station awaiting its next duties. ANDY COWARD

D5217 stands at Wolsingham station on the Weardale Railway during a working visit to the line on February 24, 2008. This locomotive is now located at Nemesis Rail's Burton-on-Trent facility and has not worked for a number of years. Former Great Central Railway-based 25265 is also located at Burton. STEVE KEMP

when 25072 or 25083 will return to use.

There are two Class 25s located at Nemesis Rail's Burton upon Trent depot. The Rodent Traction Group's 25265 saw use on Peak Rail and the Great Central Railway, but moved to Burton for storage, awaiting an overhaul. D5217 is owned by the owner of Nemesis Rail and last saw use on the Battlefield Railway.

The Battlefield Railway is currently the home to D7523. The Class 25 is usually based on the Epping Ongar Railway, but it has been at Shackerstone undergoing a contract overhaul, which is progressing well and it is expected to return to the EOR following completion of works.

D7633 spent its early years in preservation based on the Severn Valley Railway, where it was used mainly on engineering trains, as well the occasional passenger turn. It was subsequently taken out of traffic for an overhaul and moved to the Dean Forest Railway in 2003, where work on its restoration began. In 2018, the locomotive moved to a private site for the restoration work to be completed, although it is unknown when it may return to use.

The final Class 25 to be in service on BR is 25322 *Tamworth Castle*, which is based on the Churnet Valley Railway. As with several other examples, it is now many years since 25322 last saw use and it has been out of use at Cheddleton since 2002. Now repainted in BR blue with wrap-round yellow cab panels, the locomotive awaits reactivation by its owners, although again there is no target

25057 is currently located on the North Norfolk Railway, where it has been based for many years, but it has been sold to Harry Needle and is expected to move to Barrow Hill at some stage in the future for restoration work. On November 17, 2012, 25057 stands at Sheringham station. STEVE KEMP

date set for its return to use.

Stored for many years in an increasingly derelict condition has been 25244, on the Kent & East Sussex Railway. The locomotive was cosmetically restored following its purchase from BR and was displayed at a number of open days, but it has never been returned to working order and is now in a very poor condition after more than three decades out of use.

In 2018 it underwent initial

assessment to see what level of work was required to restore it, but at this stage it is not known whether restoration work will be carried out.

BELOW: Owned by Derby Industrial Museum, D7671 stands on display at an open day event at Derby on September 13, 2014. The locomotive is usually based on the Midland Railway Butterley and is currently out of service awaiting repairs and a repaint. MARTIN HART

LOCO	NAME	BR IDENTITIES	OWNER	LOCATION
D5185		D5185, 25035	NT2G	GCR
25057		D5207, 25057	Private	NNR
25059		D5209, 25059	Private	KWVR
D5217		D5217, 25067	Private	Nemesis
25072		D5222, 25072	CRDG	CR
25083		D5233, 25083	CRDG	CR
D7523		D7523, 25173	Private	BFL
D7535		D7535, 25185	SDDT	SDR
D7541		D7541, 25191	SDDT	SDR
25235		D7585, 25235	SRPSDG	BKR
25244		D7594, 25244	Private	KESR
D7612		D7612, 25262, 25901	SDDT	SDR
25265		D7615, 25265	RTG	Nemesis
D7628	Sybilla	D7628, 25278	Private	NYMR
D7629		D7629, 25279	Private	ELR
D7633		D7633, 25283, 25904	Private	Private
D7659		D7659, 25309, 25909	Private	PKR
25313		D7663, 25313	Private	WR
D7671		D7671, 25321	DIM	MRB
25322	Tamworth Castle	D7672, 25322, 25912	NSDG	CVR

OWNER KEY: CRDG – Caledonian Railway Diesel Group, DIM – Derby Industrial Museum, NSDG – North Staffordshire Diesel Group, NT2G – Northampton Type Two Group, RTG – Rodent Traction Group, SDDT – South Devon Diesel Traction, SRPSDG – Scottish Railway Preservation Society Diesel Group

LOCATION KEY: BFL- Battlefield Railway, BKR – Bo'ness & Kinneil Railway, CR – Caledonian Railway, CVR – Churnet Valley Railway, ELR – East Lancashire Railway, GCR – Great Central Railway, KESR – Kent & East Sussex Railway, KWVR – Keighley & Worth Valley Railway, MRB – Midland Railway Butterley, Nemesis – Nemesis Rail Burton-on-Trent, NNR – North Norfolk Railway, NYMR – North Yorkshire Moors Railway, PKR – Peak Rail Rowsley South, SDR – South Devon Railway, WR – Wensleydale Railway

MAIN LINE PRESERVED CLASS 25s

At the present time there is only one Class 25 which is certified for operating over Network Rail and this is D7628 *Sybilla* on the North Yorkshire Moors Railway. Since the NYMR started running services from Grosmont to Whitby, a number of NYMR locomotives have been certified for use over the line and D7628 is one such locomotive. It is also one of the hardest-working Class 25s in preservation at the present time and is a regular performer on NYMR services.

MAIN LINE REGISTERED PRESERVED CLASS 25s

Loco	Owner	National Network Certification Status
D7628	Private	Main Line Certified

The pioneer Class 26, 26007, has recently returned to service after a bodywork overhaul and repaint into Railfreight livery. The locomotive is usually based at Barrow Hill, but on May 11, 2019, it was one of the visitors to the 2019 Swanage Railway diesel and real ale festival. PAUL HADFIELD

During the final year of Class 26 operation on British Rail, 26001 and 26007 were repainted into BR green and regained their D5300 and D5301 identities. Following their preservation D5301 was initially based at the Lakeside & Haverthwaite Railway, where it was pictured at Haverthwaite Station in the company of 20214 on April 10, 2005. D5301 subsequently moved to the Caledonian Railway and is now permanently based on that line, where it remains in operational condition. NIGEL VALENTINE

CLASS 26

The Class 26 'McRats' were another Type Two locomotive design that came from the British Railways Modernisation Plan of 1955. This saw 20 Type Two locomotives ordered, to be numbered D5300-D5319, from the Birmingham Railway Carriage & Wagon Company. The locomotives would be fitted with a Sulzer 6LDA28A power unit and Crompton Parkinson main generator and traction motors. They would be capable of running at up to 80mph.

The first locomotive, D5300, was delivered to BR in July 1958 and after a follow-up order saw the total number of locomotives increased to 47, with deliveries continuing until October 1959. They were finished in BR dark green, with white window surrounds and a thin white band running around the locomotive at mid-height.

The second batch of locomotives (D5320-D5346) were some five tonnes lighter than the pilot examples, as they featured lighter traction motors and were constructed using lighter construction methods. The production locomotives were moved to Scotland after acceptance by BR and the type became synonymous with operating around Scotland throughout their working lives on both passenger and freight services. The first seven pilot locomotives were modified for use on coal services and had their steam heat boilers and water tanks removed so that a second compressor could be added. They were also fitted with air brakes and slow-speed controls.

Under TOPS the locomotives became Class 26, the pilot scheme locomotives were classified as Class 26/0 and the production examples were classified as Class 26/1. Renumbering of the fleet was largely straightforward, with most having the D53XX prefix replaced with 260XX, although there were a few exceptions to this rule. Pioneer D5300 became 26007, while D5307 became 26020 and D5320 was renumbered 26028. The first member of the class to be withdrawn was D5328 in 1972, which made it the only example not to gain a TOPS identity. Pilot scheme 26016 was withdrawn three years later and then the rundown of the fleet got under way in 1977 with another three losses, although the remainder of the withdrawals were gradual.

However, with most of the fleet surviving into the 1990s, the writing was on the wall and BR had decided that the remaining Class 26s would be withdrawn in phases during the early 1990s. As with other designs, there was an enthusiastic following of the locomotives as they were being prepared for final removal from the BR network and to acknowledge the forthcoming demise of the locomotives, 26001 and 26007 (the original D5301 and D5300 respectively) were repainted into BR green and regained their original fleet numbers in July 1992.

26038 *Tom Clift 1954-2012* stands at Keighley station during a working visit to the Keighley & Worth Valley Railway on April 27, 2013. Preserved by the late Tom Clift, 26038 was restored over several years at Cardiff Canton depot. After Mr Clift suddenly passed away in 2012, the locomotive was sold to 6LDA Locomotives on the Bo'ness & Kinneil Railway, but it has spent several years based on the North Yorkshire Moors Railway where it remains. ANDY COWARD

LOCO	NAME	PREVIOUS IDENTITIES	OWNER	LOCATION
D5301		D5301, 26001	Private	CR
D5302		D5302, 26002	STR	STR
26004		D5304, 26004	Private	Nemesis
26007		D5300, 26007	Private	BHR
D5310		D5310, 26010	LDG	GWR
26011		D5311, 26011	RTG	Nemesis
D5314		D5314, 26014	CRDG	CR
26024		D5324, 26024	6LDAL	BKR
D5325		D5325, 26025	STR	STR
26035		D5335, 26035	CRDG	CR
26038	*Tom Clift 1954-2012*	D5338, 26038	6LDAL	NYMR
26040		D5340, 26040	Private	WHC
5343		D5343, 26043	CMDG	GWR

OWNERS KEY: 6LDAL – 6LDA Locomotives, CMDG – Cotswold Mainline Diesel Group, CRDG – Caledonian Railway Diesel Group, LDG – Llangollen Diesel Group, RTG – Rodent Traction Group, STR – Strathspey Railway

LOCATION KEY: BHR – Barrow Hill Roundhouse, BKR – Bo'ness & Kinneil Railway, CR – Caledonian Railway, GWR – Gloucestershire Warwickshire Railway, NYMR – North Yorkshire Moors Railway, STR – Strathspey Railway, WHC – Whitrope Heritage Centre

D5301 was also named *Eastfield* after the Scottish Depot that had been so closely associated with the locomotives. The pair were used on railtours and special workings.

The final year in service for the Class 26s was 1993, which had 11 active members at the start of the year, but in October 1993 the number of locomotives was down to eight and these were all withdrawn, bringing down the curtain on the Class 26s after a working life of 35 years.

5343 was restored at Toddington on the Gloucestershire & Warwickshire Railway by the Cotswold Mainline Diesel Group. On October 8, 2017, 5343 nears Toddington on its home railway during a diesel event. KEVIN DELANEY

D5310 was restored to a very high standard at the Great Central Railway in 2006 and moved to a new base on the Bo'ness & Kinneil Railway at the end of the year. It has since been sold to the Llangollen Diesel Group and is usually based on the Llangollen Railway, although it is currently on a short-term visit to the Gloucestershire & Warwickshire Railway, where it is undergoing traction motor repairs before returning to North Wales. On March 1, 2009, D5310 stands in the yard at Bo'ness in the company of other members of the railways diesel fleet. TERRY EYRES

26004 was preserved on the Bo'ness and Kinneil Railway by 6LDA Locomotives and returned to service painted in Coal Sector livery, visiting several other heritage railways. However, after being taken out of service for repairs, the owning group decided to sell the locomotive and it was bought by a private individual and moved to Nemesis Rail at Burton-on-Trent for storage pending possible reactivation. On March 1, 2009, 26004 stands in the yard at Bo'ness, having clearly seen better days. TERRY EYRES

THE PRESERVED CLASS 26s

The Class 26s were another type that proved to be popular with preservationists and 12 of the locomotives managed to survive, representing just over a quarter of the original fleet. While some of these locomotives are now regular performers on heritage railways, several of them are out of service and have been for many years.

One of the major problems with the Class 26s was the presence of asbestos in the locomotives, which meant that any preservationists buying the locomotives had to agree to get the deadly insulation material removed from their '26' before it was delivered to its new home. This saw most of the locomotives bought for preservation move to scrap metal processor and asbestos contractor MC Metals in Glasgow for asbestos removal, which involved a lot of work and in many cases rendered perfectly serviceable locomotives inoperable and in need of extensive rebuilding after delivery to their new homes. It also saw many Class 26s spend a long period of time awaiting processing, delaying their restoration to working order.

The pioneer locomotive, D5300, first saw use on the East Lancashire Railway, but then moved to Barrow Hill Roundhouse, which has been its home base ever since. It has spent long spells in BR blue as 26007 and during 2018 it has been repainted into Railfreight grey livery, making its debut in its new guise at the 2019 Swanage Railway diesel weekend and real ale festival.

D5301 was originally preserved on the Lakeside & Haverthwaite Railway,

where it saw occasional use on off-peak services. However, in 2008 it paid a working visit to the Nene Valley Railway and then moved to the Caledonian Railway, where it has remained ever since. It has retained original BR green livery throughout its time in preservation.

Also based on the CR is D5314 and 26035, with D5314 being operational, sharing duties with D5301 on the line. BR blue-liveried 26035 is currently stored out of use.

26010 spent several years in store on the Northampton & Lamport Railway until it was sold to a new owner in 2005 and moved to the Great Central Railway in early 2006 for an extensive contract bodywork restoration, emerging a few months later in immaculate condition in BR green with small yellow warning panels as D5310. It then moved to Bo'ness for the completion of repairs to allow it to return to service and it ran on the Bo'ness & Kinneil Railway (BKR) between 2007 and 2009.

In 2009 it was sold to the Llangollen Diesel Group and moved to the Llangollen Railway, where it has remained a regular performer on the line. However, in early 2019 the locomotive was out of service awaiting traction motor repairs and was repainted into plain green livery with full yellow ends, before moving to the Gloucestershire & Warwickshire Railway (GWR) for contract repairs by the Cotswold Mainline Diesel Group, which also owns 5343. It is expected that D5310 will return to the Llangollen Railway towards the end of the year.

26038 was restored over a number of years at Cardiff Canton under the auspices of respected railway manager Tom Clift. After returning the locomotive to service it made working visits to several railways and was then based at the BKR alongside the 6LDA Locomotives, 26004 and 26024, which were also based on that railway.

Sadly, Tom Clift passed away unexpectedly in 2012 and 26038 was then sold to 6LDA Locomotives. 26038 was subsequently named in tribute to its former owner and has spent the past few years on hire to the North Yorkshire Moors Railway, where it regularly sees use.

6LDA Locomotives bought 26004 and 26024 following withdrawal and both were moved to the BKR. 26004 was returned to service in 1998 resplendent in Coal Sector livery and visited several other railways for diesel events. However, it was taken out of service in 2006 and after many years in store it was sold to a new owner and moved to Nemesis Rail at Burton-upon-Trent, where it remains with its future unknown.

26024 was also restored to working order by 6LDA Locomotives, but is currently out of service undergoing an overhaul. The owning group has touted the idea of returning 26024 to main line running on Network Rail metals at some stage in the future.

5343 underwent a lengthy restoration by the Cotswold Mainline Diesel Group on the GWR. The owning group's efforts were rewarded when the locomotive returned to service on the GWR in 2013 and it remains a regular and reliable performer.

Class 26s out of service for extended periods are D5302, 26004, 26011, D5325, 26035 and 26040. While some of these locomotives, such as 26040 which is nearing the end of an extensive rebuild, will undoubtedly be returned to service at some stage in the future, some of these might never run again.

CLASS 26

BUILT:	Birmingham Railway Carriage & Wagon Company, 1958-1959
ENGINE:	Sulzer 6LDA28A
NO. BUILT:	47
NO. PRESERVED:	12
OTHER SURVIVORS:	0

CLASS 27

The locomotive design that went on to become the Class 27 was a further development of the earlier Sulzer Type Two (Class 26) locomotives. Sixty-nine locomotives, to be numbered D5347-D5415, were built by the Birmingham Railway Carriage & Wagon Company at their Smethwick Works between 1961 and 1962. Indeed the number sequencing of the new locomotive order continued directly on from the final Class 26 locomotive, D5346.

The locomotives were fitted with a Sulzer 6LDA28-B power unit, which was slightly more powerful than that which had been fitted in the earlier fleet. The locomotives could be operated at speeds of up to 90mph.

They were delivered to BR in a dark green livery, with a thin white stripe along the bodyside at mid-height level and the window surrounds were also painted white, with the livery being almost identical to that which had been applied to the other BRCW diesel locomotive designs (Classes 26 and 33). They later received small yellow warning panels on the cab fronts when they became mandatory before these too were replaced by full yellow warning panels and then repaints into BR blue livery. Under the TOPS numbering scheme, the fleet became Class 27.

While the Class 27s spent a lot of their working lives in Scotland based at Eastfield Depot, a number of the locomotives were originally allocated to Thornaby Depot, Leicester and Cricklewood in London. However, by the start of the 1970s the whole fleet had moved north to Scotland and they remained there for the rest of their working lives.

As a result of service requirements, there were eventually three Class 27 sub-classes created. The unmodified locomotives were classified as Class 27/0, while those modified for working push-pull services were given the Class 27/1 sub-class and those equipped with electric train heating became Class 27/2.

The Class 27s are perhaps most well remembered for operating services between Glasgow and Edinburgh, which they operated to an intensive timetable which worked the locomotives hard. For these services a number of locomotives were equipped for push-pull workings and many had their steam heat generators replaced by electric train heating equipment.

Despite being built as a further development of the Class 26 design, it would prove that the original design would outlive the Class 27s. The first Class 27 to be withdrawn was D5383 in January 1966 after being involved in a collision and this

27005 undergoes attention inside the excellent diesel depot at Bo'ness on January 3, 2016. This is one of two Class 27s to be based on the Bo'ness & Kinneil Railway, which has a very pro-diesel attitude and an enviable fleet of modern traction locomotives. KEVIN DELANEY

locomotive was the only member of the fleet to be withdrawn before receiving TOPS numbers.

A small number of Class 27s were withdrawn during the second half of the 1970s, but it would be the mid-1980s when serious inroads into the fleet were made, with many locomotives from the Class 27 fleet being withdrawn until 27008 became the final example to be withdrawn from service in August 1987. Unusually, the final locomotive to see service on BR was not one of those members of the fleet to be saved for a further working life in preservation.

Class 27, D5401, has been based on the Great Central Railway for many years now, but is currently out of service undergoing a bodywork overhaul and other repairs. On September 8, 2012, D5401 stands at Leicester North station, as it prepares to run around its train prior to working back to Loughborough Central station. ANDREW SEWELL.

Freshly repainted into original BR green livery and shining like it did the day it was delivered to British Railways, D5370 stands inside the exhibition shed at Haverthwaite during an extended visit to the Lakeside & Haverthwaite Railway on June 17, 2012, with 20214 stabled behind it. MARTIN HART

Owned by Sandwell Council, D5410 saw use on the Severn Valley Railway for a number of years before being taken out of service in the mid-1990s for an overhaul. The locomotive has undergone an extensive bodywork overhaul at Cranmore Traincare on the East Somerset Railway and is pictured at Tyseley Locomotive Works on April 10, 2018. RICHARD THOMPSON

During an autumn 2007 visit to the Llangollen Railway, D5401 makes its way along the North Wales heritage line on October 6, 2007, during a diesel event on the line. TERRY EYRES

THE PRESERVED CLASS 27s

There are eight Class 27s in preservation, with four of them currently based in Scotland and the other four in England.

The Bo'ness & Kinneil Railway is home to two Class 27s, with 27001 and 27005 both located on the line. 27001 is currently serviceable on the railway, but 27005 is undergoing a bodywork overhaul at Bo'ness.

At the Caledonian Railway, D5370 is in regular use on the railway and is painted in BR green livery with small yellow warning panels, while D5394 on the Strathspey Railway is also in regular use and also carries original BR green, but without any cab warning panels.

With three of the Class 27s based in Scotland in operational condition, the current status of the type in England isn't as bright, with all four currently out of service. On the Great Central Railway, D5401 is currently undergoing repairs and a bodywork overhaul at Loughborough Shed after operating on the GCR for a number of years, along with visits to various other heritage

railway events. It last operated in 2016 and it is expected to return to use on the GCR following the completion of works.

D5410 was preserved by Sandwell Council in the West Midlands and was moved to the Severn Valley Railway, where it saw use on the railway until 1995, when it was taken out of service. The locomotive then spent more than 15 years in store awaiting repairs. A move to UK Rail Leasing's Leicester Depot then took place and it was subsequently moved to Cranmore Traincare on the East Somerset Railway, where it underwent a comprehensive bodywork overhaul, and it was then returned to Tyseley Locomotive Works in the spring of 2018, painted in green undercoat. It

has since returned to Leicester Depot for further attention before it returns to its home base on the SVR.

27066 was originally preserved on the North Norfolk Railway, before moving to the East Lancashire Railway for an extended visit and then on to the Dean Forest Railway, which became its home base. It was sold to Harry Needle in 2015 and moved to Barrow Hill Roundhouse, where it remains. The locomotive has worked trains since moving to Derbyshire.

Which brings us to D5353. The locomotive was based on the Mid Hants Railway for a number of years, but has been out of use for more than 20 years. An attempt to deal with bodywork corrosion ended with large sections of the locomotive's bodywork removed and the locomotive is now in very poor condition. It was sold to a new owner in 2017 and moved to a private site. At one time, it was considered that the chassis would be used to construct a lost locomotive type, but it is unknown what the future holds for this locomotive.

CLASS 27

BUILT:	Birmingham Railway Carriage & Wagon Company, 1961-1962.
ENGINE:	Sulzer 6LDA28-B
NO. BUILT:	69
NO. PRESERVED:	8
OTHER SURVIVORS:	0

Stored at Barrow Hill, 27066 is awaiting its turn for an overhaul in the workshops of its new owner, Harry Needle, who bought the locomotive from its previous owners on the Dean Forest Railway. The locomotive is pictured alongside 45060 *Sherwood Forester* at Barrow Hill Halt on June 1, 2019. ANDY COWARD

LOCO	PREVIOUS IDENTITIES	OWNER	LOCATION
27001	D5347, 27001	C27LG	BKR
27005	D5351, 27005	SRPSDG	BKR
D5353	D5353, 27007	Private	Private
D5370	D5370, 27024	CRDG	CR
D5394	D5394, 27050, 27106	STR	STR
D5401	D5401, 27056, 27112	NT2G	GCR
27059	D5410, 27059, 27123, 27205	SWC	Leicester
27066	D5386, 27066, 27103, 27212	Private	BHR

OWNER KEY: C27LG – Class 27 Locomotive Group, CRDG – Caledonian Railway Diesel Group, NT2G – Northampton Type Two Group, SRPSDG – Scottish Railway Preservation Society Diesel Group, STC – Strathspey Railway, SWC – Sandwell Council

LOCATION KEY: BHR – Barrow Hill Roundhouse, BKR – Bo'ness & Kinneil Railway, CR – Caledonian Railway, GCR – Great Central Railway, Leicester – UK Rail Leasing Leicester Depot, STR – Strathspey Railway

On September 10-11, 2005, D5705 made a visit to Crewe Works for an Open Weekend event, with the locomotive displayed in the shed on the Saturday of the event. On the Sunday it was lifted off its bogies and suspended in the air, giving a unique view of this classic locomotive. On September 10, D5705 stands on display inside the Works building. NIGEL VALENTINE

On September 11, 2005, D5705 is hoisted off its bogies and suspended in the air courtesy of the overhead cranes inside the Crewe Works complex. This exercise proved to be a popular attraction for visitors to the Open Weekend event. NIGEL VALENTINE

Its return to service is one of the most eagerly anticipated events in modern traction preservation. The team of volunteers working on sole-surviving Class 15 locomotive, D8233, are also working on the revival of D5705. Work on the locomotive is progressing well, but there is still a lot of work to be completed before it can run again. On July 9, 2019, D5705 stands inside the East Lancashire Railway Locomotive Works where its overhaul is progressing. ANDY COWARD

CLASS 28

British Railways ordered 20 pilot scheme locomotives from Metropolitan Vickers in Stockton-on-Tees and they were another design created as a result of the 1955 British Railways Modernisation Plan. The locomotives were all delivered to BR between 1958 and 1959 and were all allocated to the Midland Region. They were often referred to as 'MetroVicks' or 'Co-Bo' due to their unusual Co-Bo bogie configuration.

The locomotives had a distinctive flat-fronted look with three cab windows and had a box-like shape to them, which made them stand out somewhat from the other locomotive designs that were emerging at the time of their introduction. They were powered by a Crossley HST V8 engine and could operate at speeds of up to 75mph.

They were painted in dark green livery with a thin grey band along the bodyside towards the base of the body at solebar level. They subsequently gained small yellow warning panels on the cab fronts and a few received full yellow ends. Just one locomotive out of the fleet, D5701, received BR blue livery before being withdrawn from service.

The locomotives saw use extensively, operating in pairs on the London-Glasgow overnight Condor freight service. They also made regular appearances operating over the Midland Main Line through the Derbyshire Peak District.

The 'MetroVicks' were not a great success, with continued problems experienced with their Crossley engines. In 1961, BR returned the locomotives to Metropolitan Vickers for repairs, modifications and overhaul. While consideration was given to fitting new engines into the locomotives, this did not happen and they were returned to BR after attention and later moved to Cumbria. However, their engines still proved to be problematical, even after the manufacturer had tried to rectify the defects. Under the TOPS numbering scheme, the 'MetroVicks' were given the Class 28 classification, although none of the locomotives survived in traffic long enough to gain BR five-figure TOPS identifications.

Deemed as being non-standard and troublesome, BR gave up on the MetroVicks after less than a decade in service, with six locomotives withdrawn from service in December 1967. The remainder were all taken out of service over the next few months, with the final examples surviving until September 1968.

Thankfully, one locomotive, D5705, managed to survive the cutter's torch as it was taken on by the Research Department of BR at the Railway Technical Centre in Derby following its withdrawal from normal service. It was then used as a carriage heating unit prior to being stored out of use awaiting scrapping. It then moved to Swindon for storage and was subsequently sold into preservation.

LOCO	PREVIOUS IDENTITIES	OWNER	LOCATION
D5705	D5705, S15705, TDB968006	C-BLG	ELR

OWNER KEY: C-BLG – Co-Bo Locomotive Group

LOCATION KEY: ELR – East Lancashire Railway

THE PRESERVED CLASS 28

Following its preservation in the early 1980s, D5705 was stored at Swindon for a while, but suffered fire damage after debris was lit beneath the locomotive, causing extensive damage to the cabling under the locomotive. It also was suffering from severe bodywork corrosion.

The locomotive then moved to a new base in the goods yard alongside Matlock station in Derbyshire, which was linked to Peak Rail. The Co-Bo was based on the site alongside a number of preserved 'Peak' locomotives that were also undergoing restoration work in the yard.

In 1996, D5705 moved away again from its Peak Rail base at Matlock and was relocated to the East Lancashire Railway. Agreement had been reached for the locomotive to be based on the ELR and volunteers would assist in the revival of the locomotive, although work

CLASS 28

BUILT:	Metropolitan Vickers, Stockton-on-Tees, 1958-1959.
ENGINE:	Crossley HST V8 Power Unit
NO. BUILT:	20
NO. PRESERVED:	1
OTHER SURVIVORS:	0

did not progress as quickly as originally intended and it spent quite some time stored without seeing any attention inside Bury Transport Museum.

Its restoration is now progressing well and an agreement between the owners and the Class 15 Preservation Society has seen the C15PS working on the restoration of D5705 alongside that of D8233. While restoration work has been progressing well, D5705 has still not returned to operational condition. The return to service of both D8233 and D5705 are sure to be greeted with much enthusiasm when their respective restorations are completed.

CLASS 31

The locomotives that went on to become Class 31 were built by Brush Traction as a Type Two locomotive and were built between 1957 and 1962. With some of the surviving locomotives now well over 60 years old, the design has proved once again to be built to last, even if there is now just a solitary example operating on the Network Rail system. However, the locomotive which has served the railway so well over the past six decades wasn't without its problems during its infancy.

As with several other designs, the initial order from British Railways was for 20 prototype pilot locomotives, to be numbered D5500-D5519. The locomotives were fitted with a Mirrlees JVS12T power unit and Brush electrical equipment. The pilot locomotives were also fitted with steam heating boilers and did not feature route indicator boxes above their cabs. They were able to operate at a maximum speed of 80mph.

When delivered, the locomotives were painted in dark green, with a thin white band running the length of the locomotive halfway up the bodyside, with a thicker white band running along the solebar level. As with other types introduced at the same time, locomotives subsequently gained half yellow warning panels on the cab fronts.

Trials of the locomotives were successful and eventually the type would go on to number 263. The subsequent locomotives had various differences from the pilot examples. One noticeable difference was the addition of headcode boxes above the cabs on all the production locomotives, with the exception of the first 20 production examples.

However, problems were found with the Mirrlees power

units fitted inside the locomotives and it was decided that a trial should be carried out by fitting an English Electric 12SVT power unit into one of the locomotives. After trials, the decision was taken to fit English Electric power units into all the Brush Type Two fleet and the work was carried out over a couple of years. Under TOPS, the Mirrlees-engined examples were classified as Class 30, while those with English Electric power units were Class 31. Once the power unit replacement programme was complete, the Class 30 designation became redundant. The pilot scheme locomotives were known as Class 31/0, while the production examples were Class 31/1.

Seventy Class 31/1 locomotives were equipped with electric train heating equipment and these became Class 31/4. In the late 1980s a number of Class 31/4 locomotives which had moved to freight companies had their ETH cables isolated as the equipment was not required for freight and these locomotives were classified as Class 31/5. The final classification came after privatisation when spot hire company Fragonset equipped two Class 31/1 locomotives with through wiring for electric train heating and these two became Class 31/6.

Unlike many of the other designs, it would be nearly 20 years before the first Class 31 was withdrawn from service, with 31150 being their first in 1975 when it was hit by a runaway train, causing severe damage to the Class 31, which was not authorised for repair.

The 20 pilot scheme Class 31/0 locomotives were the first of the type to be dispensed with in any quantity, as they were deemed to be non-standard. They were withdrawn in stages between 1976 and 1980, with the exception of 31101, which was originally D5518 but had been extensively rebuilt following a

Class 31, D5830, is owned by the Type One Locomotive Company at the Great Central Railway and is painted into golden ochre livery, which was originally carried by long-scrapped D5579 experimentally. On June 8, 2014, D5830 heads a train towards Ingrow West during a working visit to the Keighley & Worth Valley Railway. KEVIN DELANEY

One of the most travelled Class 31s in preservation is 31466, which is usually based on the Dean Forest Railway and painted into EWS maroon and gold colours, as applied for its final years in service. During a visit to the Keighley & Worth Valley Railway on May 27, 2012, 31466 heads past Haworth Top Field in glorious sunshine. The locomotive is currently undergoing a bodywork overhaul at its DFR base. TERRY EYRES

D5600 was originally preserved on the East Lancashire Railway where it was repainted into original BR green livery with small yellow warning panels, complete with reinstated headcode blinds. It later moved to the Embsay & Bolton Abbey Railway, but has now been stored out of use at Bolton Abbey station for a number of years and its future is unknown. On July 25, 2009, D5600 stands at Embsay station awaiting its next duties. NIGEL VALENTINE

CLASS 31

BUILT:	Brush Traction, 1957-1962
ENGINE:	English Electric 12SVT
NO. BUILT:	263
NO. PRESERVED:	26
OTHER SURVIVORS:	10

serious collision. This locomotive was returned to service as a standard Class 31/1. Of the other pilot scheme locomotives 31018 (the original D5500) was preserved by the National Railway Museum and four were taken into Departmental service as train heating locomotives prior to being scrapped in the mid-1980s.

A steady flow of withdrawals took place throughout the 1980s and early 1990s, with the withdrawal programme accelerating towards the late 1990s, although there were still a number of Class 31s in service after British Rail had been privatised, with the surviving Class 31s being inherited by freight company English Welsh & Scottish Railways (EWS).

Post privatisation, the Class 31s continued to be popular, although EWS quickly dispensed with its final Class 31s, as it sought to replace its ageing fleets with the new Class 66 and Class 67 locomotives.

Open access spot-hire operator Fragonset set up its base at Derby in the former Railway Technical Centre, re-certified a number of Class 47s for spot-hire basis and then also started to see the benefits of having a small fleet of Class 31s for spot-hire use. Fragonset reactivated a number of Class 31s for main line use and also bought numerous other withdrawn examples. However, after merging with Merlin Rail to form a new company, FM Rail, the company got into financial difficulties and subsequently fell into administration, with many of the stored Class 31s being sent for scrapping, while the operational examples were split between RVEL or Nemesis Rail and those which had been privately owned but operated by FM Rail were returned to their owners.

Network Rail operated a fleet of Class 31 locomotives, with the company operating 31105, 31233, 31285 and 31465 on a range of workings, although these have now been retired.

There is now just one Class 31 operating on the main line, with 31128 making occasional trips out on behalf of Nemesis Rail, making it the sole survivor on the National Network out of the 263 locomotives built.

Following preservation on the North Norfolk Railway, 31207 was repainted into BR green and regained its original D5631 number. However, the locomotive has now been taken out of service for a bodywork overhaul, which has seen the original bodywork skirting reinstated and returning the locomotive to as-built condition. On September 21, 2016, D5631 stands at Sheringham on its home railway. MARTIN HART

Looking suitably weathered, Regional Railway liveried 31270 *Athena* departs from Matlock, with a service to Rowsley South on Peak Rail on September 13, 2015. The livery for this locomotive is unauthentic, but was carried by four Class 31/4s during BR operations. 31270 has since moved to Nemesis Rail at Burton-upon-Trent for an extensive overhaul. KEVIN DELANEY

THE PRESERVED CLASS 31s

By far the most prolific owner of preserved Class 31s is A1A Locomotives, based at the Midland Railway Butterley. The group owns 31108, 31162, 31271 *Stratford 1840-2001*, 31414 and 31418, with all except 31271 currently located on the MRB in A1A's own restoration and maintenance facility. The group has an enviable reputation for the standard of its restoration work and its locomotives are popular as guests at diesel events and for hire to other lines. 31271 is currently based on the Llangollen Railway and is expected to stay in North Wales until the end of the 2020 season.

Current restoration efforts by A1A are being concentrated on 31414, which was bought from its former owner on the Ecclesbourne Valley Railway and is now being restored to the usual high standard achieved by the group. Once work on 31414 has been completed, attention is likely to turn to reviving 31418 which has yet to run in preservation.

The National Railway Museum is home to the pioneer Class 31, 31018 (D5500), which is usually on display in the Great Hall at York. During the 1990s the locomotive was a regular on the diesel gala circuit and spent several periods working on the East Lancashire Railway and the North Yorkshire Moors Railway, among others.

However, it has not run for a number of years and the NRM has no plans at the present time for the locomotive to be returned to operational condition for the foreseeable future.

The most recent Class 31s to be preserved are former Network Rail 31105 and 31233, which were bought in late 2018 by John Jolly and moved to the Mangapps Railway Museum. Both were found to be in excellent condition and 31105 was quickly revived by its new owner, while 31233 was brought back to life in June 2019 following the fitment of a new set of batteries. These two locomotives are being restored at Mangapps and are then expected to be made available for hire to other heritage lines that may be able to make use of them.

The Ecclesbourne Valley Railway is currently home to two Class 31s, with 31206 and 31601 *Devon Diesel Society* both based on the line. 31206 was originally located at Rushden Station Museum, where it was restored to operational condition and repainted into yellow and grey Civil Engineers 'Dutch' livery, while 31601 was bought from RMS Locotec in 2018 and moved to the railway after being retired from main line running.

In early 2019, Chinnor & Princes Risborough Railway volunteers repainted 31163 into BR Research Department livery, as once carried by 31326 which was renumbered 97204 during its time with the Research Department at Derby. As such, 31163 has been renumbered 97205 and the locomotive is pictured approaching Corfe Castle on the Swanage Railway on May 11, 2019. PAUL HADFIELD

On May 26, 2012, a weathered 31438 stands at North Weald station on the Epping Ongar Railway. Originally preserved on the Mid Norfolk Railway, 31438 moved to the EOR in October 2011 and has since had a bodywork overhaul and repaint into another coat of BR blue. STEVE KEMP

The Avon Valley Railway is home to the two Class 31s owned by Suburban Preservation, 31101 and 31130 *Calder Hall Power Station*. 31101 was originally preserved by Pete Waterman, but was purchased by Suburban Preservation in 1995 and was moved to the Battlefield Railway, where it was later joined by 31130. Both locomotives became regular performers at Shackerstone, but were relocated to Bitton in 2014.

Two Class 31s are based on the Embsay & Bolton Abbey Railway, although both are currently stored out of use at Bolton Abbey and the future for 31119 and D5600 is unknown, despite both locomotives having previously been operational.

Another Class 31 now in need of repairs is 31270 *Athena*, which recently moved from Peak Rail to Nemesis Rail at Burton upon Trent. The locomotive was originally preserved on the Colne Valley Railway, before moving to Peak Rail in 2004.

In need of a repaint to replace its worn Coal Sector livery, a poll of enthusiasts was held and it was subsequently repainted into Regional Railways livery, which was unauthentic for 31270 but had been carried by a number of Class 31/4s during the 1990s. Regularly used on Peak Rail until a couple of years ago, the locomotive is known to require engine repairs and a bodywork overhaul before it can return to use.

Another locomotive currently carrying an authentic livery for Class 31s, but not for the locomotive in question, is 31163 on the Chinnor & Princes Risborough. The locomotive has recently been outshopped in the former Research Department livery of red, black and cream, as once carried by 31326 which was renumbered 97204 during its time with the Research Department at Derby. As such, 31163

5580 is preserved by A1A Locomotives and is usually based on the Midland Railway Butterley. On March 26, 2011, 5580 stands at Llangollen station awaiting departure with a service to Carrog. KEVIN DELANEY

has been renumbered 97205 and the distinctive new look was unveiled in spring 2019, with the locomotive making a number of visits to other heritage lines.

31210 has been under restoration at the Dean Forest Railway (DFR) for a number of years and its restoration is now nearing completion at Lydney. The locomotive has been painted into Railfreight grey livery and it is anticipated that it may return to use in the near future.

The DFR is also home to EWS-liveried 31466, which has been another popular locomotive on the heritage railway gala circuit. During 2019 the locomotive has been back at its Lydney base where it is undergoing a bodywork overhaul to address corrosion.

31289 *Phoenix* is based on the Northampton & Lamport Railway and the locomotive remains in original

body condition, with front skirts and a bodyside metal band. The locomotive carried workworn BR blue for a number of years but has been painted in a version of electric blue livery.

The Pontypool & Blaenavon Railway (PBR) is home to D5627 *Steve Organ G.M.* where it has been based since being preserved. However, the locomotive was involved in a runaway incident in 2011 when it was struck by an errant Class 37, resulting in the Class 31 needing to be sent away to Nemesis Rail for repairs to a damaged cab. It has since returned to the PBR.

The North Norfolk Railway is home to D5631 which is currently undergoing a bodywork overhaul and repaint at Weybourne.

31430 *Sister Dora* and 31438 are both operational and painted in BR blue and are located at the Spa Valley Railway

The pioneer Class 31, D5500, is pictured at the former Steamtown Museum at Carnforth in 1989. This locomotive is now a static exhibit at the National Railway Museum in York, painted into BR blue livery. STEVE KEMP

Recently retired from main line running 31106 *Spalding Town* is now located on the Weardale Railway, where it is used alongside Class 31s belonging to Harry Needle Railroad Company and RMS Locotec on passenger services on the railway. On April 12, 2019, 31106 stands at Wolsingham station during a Class 31 running day, with 31465 in the background. KEVIN DELANEY

'Skinhead' 31108 is another Class 31 owned by A1A Locomotives and based on the Midland Railway Butterley. It is also another locomotive that has travelled extensively around various heritage railways during its time in preservation and is painted in the classic 1980s railfreight grey livery. 31108 is displayed at Eastleigh Works during an open day on May 23, 2009. MARTIN HART

Preserved in the attractive yellow and grey civil engineers 'Dutch' livery, 31206 is based on the Ecclesbourne Valley Railway after initially being restored at Rushden Station Museum. The immaculate '31' awaits departure from Wirksworth on August 12, 2017. ANDREW SEWELL

and Epping Ongar Railway respectively.

The Weardale Railway is now the home line of 31106 *Spalding Town*, which was a main line performer until a couple of years ago. It is now based at Wolsingham and used on the railway alongside other non-preserved Class 31s which are also based on the line.

The last-built 31327 is located on the Strathspey Railway, where it is often used for shunting the coaching stock from the 'Royal Scotsman' train. This is the only Class 31 to be based in Scotland.

There are no preserved Class 31s that have been passed for main line running on Network Rail metals, although several locomotives which have operated on the main line until recently, such as those previously owned by Network Rail and the RMS Locotec fleet, are now based on heritage lines where they are used on passenger services, although those owned by RMS Locotec, Harry Needle Railroad Company and Nemesis Rail cannot be classed as preserved.

31271 *Stratford 1840-2001* departs from Consall station on the Churnet Valley Railway on May 5, 2019. This locomotive was visiting the CVR on its way to the Llangollen Railway in North Wales where it has moved on a two season loan period after spending a number of years based on the Nene Valley Railway. 31271 is another locomotive owned and maintained by A1A Locomotives. KEVIN DELANEY

Another recently preserved Class 31 is 31601 *Devon Diesel Society*, which is painted in the colours of its former owners, Devon & Cornwall Railways. The locomotive was purchased in 2018 and has moved to the Ecclesbourne Valley Railway where it is pictured at Wirksworth awaiting departure on August 18, 2018. KEVIN DELANEY

LOCO	NAME	BR IDENTITIES	OWNER	LOCATION
31101		D5518, 31101	SP	AVR
31105		D5523, 31105	MRM	MRM
31106	Spalding Town	D5524, 31106	Private	WR
31108		D5526, 31108	A1A	MRB
31119		D5537, 31119	Private	EBAR
31130	Calder Hall Power Station	D5548, 31130	SP	AVR
31162		D5580, 31162	A1A	MRB
97205		D5581, 31163	Private	CPRR
D5627	Steve Organ G.M.	D5627, 31203	Private	PBR
31206		D5630, 31206	Private	EVR
D5631		D5631, 31207	Private	NNR
31210		D5634, 31210	Private	DFR
31233		D5660, 31233	MRM	MRM
31270	Athena	D5800, 31270	Private	Nemesis
31271	Stratford 1840-2001	D5801, 31271	A1A	MRB
31289	Phoenix	D5821, 31289	Private	NLR
31327		D5862, 31327	Private	SPR
31414		D5814, 31414, 31514	A1A	MRB
31418		D5522, 31418	A1A	MRB
31430	Sister Dora	D5695, 31265, 31430, 31530	Private	SPVA
D5600		D5600, 31179, 31435	Private	EBAR
31438		D5557, 31139, 31438, 31538	Private	EOR
D5830		D5830, 31297, 31463, 31563	T1LC	GCR
31466		D5533, 31115, 31466	Private	DFR
31601	Devon Diesel Society	D5609, 31186	Private	EVR

OWNERS KEY: A1A – A1A Locomotives, MRM – Mangapps Railway Museum, NRM – National Railway Museum, SP – Suburban Preservation, T1LC – Type One Locomotive Company

LOCATION KEY: AVR – Avon Valley Railway, CPRR – Chinnor & Princes Risborough Railway, DFR – Dean Forest Railway, EBAR – Embsay & Bolton Abbey Railway, EOR – Epping Ongar Railway, EVR – Ecclesbourne Valley Railway, GCR – Great Central Railway, MRB – Midland Railway Butterley, MRM – Mangapps Railway Museum, Nemesis – Nemesis Rail Burton-on-Trent, NLR – Northampton & Lamport Railway, NNR – North Norfolk Railway, PBR – Pontypool & Blaenavon Railway, RMY – Railway Museum York, SPA – Strathspey Railway, SPVA – Spa Valley Railway, WR – Weardale Railway

OTHER CLASS 31s

Class 31s running on the main line network is now largely a thing of the past, with just Nemesis Rail's 31128 the only example of the type to still see occasional use on Network Rail. Nemesis Rail also owns 31461 at Burton upon Trent but this locomotive has never been returned to a serviceable condition.

Following rail privatisation, several Class 31s were used by open access operators, such as the erstwhile FM Rail, RVEL at Derby, Nemesis Rail, West Coast Railway Company and Network Rail.

RMS Locotec currently owns three Class 31s, with 31190 and 31454 (being used as a spares donor) based on the Weardale Railway and 31452 on the Dartmoor Railway.

Network Rail was also a regular user of Class 31s, with the infrastructure company previously owning 31105, 31233, 31285 and 31465, which were all operated on a variety of trains across the country. The Network Rail Class 31 fleet was withdrawn during 2017 and 2018, with 31285 and 31465 acquired by Harry Needle Railroad Company, while 31105 and 31233 were secured for preservation by John Jolly, the owner of the Mangapps Railway Museum in Essex.

Harry Needle Railroad Company has also bought 31235 and 31255 out of preservation, while 31459 was acquired from RVEL at Derby.

With only one locomotive now registered for use on Network Rail, the future for Class 31s on the main line network looks uncertain and whether any more examples return to main line use in the future remains to be seen. They have proved to be a useful workhorse on the railway for many years, but it does appear that their reign on main line workings is drawing to a close.

HARRY NEEDLE RAILROAD COMPANY:	31235, 31255, 31285, 31459, 31465
NEMESIS RAIL:	31128, 31461
RMS LOCOTEC:	31190, 31452, 31454

CLASS 33

Introduced on to the railway network as a Type Three design to be based on the Southern Region, an order was placed for 98 locomotives with the Birmingham Railway Carriage & Wagon Company. Built between 1960 and 1962, the locomotives were designed with a Sulzer 8LDA28A power unit and were known to many railwaymen as 'Cromptons'.

Eighty-six standard locomotives were built, while 12 of the fleet were built with a narrower body profile to allow them to work on the Hastings line, which had lower gauging tolerances than other routes on the Southern Region.

They were delivered to BR in a dark green livery with a thin cream band midway along the bodyside and cream window surrounds on the cab windows. Yellow warning panels were subsequently added and, as with all other types that survived into the 1970s, they all then succumbed to corporate BR blue colours.

During the 1960s the electrification of the line into Bournemouth saw 19 of the locomotives modified for push-pull operation alongside 4TC units, ensuring that the locomotives could be used for onward travel towards Weymouth. The push-pull examples proved to be extremely useful for BR and their sphere of operation was expanded to cover other routes in later years.

Under TOPS the locomotives became Class 33, with the standard locomotives becoming Class 33/0, the push-pull equipped examples Class 33/1 and the narrow Hastings-profiled locomotives became Class 33/2. The Class 33s had gained an enviable reputation as a reliable design that was powerful and versatile.

As BR blue livery was replaced with an assortment of other liveries, it is fair to say that the Class 33s have carried their fair share of colour schemes, with Civil Engineers grey, yellow and grey 'Dutch', EWS red and gold (in the case of 33030), Direct Rail Services and West Coast Railway Company maroon all making appearances on various examples.

The first locomotive to be withdrawn from the fleet was D6502 in May 1964, following a serious collision two months earlier which caused substantial damage to the locomotive. The next withdrawal was D6576 in November 1968, also as a result of the locomotive suffering serious collision damage. Neither of these locomotives survived in traffic long enough to receive TOPS numbers.

Apart from a couple of other losses during the 1970s, it would be 1986 before the first Class 33s were removed from traffic and withdrawn. As the 1990s approached, the rate of withdrawals increased and following privatisation the surviving locomotives all became the property of English Welsh & Scottish Railways (EWS). By 1998, the final locomotives, 33051, 33109 and 33116, were being used on various charters and tours around the network, before they too were withdrawn.

A subsequent shortage of locomotives for use in Scotland saw EWS send a couple of Class 33s north of the border for a short time, before they were stood down again.

The withdrawal of the fleet by EWS was not the end of the story and other private operators, such as Direct Rail Services, Fragonset Railways (later FM Rail) and West Coast Railway Company all operated various Class 33s on the main line following privatisation, although WCRC is now the only main line operator to still use Class 33s on some of its services.

The Pioneer Diesel Group's 33035 hauls a Keighley to Oxenhope service towards Oakworth on the Keighley & Worth Valley Railway on June 8, 2014, during one of the popular KWVR diesel events at which the Class 33 was one of the visitors. TOM MCATEE

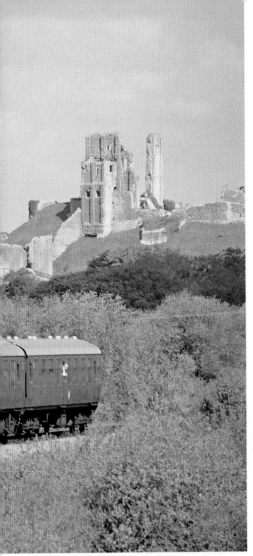

With the unmistakable landmark of Corfe Castle ruins dominating the background, D6515 *Lt Jenny Lewis RN* hauls its train along the Swanage Railway on May 11, 2019. This locomotive is based on the Swanage Railway, but is also registered for operating under its own power on Network Rail and occasionally ventures away from its home line. PAUL HADFIELD

CLASS 33

BUILT:	Birmingham Railway Carriage & Wagon Company, 1960-1962.
ENGINE:	Sulzer 8LDA28A
NO. BUILT:	98
NO. PRESERVED:	23
OTHER SURVIVORS:	5

THE PRESERVED CLASS 33s

The Class 33s are another diesel design to be well represented in preservation, with 12 Class 33/0s, eight Class 33/1s and three of the slimline Class 33/2s surviving and many of the survivors are operational.

The first Class 33 to run in preservation was 33117 on the East Lancashire Railway (ELR) in 1997. It had been a race between 33117 and 33208 on the Mid Hants Railway to be the first, with 33117 winning the race. Ironically, both of these locomotives

have now been out of service for well over a decade awaiting major overhauls. 33117 is now undergoing an extensive bodywork overhaul and mechanical repairs, while 33208 is now based at Shackerstone, where it is due to be reactivated at some stage.

There are three Class 33s on the Spa Valley Railway, with 33063 *R J Mitchell* and 33065 owned by the South East Locomotive Group and the Birmingham Railway Carriage & Wagon Groups 33201 also on the line. Of the three, 33065 is

33108 is mainly used on engineering duties on the Severn Valley Railway, but does occasionally see passenger use on the railway. On May 19, 2018, 33108 approaches Bewdley during the railway's spring diesel gala. KEVIN DELANEY

Making a working visit away from its home on the South Devon Railway, 33002 *Sea King* stands at Leicester North on the Great Central Railway on September 8, 2012. The locomotive has since been repainted out of its BR Civil Engineers yellow and grey 'Dutch' livery and now carries BR green as D6501. ANDREW SEWELL

33063 *R J Mitchell* is one of three Class 33s currently based on the Spa Valley Railway. On October 19, 2013, the locomotive departs from Groombridge station while painted in the attractive Trainload Freight grey and with Railfreight General sector decals applied. KEVIN DELANEY

On April 20, 2019, 33103 *Swordfish* powers its way along the Ecclesbourne Valley Railway. The locomotive is painted into BR's Civil Engineers grey livery, which when originally applied was generally unpopular, but it is now carried by three of the preserved Class 33s, 33103, 33109 and 33110, although 33110 is in the process of being repainted green in summer 2019. NIGEL VALENTINE

undergoing an extensive overhaul, while the other two are operational.

The Swanage Railway is another heritage line that is home to two of the surviving '33s' with 33111 and main line registered D6515 *Lt Jenny Lewis RN* based on the line. 33111 is owned by the Class 33/1 Preservation Company and represents the BR blue era, while D6515 belongs to the 71A Locomotive Group and is painted in BR green with small yellow warning panels. Both Class 33s at Swanage are operational.

Another line to boast two operational Class 33s is the West Somerset Railway (WSR), which is home to D6566 and D6575, both of which are owned by a private individual who is actively involved in the Diesel & Electric Preservation Group and they are regularly in use on the WSR, with both carrying matching BR green liveries.

33021 *Eastleigh* and 33102 *Sophie* both call the Churnet Valley Railway home and are both operational. 33021 carries a very distinctive post office red livery, while 33102 carries a more traditional coat of BR blue.

When BR applied Civil Engineers grey livery to various locomotives in its fleet, the choice of colour scheme was not universally popular and most subsequently had their bodywork livery altered to the brighter yellow and grey 'Dutch' colours. However, in preservation three operational Class 33/1s currently wear the previously unpopular livery, which does suit the design well. 33103 *Swordfish* on the Ecclesbourne Valley Railway, 33109 *Captain Bill Smith RNR* on the ELR and 33110 on the Bodmin & Wenford Railway all carry Civil Engineers grey livery, although the weatherworn paintwork on 33110 is being attended to during summer 2019 and 33110 is expected to receive a variation of BR green livery.

33108 is another locomotive belonging to the Class 33/1 Preservation Company and is based on the Severn Valley Railway, where it occasionally sees use

Following its original preservation, 33021 *Eastleigh* was returned to main line service by Fragonset Railway and painted into post office red livery before being repainted into the operator's standard black and red stripe livery. Now retired from main line running, the locomotive is based at the Churnet Valley Railway and has recently had its distinctive red livery reapplied. On May 5, 2019, 33021 stands at Cheddleton station. KEVIN DELANEY

on passenger workings, but is mainly used by the railway's Civil Engineering department for hauling works trains on the railway.

33202 *Dennis G Robinson* was the final Class 33/2 to be sold by English Welsh & Scottish Railways and although it has a number of different home railways since entering preservation, it is currently based at the Mid Norfolk Railway.

The other operational Class 33s are D6501 *Sea King* on the South Devon Railway, 33035 on the Wensleydale Railway, D6535 on the Great Central Railway and D6570 on the Kent & East Sussex Railway.

Of the non-operational Class 33s, D6508 *Eastleigh* was a celebrity during its final years in service with British Rail, but has never operated in preservation and is undergoing an extensive contract overhaul at Shackerstone on the Battlefield Railway, which is progressing well. 33208 is also at Shackerstone for an overhaul, while 33018 is now stored at a private site and nothing is known as to its current condition, or whether it is being restored to working order.

33053 left its previous home at the Mid Hants Railway in 2018 for a new home at UK Rail Leasing's Leicester Depot, where it remains in store. As

already mentioned, 33065 and 33117 are both out of service undergoing overhaul at their respective home railways.

One locomotive destined to leave the list of preserved Class 33s is 33046 on the ELR. The locomotive has spent the past 10 years being used as a source of spares both for the Class 33/1s based on the railway and, prior to that, it served the same purpose on the Midland Railway Butterley for the owners of 33201. Component recovery has been advancing in recent months and it is anticipated that 33046 will be scrapped over the coming months. It is believed that one of the cabs has been secured for preservation at The Cab Yard in Wales.

During a visit to the Midland Railway Butterley, South Devon Diesel Traction's D6501 stands at Swanwick Junction station on July 8, 2017. RICHARD THOMPSON

D6566 is one of two Class 33s maintained in immaculate condition on the West Somerset Railway, both wearing original BR green livery with small yellow warning panels. The two Class 33s are owned by a prominent member of the Diesel & Electric Preservation Group and are maintained and operated on the WSR by the DEPG. D6566 stands at Minehead between duties on June 21, 2019. STEVE KEMP

33111 is the second Class 33 to be permanently resident on the Swanage Railway. Owned by the Class 33/1 Preservation Company, the locomotive carries BR blue livery and is pictured at the head of a train approaching Corfe Castle on May 11, 2019. PAUL HADFIELD

LOCO	NAME	BR IDENTITIES	OWNER	LOCATION
D6508	*Eastleigh*	D6508, 33008	Private	BFL
D6515	*Lt Jenny Lewis RN*	D6515, 33012	71ALG	SR
33018		D6530, 33018	Private	Private
33021	*Eastleigh*	D6539, 33021	Private	CVR
33035		D6553, 33035	PDG	WR
33046		D6564, 33046	Private	ELR
D6566		D6566, 33048	DEPG	WSR
D6570	*Ashford*	D6570, 33052	Private	KESR
33053		D6571, 33053	Private	Leicester
D6575		D6575, 33057	DEPG	WSR
33063	*R J Mitchell*	D6583, 33063	SELG	SPVR
33065		D6585, 33065	SELG	SPVR
33102	*Sophie*	D6513, 33102	NSDG	CVR
33103	*Swordfish*	D6514, 33103	Private	EVR
33108		D6521, 33108	C33/1PC	SVR
33109	*Captain Bill Smith RNR*	D6525, 33109	Private	ELR
33110		D6527, 33110	Private	BWR
33111		D6528, 33111	C33/1PC	SR
D6535		D6535, 33116	NRM	GCR
D6536		D6536, 33117	Private	ELR
33201		D6586, 33201	BRCWG	SPVR
33202	*Dennis G Robinson*	D6587, 33202	Private	MNR
D6593		D6593, 33208	Private	BFL

OWNER KEY: 71ALG – 71A Locomotive Group, BRCWG – Birmingham Railway Carriage & Wagon Group, C33/1PC – Class 33/1 Preservation Company, DEPG – Diesel & Electric Preservation Group, NRM – National Railway Museum, NSDG – North Staffordshire Diesel Group, PDG – Pioneer Diesel Group, SDDT – South Devon Diesel Traction, SELG – South East Locomotive Group

LOCATION KEY: BFL – Battlefield Railway, BWR – Bodmin & Wenford Railway, CVR – Churnet Valley Railway, ELR – East Lancashire Railway, EVR – Ecclesbourne Valley Railway, GCR – Great Central Railway, KESR – Kent & East Sussex Railway, Leicester – UK Rail Leasing Leicester Depot, MNR – Mid Norfolk Railway, SDR – South Devon Railway, SPVR – Spa Valley Railway, SR – Swanage Railway, SVR – Severn Valley Railway, WSR – West Somerset Railway, WR – Wensleydale Railway

12 Class 33s were built to a narrower body profile for working on the Hastings line loading gauge and these were given the Class 33/2 classification. 33202 *Dennis G Robinson* stands at Norden Gates on the Swanage Railway during a visit to the line on May 10, 2014. MARTIN HART

RIGHT: Looking rather work-weary is D6535 as it runs around its train at Leicester North on the Great Central Railway on September 11, 2016. This locomotive belongs to the National Railway Museum collection, but has been based at the GCR since it first entered preservation. ANDREW SEWELL

33053 is currently located at UK Rail Leasing's Leicester Depot, but spent several years working services on the Mid Hants Railway. On October 20, 2017, the locomotive is pictured coupled to visiting 33202 *Dennis G Robinson* at Alresford. MARTIN HART

33102 *Sophie* is one of two Class 33s to be based on the Churnet Valley Railway. Preserved by the North Staffordshire Diesel Group, the locomotive has recently returned to service after an extensive bodywork overhaul and repaint into BR blue livery and the locomotive is captured in action on its home railway on May 5, 2019. KEVIN DELANEY

MAIN LINE PRESERVED CLASS 33s

At the time of writing, there is currently only one preserved Class 33 that is main line registered and that is Swanage Railway-based D6515 *Lt Jenny Lewis RN*. The locomotive is owned by the 71A Locomotive Group. While it primarily sees use on its home railway, it is not unknown for D6515 to venture away from Swanage to haul a main line charter or for other hire contracts.

Mid Hants Railway-based D6593 was the first Class 33 to be re-registered for main line running, but has not operated over Network Rail metals for many years now and it is currently stored on the Battlefield Railway awaiting reactivation.

33021, 33103 and 33108 were all registered for main line running with Fragonset Railways for several years, but following the collapse of FM Rail (as Fragonset became known following a merger with Merlin Rail) at the end of 2006, the locomotives were returned to operating within the heritage sector.

MAIN LINE REGISTERED PRESERVED CLASS 33s

Loco	Owner	National Network Certification Status
D6515	71A Locomotive Group	Main Line Certified
33021	Private	Main Line Certification Expired
33103	Private	Main Line Certification Expired
33108	Class 33/1 Preservation Company	Main Line Certification Expired
D6593	Private	Main Line Certification Expired

OTHER CLASS 33s

There are five Class 33s that are owned by commercial organisations, with three of these being active on Network Rail metals, one based on a heritage line and the fifth being used as a component donor.

Nemesis Rail own 33019 *Griffon*, but this locomotive has been based on the Battlefield Railway for a number of years and has been used on the railway's passenger services alongside their other diesel locomotives, although it is currently out of service.

While a number of Nemesis Rail locomotives have moved to their Burton upon Trent depot facility, 33019 has remained at Shackerstone.

West Coast Railway Company at Carnforth own 33025, 33029, 33030 and 33207 *Jim Martin*.

Of these, 33030 is currently a spares donor locomotive and is unlikely to ever be returned to main line use, while the other three locomotives are painted in the WCRC maroon livery and are all still active on the main line, hauling various charter services across the country.

NON-PRESERVED SURVIVING CLASS 33s

NEMESIS RAIL: 33019

WEST COAST RAILWAY COMPANY: 33025, 33029, 33030, 33207

After undergoing an extensive bodywork overhaul for a proposed use by South West Trains, work was suspended on the refurbishment of 33046 and it was subsequently sold to the owners of 33201 as a spares donor. It has since been sold again to the owners of 33109 and 33117 on the East Lancashire Railway and once final spares recovery has been completed 33046 is expected to be scrapped. On July 15, 2019, 33046 awaits its fate at Baron Street Locomotive Works. ANDY COWARD

CLASS 35

Built by Beyer Peacock at Gorton Works in Manchester, the 'Hymek' was the Western Region's (WR) choice for a medium-powered Type Three design. They were fitted with a single Maybach MD870 power unit, as opposed to the other main WC diesel-hydraulic 'Western' and 'Warship' designs which featured twin engines.

The 'Hymek' was another design to emerge following the publication of the 1955 British Railways Modernisation Plan. BR placed an initial order for 45 locomotives in 1959, with a further 50 ordered in 1960 and another six in 1961. The locomotives were numbered D7000-D7100 and they were allocated to Bristol Bath Road, Cardiff Canton, Newton Abbot and Old Oak Common.

The first example, D7000, entered service in January 1961 and the final locomotive was accepted in February 1964. They were delivered in two-tone green livery, with the majority of the bodysides painted dark green, with a thin lighter green band along the lower bodysides and skirting, similar to that which had been applied to the 'Deltics' and featuring white cab window surrounds. As with most other types, they gained half yellow warning panels on the cab fronts as these became mandatory, with them later having full yellow cab fronts applied, before they were repainted into BR blue in the late 1960s and early 1970s.

The 'Hymeks' carried cast alloy numbers on each cabside and these remained on them throughout their working lives. Unlike the 'Westerns' and 'Warships', BR decided that the 'Hymeks' would not carry names.

Under TOPS classification in 1973 they were allocated

Class 35, but none of them received five-figure fleet numbers, with some having the 'D' prefix alloy letter painted blue, as these were no longer recognised by BR. In preservation one locomotive, D7017, did carry a BR identity of 35017 while painted in fictitious yellow and grey 'Dutch' Civil Engineers livery for a brief period.

They were designed as a mixed-traffic locomotive capable of working passenger and freight services across the WR, although they occasionally ventured on to the Southern Region.

The decision by BR to dispense with the diesel-hydraulic designs meant that the 'Hymeks' were another class to be withdrawn long before their time. BR had introduced the Class 37s as their Type Three design of choice and the large number of these locomotives in traffic would allow the 'Hymeks' to be withdrawn.

First to be withdrawn were D7006 and D7081 in September 1971, with the rundown of the remainder taking three-and-a-half years to complete when the final example was stood down in March 1975. As with several other designs, some examples had been in service for less than a decade when they were withdrawn.

Two locomotives, D7076 and D7096, were moved to the Research Department at the Railway Technical Centre in Derby, where they were used as dead loads for testing other locomotives. This move ensured the survival of both locomotives into the 1980s and allowed the preservation of D7076 to take place long after the remaining 'Hymeks' had been scrapped, with D7096 providing many valuable spare parts prior to scrapping.

The stylish and attractive lines of the Beyer Peacock 'Hymek' design are shown to good effect on D7017 at Minehead on the West Somerset Railway on July 26, 2014. STEVE KEMP

Oozing with atmosphere, D7076 hauls a demonstration goods train through Little Burrs on the East Lancashire Railway on March 7, 2015. The locomotive was repainted into BR blue in 2014, having carried green throughout its time in preservation since returning to traffic in October 1988. NIGEL VALENTINE

THE PRESERVED CLASS 35s

Four Class 35s have survived into preservation, with two, D7017 and D7018, based on the West Somerset Railway (WSR), one, D7029, on the Severn Valley Railway (SVR), and the fourth, D7076, on the East Lancashire Railway (ELR).

D7017 was purchased by the Diesel and Electric Preservation Group (DEPG)

CLASS 35

BUILT:	Beyer Peacock, Gorton Works, Manchester, 1961-1964
ENGINE:	Maybach MD870
NO. BUILT:	101
NO. PRESERVED:	4
OTHER SURVIVORS:	0

from BR in July 1975 and was moved to the WSR for restoration, which was completed in March 1977 when it re-entered traffic on the railway. Over the past 42 years D7017 has proved itself to be a reliable and consistent workhorse for its owners and the WSR and it remains a popular and regular performer.

In the autumn of 1992, D7017 was repainted into a variation of BR's yellow and grey 'Dutch' Civil Engineers livery, which was applied to a number of BR locomotives during the early 1990s. It was also renumbered as 35017 and named *Williton* after the WSR base where the DEPG maintains its

Prior to failing with a serious engine fault in 1995, D7018 was a consistent performer on the West Somerset Railway. In this undated view, D7018 departs from Williton station hauling a Minehead to Bishops Lydeard service. RICHARD HOLMES

Fictitious 35017 in BR Civil Engineers 'Dutch' livery stands at Minehead awaiting its next duties in October 1992. In the background, D7018 can be seen wearing a more traditional 'Hymek' colour scheme. RICHARD HOLMES

For a period in 1995, D7076 on the East Lancashire Railway was disguised as now-scrapped D7096. The scrapped 'Hymek' accompanied D7076 to the Railway Technical Centre in Derby when both were used as dead loads for testing purposes and when D7076 was bought for preservation, D7096 was used to donate many spare parts to aid the restoration of D7076 before scrapping. STEVE KEMP

fleet of locomotives. While this was completely inauthentic for the 'Hymeks', it suited the locomotive well, although it was relatively short-lived and the following year it was returned to a more traditional 'Hymek' livery, with it being painted into BR blue with small yellow warning panels.

D7018 was also purchased by the DEPG in 1977 and initially moved to the Didcot Railway Centre for restoration. It returned to service in 1985 and was later moved across to the WSR to join D7017.

In 1995, D7018 suffered from a serious engine failure and the DEPG took the locomotive out of service to carry out repairs and then decided to completely overhaul the locomotive. The immaculate locomotive was returned to service in June 2019 at the WSR 'Diesels to the Seaside' event and provided a matching pair along with an equally well turned-out D7017, with the 'Hymeks' double-heading on a number of trains.

D7029 is another locomotive owned by the Diesel Traction Group and is now based on the SVR. Upon preservation in 1975, it was initially moved to the former Reading Gas Works along with D821 *Greyhound*, before moving on to Swindon Works two years later. In 1981 it moved to the North Yorkshire Moors Railway (NYMR), again with D821 keeping it company.

D7029 was withdrawn from service on the NYMR in July 1987 and has been undergoing an overhaul and rebuild ever since. A lot of bodywork, mechanical and electrical restoration work has been carried out on the locomotive, but its overhaul is not yet complete and no target date has been announced as to when it may return to service on the SVR. After more than 30 years since it last hauled a train, its return is eagerly awaited by many diesel-hydraulic followers.

After spending a number of years at the Railway Technical Centre in Derby, D7076 was privately purchased in 1983 and placed under the care of the Bury Hydraulic Group on the ELR.

By the time of its purchase D7076 was in poor condition and in order to assist with its restoration, the owner was able to recover a large quantity of spare parts from D7096 prior to that locomotive being scrapped. Restoration was completed in autumn 1988, with the locomotive freshly repainted into BR green, and it has remained an important part of the ELR's diesel collection ever since. The B End of the locomotive bears the D7096 identification inside the cab as a tribute to the lost donor 'Hymek'.

In 2009 D7076 had been suffering from engine problems and the BHG volunteers came up with a unique way of returning the 'Hymek' to service quickly while a replacement Maybach MD680 was prepared for the locomotive.

With D1041 *Western Prince* out of service undergoing a major overhaul, the BHG volunteers decided to fit a serviceable Maybach MD655 engine out of D1041 into D7076. The engine could

D7017 passes through Eastcombe on the West Somerset Railway while carrying BR blue with small yellow warning panels during the mid-1990s. RICHARD HOLMES

be accommodated inside the 'Hymek' with some alterations made to the roof sections. The experiment was a success and the modified locomotive, nicknamed as a 'Wesmek', ran on a number of occasions with its temporary engine.

A replacement MD870 engine was subsequently sourced for D7076 to replace the original defective engine and this was fitted into D7076 in 2011. It was also repainted into BR blue for the first time in preservation after spending the previous 23 years in green livery. At the time of writing the locomotive is out of service undergoing engine repairs.

There are no known plans for any of the preserved 'Hymeks' to ever return to main line use and it seems unlikely that a Class 35 will ever haul a train on the main line under its own power again.

Repainted into BR blue, D7076 approaches Burrs foot crossing between Bury and Summerseat on the East Lancashire Railway on July 4, 2015. The locomotive has been paired with a matching rake of blue and grey Mark 1 coaches, helping to recreate a scene that could be straight out of the early 1970s. TERRY EYRES

BELOW: The DEPG pair of 'Hymeks' stand in the wet at Minehead on the West Somerset Railway on June 23, 2019. DAVID STERRY

LOCO	BR IDENTITIES	OWNER	LOCATION
D7017	D7017	DEPG	WSR
D7018	D7018	DEPG	WSR
D7029	D7029	DTG	SVR
D7076	D7076	BHG	ELR

OWNERS KEY: BHG – Bury Hydraulic Group, DEPG – Diesel & Electric Preservation Group, DTG – Diesel Traction Group

LOCATION KEY: ELR – East Lancashire Railway, SVR – Severn Valley Railway Railway, WSR – West Somerset Railway

After an extensive overhaul and rebuild which took almost 25 years to complete, D7018 returned to service on the West Somerset Railway during their 'Diesels to the Seaside' event. On June 20, 2019, D7018 prepares to depart from Minehead during its inaugural weekend back in traffic. DAVID STERRY

A study of a 'what might have been' livery applied to D7017. DEPG repainted the locomotive in the autumn of 1992 into BR's yellow and grey Civil Engineers 'Dutch' colours, renumbered it 35017 and fitted *Williton* nameplates, in tribute to the DEPG's maintenance base on the West Somerset Railway. The livery was short-lived and it had been repainted into BR blue by the following year. RICHARD HOLMES

CLASS 37

The English Electric Type Three, or Class 37 as it is more commonly known, has proved to be one of the most successful locomotive designs to emerge as a result of the 1955 British Railways Modernisation Plan. Between 1960 and 1965 a total of 309 Type Three locomotives were built and almost 60 years since the first locomotive emerged from the production lines there are still 99 of them in existence, with most of the survivors still operational.

Similar in appearance to the English Electric Type Four (Class 40), but shorter, the locomotives were fitted with an English Electric 12CSVT power unit and could operate at a maximum speed of 80mph. The newly delivered locomotives were mainly bedecked in BR green livery, although some of the later-built examples emerged in BR blue.

Numbered D6700-D6999 and D6600-D6608, they were designed as a mixed-traffic locomotive and saw use on both passenger and freight services.

All the locomotives featured headcode boxes on the cab fronts, with most having a central headcode box and the others split-headcode boxes, although following refurbishment some of the fleet had their headcode boxes removed.

Initially concentrated on the Eastern Region, as more of the fleet entered service they spread their wings across the whole of the BR network and there are few areas of the country that they have not visited at some point. During the 1980s many of the locomotives underwent refurbishment and a programme of modifications to suit different types of services saw a number of Class 37 sub-classes created.

The first sub-class of locomotives were the Class 37/3s, which were given an overhaul and fitted with CP7 bogies and were used on a variety of workings.

Probably the most useful and popular sub-class has been the electric train heat fitted Class 37/4s. Thirty-one Class 37/0 locomotives were refurbished and the main generator on these locomotives was replaced with an alternator and Electric Train Supply equipment was fitted to allow the locomotives to be used on passenger services where they could also heat the coaching stock when required. These were numbered 37401-37431.

Another popular sub-class were the Class 37/5s, which also received alternators in place of their main generators, although these were not fitted with Electric Train Supply equipment, as they were restricted to freight services. Two batches were created, numbered 37501-37521 and 37667-37699.

Newly returned to service on the Wensleydale Railway following restoration and a repaint into BR yellow and grey 'Dutch' livery, 37250 departs from Bedale station with a Leeming Bar to Redmire service on July 3, 2019. This is one of two Class 37s to be based on the pro-diesel Wensleydale Railway. KEVIN DELANEY

LEFT: During an evening photographic charter, 37264 stands at Pickering at the head of a matching rake of blue and grey coaches on the North Yorkshire Moors Railway on March 17, 2013. Originally restored at Tyseley Locomotive Works, 37264 has been based at the NYMR since 2010. TERRY EYRES

CLASS 37

BUILT:	Vulcan Foundry, Newton-le-Willows and Robert Stephenson & Hawthorn, Darlington, 1960-1965
ENGINE:	English Electric 12CSVT
NO. BUILT:	309
NO. PRESERVED:	32
OTHER SURVIVORS:	67

Pioneer Class 37, D6700, is owned by the National Railway Museum, but has been a regular on the diesel gala circuit over the years. On May 22, 2011, the locomotive approaches Oakworth on the Keighley and Worth Valley Railway. TERRY EYRES

A fleet of 12 Class 37/6s were created in 1995 for European Passenger Services at Doncaster Works. These were converted from Class 37/5 locomotives and fitted with through wiring for Electric Train Supply and could be operated in multiple. Numbered 37601-37612, this batch of locomotives was subsequently bought by Direct Rail Services, although in recent years a number of these have been sold on again to Europhoenix and Harry Needle Railroad Company.

Ballast weights were fitted to 44 locomotives and these were designed to be used for hauling heavier trains than a standard Class 37/0. This batch of locomotives was classified as Class 37/7.

Six locomotives were fitted with new engines as BR sought to investigate new locomotives that would eventually replace the Class 37s. These were to be classified as Class 37/9 and 37901-37904 were fitted with a Mirrlees power unit and 37905-37906 were fitted with a Ruston engine. The Mirrlees engine was subsequently chosen to be fitted in the then-new Class 60 locomotives.

The first locomotive to be withdrawn was D6983, which was officially condemned in April 1966 after being involved in a fatal collision at Bridgend in December 1965, the only member of the fleet not to receive TOPS numbers. It would be another 21 years before the next withdrawal, when 37011 was removed from stock in August 1987.

While a steady flow of withdrawals followed throughout the 1990s, it was the introduction of 250 brand new Class 66s for English Welsh & Scottish Railways following privatisation that saw more widespread disposals from the Class 37 fleet.

After EWS disposed of its final members of the fleet, it fell on other operators to keep the Class 37s active on the main line network. And as we approach the 60th anniversary of their introduction, it appears that Class 37s will remain active on the main line and in preservation for many years to come.

A powerful combination for a four coach train and a rather colourful convoy, as 37418 *Pectinidae* leads 37901 *Mirrlees Pioneer* and 37109 through Burrs with a Bury to Rawtenstall service on the East Lancashire Railway on May 30, 2009. 37418 is now back operating on the main line for Colas Rail on the Cardiff to Rhymney line services, while 37901 is now commercially owned by Europhoenix and is currently waiting a return to main line service. TOM MCATEE

THE PRESERVED CLASS 37s

Although there are currently a healthy 32 Class 37s in preservation, that number is somewhat smaller than it was a few years ago. A number of previously preserved locomotives have either been sold for scrap or bought by main line operators for reactivation on Network Rail metals.

The first Class 37 to enter preservation was 37029, which was bought by Pete Waterman and restored at Crewe Heritage Centre. It was subsequently sold to Direct Rail Services, but has since been sold back into preservation and is now privately owned on the Epping Ongar Railway where, as BR green-liveried D6729, it remains a popular member of the railway's fleet.

Pioneer locomotive, D6700, was donated to the National Railway Museum by EWS upon its withdrawal and it is now located at the Railway Museum in York. The NRM has recently carried out a review of its locomotive fleet and most of the fleet is now destined to remain as static exhibits at York or Shildon. However, the NRM has stated that D6700 is to be retained in operational condition and will be available to visit other heritage railways.

The Class 37 Locomotive Group owns 37003, which is currently undergoing an extensive overhaul at UK Rail Leasing's Leicester Depot.

The locomotive is being restored to original condition as D6703, although much work remains to be done before it can return to its home on the Mid Norfolk Railway and the owning group is encouraging donations towards the locomotive's restoration.

On the North Norfolk Railway, D6732 has recently returned to service after an extensive overhaul and is another Class 37 which has been restored to as-built condition. Other Class 37s restored to original condition are BR blue-liveried D6737 on the South Devon Railway and D6916 on the Pontypool & Blaenavon Railway.

D05 Preservation Ltd have recently completed a bodywork overhaul and repaint on 37688 *Great Rocks* on the Severn Valley Railway. The locomotive has also had its vacuum braking equipment reinstated to allow it to be used on passenger services on the SVR. The locomotive is painted in Trainload Freight triple grey, joining 37714 *Cardiff Canton* on the Great Central Railway and 37075 on the Keighley & Worth Valley Railway. While 37075 is unbranded, 37688 carries Metals sector blue and yellow markings and 37714 represents the Construction sector with its bodyside decals.

The Growler Group owns two Class 37s on the Gloucestershire & Warwickshire Railway. 37215 has been located at Toddington for a number of

It could well be a scene from the 1970s, as 37275 heads a rake of Mark 2 blue and grey coaches through Horncliffe on the East Lancashire Railway on August 11, 2012. The locomotive is now owned by and located at the Paignton & Dartmouth Steam Railway. NIGEL VALENTINE

years, while D6948 returned to service two years ago after a comprehensive restoration which has returned it to as-built condition. Prior to its restoration, while still running as 37248, the locomotive was on long-term hire to West Coast Railway Company for main line running, although its main line running certification has now expired.

The North Yorkshire Moors Railway has been home to 37264 since 2010 and the Large Logo Class 37 is a regular performer on the line, which has seen an increase in the number of occasions diesel traction is used to haul its services, alongside its enviable fleet of steam locomotives. It is not main line registered and is not used on the Grosmont to Whitby services, being restricted to operating between Pickering and Grosmont.

The Wensleydale Railway is also home to two Class 37s, with 37250 and 37674 both based on the line. 37250 has recently returned to service following an overhaul and repaint into BR Civil Engineers yellow and grey 'Dutch' livery.

Another locomotive which has recently returned to use after repairs is 37227, which is now based on the Chinnor & Princes Risborough Railway. At Peak Rail, 37152 was unveiled in August 2019 carrying Large Logo blue livery, regaining its former identity of 37310 *British Steel Ravenscraig*, and it is expected to return to service over the next few months.

37025 *Inverness TMD*, 37403 *Isle of Mull* and 37418 are all preserved locomotives that are main line registered and currently on hire to main line operators. 37025 and 37403's home

37688 *Great Rocks* is owned by D05 Preservation Ltd and has been recently repainted into Trainload Freight Construction sector colours on the Severn Valley Railway, where the locomotive is based. As a one-time Buxton allocated locomotive, 37688 also sports Buxton millstone depot plaques on the secondman cabsides. On May 19, 2019, 37688 approaches Bewdley with a Bridgnorth to Kidderminster service. MARTIN HART

railway is the Bo'ness & Kinneil Railway, while 37418 was formerly based on the East Lancashire Railway, but has been located at Barrow Hill more recently before returning to main line use.

Representing the BR blue era, D6737, 37097, 37109, 37142, 37215, 37275 and 37294 are all operational on their respective railways, making this livery the best represented out of the preserved operational Class 37s.

Seven Class 37s – 37009, 37023, 37042, 37108, 37261, 37263 and 37308 – have yet to haul a train in preservation, although all are subject to overhauls by their respective owners and should hopefully be returned to service.

Of the currently preserved examples

only one, 37214, is destined to be scrapped after recovery of spares. This locomotive was preserved before being bought by West Coast Railway Company and returned to main line service, although it suffered a power unit failure and has been used as a spares donor ever since. It is now owned by the Scottish 37 Group and is providing spares for the group's other locomotives at Bo'ness.

Direct Rail Services have also placed 37716 on long-term loan to the Bo'ness & Kinneil Railway, although it remains a commercial asset of the company and whether it passes into preservation after DRS has finished with it remains to be seen.

One of the most comprehensive and immaculate restorations of a Class 37 in preservation has been the transformation of D6948 on the Gloucestershire Warwickshire Railway by the Growler Group. The locomotive has been restored to as-built condition and on October 8, 2017, the spotless Class 37 passes through Gotherington station. KEVIN DELANEY

With the BR blue paintwork looking suitably worn, 37109 heads through the former Heap Bridge Junction between Bury and Heywood, while working a Rawtenstall to Heywood service on the East Lancashire Railway on September 23, 2018. TOM MCATEE

LOCO	NAME	BR IDENTITIES	OWNER	LOCATION
D6700		D6700, 37119, 37350	NRM	RMY
37003		D6703, 37003	C37LG	Leicester
37009		D6709, 37009, 37340	Private	GCRN
37023		D6723, 37023	Private	Studley
37025	Inverness TMD	D6725, 37025	S37G	On Hire
D6729		D6729, 37029	Private	EOR
D6732		D6732, 37032, 37353	Private	NNR
D6737		D6737, 37037, 37321	DDS	SDR
37042		D6742, 37042	Private	EDVR
37075		D6775, 37075	Private	KWVR
37097		D6797, 37097	CRDG	CR
37108		D6808, 37108, 37325	Private	CHC
37109		D6809, 37109	Private	ELR
37142		D6842, 37142	BWMLDG	BWR
37310	British Steel Ravenscraig	D6852, 37152, 37310	Private	PKR
37214		D6914, 37214	S37G	BKR
37215		D6915, 37215	GG	GWR
D6916		D6916, 37216	Private	PBR
37227		D6927, 37227	Private	CPRR
D6948		D6948, 37248	GG	GWR
37250		D6950, 37250	Private	WR
37261		D6961, 37261	S37G	BKR
37263		D6963, 37263	Private	TSR
37264		D6964, 37264	Private	NYMR
37275		D6975, 37275	PDSR	PDSR
37294		D6994, 37294	Private	EBAR
37308		D6608, 37308, 37274	Private	DFR
37403	Isle of Mull	D6607, 37307, 37403	SRPS	On Hire
37418		D6971, 37271, 37418	Private	On Hire
37674		D6869, 37169, 37674	Private	WR
37688	Great Rocks	D6905, 37205, 37688	D05PL	SVR
37714	Cardiff Canton	D6724, 37024, 37714	HTG	GCR

OWNERS KEY: BWMLDG – Bodmin & Wenford Main Line Diesel Group, C37LG – Class 37 Locomotive Group, CRDG – Caledonian Railway Diesel Group, D05PL – D05 Preservation Ltd, DDS – Devon Diesel Society, GG – Growler Group, HTG – Heavy Tractor Group, NRM – National Railway Museum, PDSR – Paignton & Dartmouth Steam Railway, S37G – Scottish 37 Group, SRPS – Scottish Railway Preservation Society

LOCATION KEY: BKR – Bo'ness & Kinneil Railway, BWR – Bodmin & Wenford Railway, CHC – Crewe Heritage Centre, CPRR – Chinnor & Princes Risborough Railway, CR – Caledonian Railway, DFR – Dean Forest Railway, EBAR – Embsay & Bolton Abbey Railway, EDVA – Eden Valley Railway, ELR – East Lancashire Railway, EOR – Epping Ongar Railway, GCR – Great Central Railway, GCRN – Great Central Railway (Nottingham), GWR – Gloucestershire & Warwickshire Railway, KWVR – Keighley & Worth Valley Railway, NNR – North Norfolk Railway, NYMR – North Yorkshire Moors Railway, PDSR – Paignton & Dartmouth Steam Railway, PKR – Peak Rail Rowsley South, RMY – Railway Museum York, SDR – South Devon Railway, Studley – Allelys Transport Yard Studley, SVR – Severn Valley Railway, TSR – Telford Steam Railway, WR – Wensleydale Railway

Now painted into unbranded Trainload triple grey livery, 37075 is now resident on the Keighley & Worth Valley Railway, where it is owned by a consortium of volunteers on the line. On May 4, 2019, 37075 stands in the sun at Haworth MPD Yard awaiting its next duties. KEVIN DELANEY

37294 is spending its retirement working on the Embsay & Bolton Abbey Railway, where it has been returned to operational condition and repainted into BR blue. On April 30, 2016, an un-numbered 37294 awaits departure from Embsay with a service to Bolton Abbey. ANDREW SEWELL

Restored from scrap condition at the Bo'ness & Kinneil Railway, 37403 *Isle of Mull* has spent most of the time since it returned to use on hire to Direct Rail Services. On May 23, 2017, 37403 is about to cross the pedestrian beach tunnel at Bank Yard Road as it approaches Parton with a Barrow-in-Furness to Carlisle service operated by DRS for Northern. KEVIN DELANEY

Owned by the Heavy Tractor Group and based on the Great Central Railway, 37714 *Cardiff Canton* has been immaculately restored into Trainload Freight Metals sector livery. On March 18, 2017, 37714 runs around its train at Loughborough. KEVIN DELANEY

Under restoration 37108 stands alongside Colas Rail 37219 on August 4, 2018 at Crewe Heritage Centre. While 37108 has yet to haul a train in preservation, 37219 was formerly a preserved locomotive based on the Pontypool & Blaenavon Railway before being sold to Colas for another spell of main line operation. KEVIN DELANEY

MAIN LINE PRESERVED CLASS 37s

There are currently three preserved Class 37s on hire to main line operators, two of which are normally based on the Bo'ness & Kinneil Railway. 37025 *Inverness TMD* and 37403 *Isle of Mull* were both extensively overhauled at Bo'ness and while 37025 went on hire to Colas Rail for various infrastructure workings, 37403 is currently hired by Direct Rail Services, where it is used to supplement the operator's own fleet of Class 37/4 locomotives.

37418 spent most of its time in preservation based on the East Lancashire Railway, but was moved to Barrow Hill for recertification and has now been hired to Colas Rail. The company has been awarded a contract to have a locomotive-hauled set on the Cardiff to Rhymney service for Transport for Wales, with services mainly being hauled by 37418 and Colas' own 37421.

It is expected that following their hire to Colas and DRS, these three locomotives will all be returned to their owners, although they may retain their main line operating status to allow them to be used on charters and by other operators.

As 37248, the Growler Group's D6948 ran for a number of years on hire to West Coast Railway Company. This locomotive was returned to its owner at the end of its hire period and has now been completely restored to as-built condition on the Gloucestershire & Warwickshire Railway.

Having been stripped of many components following its withdrawal by Direct Rail Services, 37261 is considered to be a long-term restoration project for its owners, the Scottish 37 Group. However, the group has also bought 37214 from West Coast Railway Company, which will also provide many spares towards 37025 and 37261 before being scrapped at some point in the future. A heavily stripped 37261 stands in the yard at Bo'ness on January 2, 2016, before restoration work got under way. KEVIN DELANEY

Leaving its previous base at Tyseley Locomotive Works, 37263 was moved to the Telford Steam Railway on May 24, 2017. Originally preserved on the Dean Forest Railway, the locomotive has been undergoing restoration for a number of years and has not yet returned to use, although its overhaul is reaching an advanced stage. RICHARD THOMPSON

MAIN LINE REGISTERED PRESERVED CLASS 37s

Loco	Owner	National Network Certification Status
37025	Scottish Thirty-Seven Group	Main Line Certified on hire to Colas
37248	Growler Group	Main Line Certification Expired
37403	Scottish Railway Preservation Society	Main Line Certified on hire to DRS
37418	Private	Main Line Certified on hire to Colas

Of all the surviving heritage diesel designs that are still in main line service with commercial operators, the Class 37 is the most numerous, with 68 examples owned by the commercial sector. By far the largest operator of the type is Direct Rail Services, which owns 24 Class 37s, most of which are still in regular use. DRS also owns the majority of the surviving members of the Class 37/4 sub-fleet, which are still in demand for passenger workings due to their Electric Train Heat capabilities.

Investment in a new locomotive fleet of Class 68 and Class 88 locomotives means that DRS is likely to dispense with some of its Class 37 fleet, while new train fleets for passenger operators Northern and Greater Anglia also mean that the diagrams that have relied on the use of Class 37/4s are now transferring to the new fleets and allowing the Class 37/4s to be retired from the services that they have been operating in recent times.

Colas Rail also owns a fleet of eight Class 37s, which are used on a variety of services. All of their locomotives were bought from the preservation sector and recertified for main line use. Colas also hires preserved 37025 and 37418 from their owners and these two locomotives are expected to return to heritage railway use following the end of their hire period.

West Coast Railway Company is another company which uses Class 37s as part of its fleet of charter and spot hire locomotives. The company owns 11 Class 37s, but not all of these are operational and a number of them are used to provide spares for the operational fleet.

Europhoenix has 10 Class 37s on its books, but as with WCRC not all of its fleet are expected to return to use and several will be scrapped after they have donated any reusable spare parts.

The company bought four previously preserved Class 37s (37146, 37188, 37207 and 37901) which had been bought by Colas for reactivation, but work on them was stopped following a review of the Colas fleet.

37188 was scrapped in August 2019 and it is possible that another of the formerly preserved Class 37s may be broken up for scrap after component recovery.

Network Rail owns five Class 37s. Four of these were extensively rebuilt by Harry Needle Railroad Company at Barrow Hill and these were given 973XX fleet numbers. The company also owns 37198, which is being used as a parts donor and is expected to be scrapped in the future.

Harry Needle Railroad Company also owns three former DRS Class 37/6 locomotives, which are to be used on a spot-hire basis, mainly being hired by Colas Rail. 37610 was originally bought from DRS by Locomotive Services Ltd before being exchanged to HNRC for Class 47, 47853.

Locomotive Services Ltd's growing diesel fleet includes a pair of Class 37s, with 37667 purchased from Direct Rail Services some time ago and 37190 has recently arrived at Crewe for reactivation after its purchase from preservation with the Class 40 Appeal at the Midland Railway Butterley.

UK Rail Leasing owns the two Ruston-engine fitted Class 37/9s, 37905 and 37906, both of which are at Leicester Depot. Although 37905 has seen use at some heritage railway events, neither has worked for some time and 37906 is now in relatively poor condition after a long period in store. Despite proposals for the pair to move to the Shackerstone Railway for reactivation, it is believed that this may not now be happening and the future of both locomotives is still unknown.

Boden Rail Engineering Ltd recently bought 37240 out of preservation from the Llangollen Diesel Group and it is currently undergoing an extensive mechanical and bodywork overhaul before an expected return to main line use based at BREL's Nottingham Eastcroft Depot.

The other commercial company to own a solitary Class 37 is Nemesis Rail, which owns 37255. While this locomotive was formerly based at the Great Central Railway, it has now been at Burton upon Trent depot for a number of years, although it is unlikely to be recertified for main line use in the future.

NON-PRESERVED SURVIVING CLASS 37s

BODEN RAIL ENGINEERING LTD: 37240

COLAS RAIL: 37057, 37099, 37116, 37175, 37219, 37254, 37421, 37521

DIRECT RAIL SERVICES: 37038, 37059, 37069, 37218, 37259, 37401, 37402, 37405, 37407, 37409, 37412, 37419, 37422, 37423, 37424, 37425, 37602, 37603, 37604, 37605, 37606, 37609, 37703, 37716

EUROPHOENIX: 37146, 37207, 37503, 37510, 37601, 37608, 37611, 37800, 37884, 37901

HARRY NEEDLE RAILROAD COMPANY: 37607, 37610, 37612

LOCOMOTIVE SERVICES LTD: 37190, 37667

NEMESIS RAIL: 37255

NETWORK RAIL: 37198, 97301, 97302, 97303, 97304

UK RAIL LEASING: 37905, 37906

WEST COAST RAILWAY COMPANY: 37165, 37516, 37517, 37518, 37668, 37669, 37676, 37685, 37706, 37710, 37712

• Please note that some of these locomotives are operational, while others are stored or being used as spares donor locomotives.

37042 was bought from EWS for preservation on the Eden Valley Railway at Warcop. Looking rather weary after a number of years out of service, it is pictured awaiting attention on April 21, 2018.
KEVIN DELANEY

CLASS 40

The Class 40, or English Electric Type Four as it was originally known, was another locomotive design which had a huge impact on the railway network, as well as gaining a large following by enthusiasts during their 30-year working career.

Under the 1955 BR Modernisation Plan, 10 Type Four locomotives were ordered from English Electric, to be numbered D200-D209. They were fitted with an English Electric 16SVT MkII power unit and built at Vulcan Foundry in Newton-le-Willows.

D200 made its debut hauling a demonstration train from London Liverpool Street to Norwich on April 18, 1958. The design was considered a success and a further 190 locomotives were ordered, numbered D210-D399. Most of the production order was built by Vulcan Foundry, although D305-D324 were built by Robert Stephenson & Hawthorn.

The EE Type Four was a mixed-traffic locomotive and worked a wide variety of freight and passenger workings, with the north of England and Scotland becoming strongholds for the type, although they could generally be found working across the country, except for the Southern and Western Regions, where appearances were rare.

Twenty-five of the locomotives (D210-D225 and D227-D235) were named after ocean liners. Mystery surrounds the proposed naming of D226, which was allocated the name *Media* and for which the nameplates were cast, but they were never fitted to the locomotive. No other locomotives were named by BR although both 40106 and 40145 have carried names in preservation.

The first withdrawal came in September 1967 when D322 was involved in a serious collision near Warrington, which was so serious the locomotive had to be scrapped. It was the only member of the fleet to never receive TOPS numbers and the vacant 40122 number was subsequently allocated to fleet pioneer D200. Under TOPS the EE Type-Four became Class 40 and they were numbered 40001-40199.

The rundown started in January 1976 when the first withdrawals took place and by 1980 a total of 17 Class 40s had been withdrawn. From 1980 withdrawals were accelerated with more Class 40s taken out of service, as BR sought to rid itself of some of its older locomotives and new Class 56s and Class 58s were on order or recently delivered.

When Crewe station was being remodelled in spring 1985 four Class 40s were reinstated into departmental service to haul trains in connection with the project. 40012 was renumbered 97407, while 40060 became 97405, 40118 became 97408 and 40135 became 97406. Of these four locomotives, three were subsequently saved for preservation after their brief stay of execution came to an end in 1987.

The final regular service examples had been taken out of service in February 1985, leaving just 'celebrity' D200 in traffic for hauling special trains, railtours and attending open days. As 40122, the pioneer had originally been withdrawn in 1981, but was resurrected using the bogies and power unit from 40076 following a campaign by Rail magazine to get the locomotive reinstated for railtour use. It was finally withdrawn in April 1988 and claimed by the National Railway Museum for preservation.

Fleet pioneer, D200, is preserved by the National Railway Museum at the Railway Museum in York, but the locomotive is now maintained as a static exhibit and requires repairs to its main generator before it could return to use. On April 18, 1998, D200 stands at Rawtenstall on the East Lancashire Railway during a period on loan to the railway, where it took part in an event to celebrate the 40th anniversary of the locomotive entering service. It returned to the ELR for a celebratory event in April 2018. STEVE KEMP

LEFT: In April 2018 the Class 40 Preservation Society organised a celebration of the 60th anniversary of the introduction into service of D200 at the East Lancashire Railway, with the event bringing together six of the surviving Class 40s. During an evening photographic event on April 11, 2018 D200, D213 *Andania*, 40106 *Atlantic Conveyor*, 40012 *Aureol*, 40135 and 40145 are displayed at Baron Street Locomotive Works. The only surviving Class 40 missing from the event was 40118, which is being restored at Tyseley Locomotive Works. TOM MCATEE

CLASS 40

BUILT: Vulcan Foundry and Robert Stephenson & Hawthorn, 1958-1962

ENGINE: English Electric 16SVT MkII

NO. BUILT: 200

NO. PRESERVED: 7

OTHER SURVIVORS: 0

THE PRESERVED CLASS 40s

Following their withdrawal by BR, seven Class 40s were secured for preservation, along with one of the cabs from 40088, which is now mounted on to a road trailer to form a mobile sales stand for the Class 40 Preservation Society (CFPS).

The first Class 40s bought for preservation were 40145, which was purchased by the CFPS in February 1984, with celebrity BR green-liveried 40106 acquired by the late Gerald Boden

the following month. Both were in generally good condition, with 40145 moving to the East Lancashire Railway (ELR) and 40106 finding a new home on the Great Central Railway (GCR).

Having been withdrawn with minor derailment damage, 40145 moved to Bury in early 1985 and the CFPS carried out the necessary works to refurbish and return the locomotive to service. It was one of the first two diesel locomotives to find passenger use on the ELR when the railway was reopened from Bury to Ramsbottom in July 1987.

40145 has remained at Bury throughout its time in preservation, but has visited many other heritage lines and in November 2002 it became the first privately owned Class 40 to be recertified for main line running. At the time of writing, the locomotive is at Barrow Hill undergoing a bogie overhaul, which will include the fitting of new tyres.

In 2007 the locomotive was repainted into fictitious BR Large Logo livery, as carried by the smaller Class 37s and was named *East Lancashire Railway* in tribute to its home railway. The nameplates had previously been carried by 37418 and remained on 40145 until it was repainted into BR blue in 2013.

40106 gained a following during its twilight years in BR service, due to it retaining BR green livery throughout its time operating in BR service, including a repaint into green long after blue had been adopted as the corporate BR identity on diesel locomotives. It was

40106 *Atlantic Conveyor* was the first Class 40 to haul a train in preservation while it was based on the Great Central Railway. Originally preserved by the late Gerald Boden, it spent long periods based on the GCR, the Nene Valley Railway and at Neil Boden's former engineering base at Washwood Heath. In November 2015 the locomotive was bought by the Class 40 Preservation Society and moved to the East Lancashire Railway, although it is currently on long-term hire to the Severn Valley Railway. On October 4, 2014, 40106 passes through Foley Park on the SVR working a Kidderminster to Bridgnorth service during a diesel event on the line. TOM MCATEE

Recreating a scene that could be straight out of the 1970s, 345 (40145) arrives at the head of a rake of blue and grey Mark 2 coaches into Bury Bolton Street station during an evening photographic charter on March 21, 2014. NIGEL VALENTINE

Main line registered Class 40, 345, hauls the 'Scarborough Spa Express' railtour through Preston on August 17, 2017. The locomotive is currently out of service undergoing a bogie overhaul and the fitting of new tyres. TERRY EYRES

withdrawn due to only being equipped with vacuum braking, when the use of air brakes on BR was becoming the norm.

Following its preservation, Gerald Boden moved 40106 to the Great Central Railway at Loughborough and it became the first Class 40 to work in preservation the following month. Mr Boden and his family kept the locomotive in immaculate condition and it continued to be a popular performer whenever it worked on the railway.

In August 1984, 40106 was named *Atlantic Conveyor* in tribute to the Cunard cargo ship and its crew after the ship had been sunk during the Falklands War. The nameplates were cast in the same style as those carried by the Class 40s that had been named by British Railways.

40106 subsequently moved to the Nene Valley Railway in the early 1990s, where it remained until 2011.

Gerald Boden passed away in

February 2011 and the locomotive was placed in the care of his son, Neil Boden, who moved 40106 to his railway engineering works at Washwood Heath where it could be kept undercover and made available for visits to heritage railways.

In November 2015 it was purchased by the CFPS and moved to the ELR in spring 2016.

In 2018 it moved to the Severn Valley Railway (SVR) in place of 40135, which was originally due to spend a season on loan to the SVR.

40013 *Andania* was used as a BR London Midland Region exhibition locomotive following withdrawal, before being purchased for preservation by the late Trevor Dean and moved to the South Yorkshire Railway at Meadowhall in 1988. It then moved to the Midland Railway Butterley in 1999 for restoration by the Class 40 Appeal, but the arrangement was subsequently ended and the locomotive was moved again to

Barrow Hill Roundhouse in 2002.

After the death of Mr Dean in October 2011 the locomotive was initially bequeathed to the Museum of Science and Industry in Manchester, but was rejected by MOSI due to its size, and it was subsequently bought by a small consortium of Barrow Hill volunteers and returned to service after a thorough restoration in 2016. It has since operated at several heritage railway events, including appearances at the ELR, Swanage Railway and North Yorkshire Moors Railway (NYMR).

Following completion by BR of the Crewe remodelling project in 1988, 40012, 40118 and 40135 were secured for preservation. 40012 was purchased by the Class 40 Appeal and moved to the Midland Railway Butterley, while 40118 had been purchased by the 16 SVT Society. 40135 became the second Class 40 to be purchased by the CFPS and it moved to Bury in early 1989 to join 40145.

The new owners of 40012 found that the locomotive had suffered engine damage while in store following withdrawal which required specialist repairs. It was repainted into BR blue as 212 and renamed *Aureol* at the Longsight Depot Open Day in 1992, before re-entering service on the MRB in July 1993 after a restoration taking some four years to complete. In 2006 the locomotive was returned to BR green, regaining its original D212 identity and was restricted to its MRB base, due to the bogies requiring welding repairs to cracks in the frames.

In recent years the locomotive has been undergoing a programme of repairs at Barrow Hill, including the outstanding bogie welding repairs and a full bodywork overhaul and repaint into BR blue livery. It then moved to the ELR in spring 2018 for an appearance at the ELR's '40s@60' event, with it remaining at the railway for several months, before returning to the MRB for repairs to a failed turbo and the overhaul of 40012's

D212 *Aureol* stands awaiting its next duties at Swanwick Junction on the Midland Railway Butterley on September 11, 2006, shortly after the locomotive had been repainted into BR green livery with small yellow warning panels. The Class 40 Appeal owns this locomotive and in 2018 it returned to service after several years out of use undergoing repairs at Barrow Hill. ANDY COWARD

D335 was preserved by the Class 40 Preservation Society in 1988 and has been based at the East Lancashire Railway ever since, although it has paid working visits to other railways on occasions. On July 23, 2016, 40135 rounds the Forth Estuary with a Bo'ness to Manuel service while visiting the Bo'ness & Kinneil Railway, hauling a mixed train, which included pioneer HST power car 41001, 37714 and 33109 *Captain Bill Smith RNR*. TOM MCATEE

Disguised as Great Train Robbery locomotive D326, the CFPS-owned D335 hauls a short train of matching maroon coaches into Irwell Vale on the East Lancashire Railway on March 24, 2012. The locomotive has been used on a number of occasions for filming contracts in connection with the infamous robbery, as the locomotive is from the same batch of split-headcode Class 40s as the original D326. On this occasion it had been used for filming scenes for the ITV drama Mrs Biggs. TOM MCATEE

other turbos. Following a repaint by BR for open day appearances, 40135 avoided scrapping and was subsequently purchased by the CFPS. After asbestos removal, it arrived at Bury in 1989 and made its preservation debut in October 1989.

As with 40145, the CFPS's second 'Whistler' has been loaned out to several other heritage lines for special events. It has been a consistent performer, but is currently out of service following the discovery of damaged segmental bearings, which require replacing before the locomotive can return to regular use. A planned loan of 40135 to the SVR had to be cancelled, with 40106 sent as a replacement. 40135 was repainted into BR blue by Loram at Derby during 2017.

40118 was moved to Birmingham Railway Museum in Tyseley (now Tyseley Locomotive Works) following its purchase from BR and is receiving a complete rebuild by its owners. Work completed so far has been carried out to a very high standard, but is not yet complete and 40118 is now the only preserved Class 40 which has not yet hauled a train in preservation. There is no known target date for the completion of its restoration.

The final Class 40 to be withdrawn was fleet pioneer 40122 (D200), which had been retained by BR until April 1988. It was then claimed by the National Railway Museum and moved to York as part of the National Collection.

Over the following two decades, D200 spent long periods on display at York, but also spent extended periods on loan to the ELR and the NYMR, as well as occasional working visits to other heritage lines. However, in 2007 the locomotive suffered a generator failure while at the NYMR and returned to York for repairs, which have not yet

been carried out. In 2017 the locomotive was repainted into BR green livery by Heritage Painting to address the deteriorating condition of the bodywork and paintwork.

In April 2018 it made another return to the ELR, where it was displayed as a static exhibit on Platform 1 at Bury Bolton Street as part of the CFPS' '40s@60' event to commemorate the 60th anniversary of D200 entering service on BR – an event which brought together six of the seven survivors, with under-restoration 40118 being the only example missing from the party.

Now repainted into BR blue, 40012 *Aureol* visited the East Lancashire Railway for six months during 2018. On May 7, 2018, 40012 heads into Ramsbottom with a Rawtenstall to Heywood service. It has since returned to the Midland Railway Butterley for repairs to its turbos. NIGEL VALENTINE

In 2007, the CFPS repainted 40145 into Large Logo blue livery, which was unauthentic for Class 40s. While somewhat controversial, the new look certainly attracted attention and the main line-registered 40145 was also named *East Lancashire Railway*, carrying the nameplates once carried by 37418. The locomotive passes Cockwood while working the Penzance to Portsmouth 'Cornish Explorer' railtour on June 27, 2009. TERRY EYRES

The second preserved Class 40 to return to the main line has been D213 *Andania*, which was recertified for operating over Network Rail metals in 2018. The locomotive is privately owned but has been hired to Locomotive Services Ltd at Crewe for three years. On August 9, 2018, D213 works a loaded test run from Crewe to Telford Central through Croes Newydd. TERRY EYRES

Still awaiting its return to active service, the owners of 40118 at Tyseley Locomotive Works are carrying out a comprehensive rebuild of the locomotive to a very high standard. On a snowy December 12, 2017, 40118 stands at Tyseley Locomotive Works, with the other end of the locomotive housed beneath a makeshift restoration shelter. RICHARD THOMPSON

LOCO	NAME	PREVIOUS NUMBERS	OWNER	LOCATION
D200		D200, 40122	NRM	RMY
D212	*Aureol*	D212, 40012, 97407	C40A	MRB
D213	*Andania*	D213, 40013	Private	BHR
40106	*Atlantic Conveyor*	D306, 40106	CFPS	SVR
40118		D318, 40118, 97408	16SVTS	TLW
40135		D335, 40135, 97406	CFPS	ELR
40145		D345, 40145	CFPS	BHR

OWNERS KEY: 16SVTS – 16SVT Society, C40A – Class 40 Appeal, CFPS – Class 40 Preservation Society, NRM – National Railway Museum

LOCATION KEY: BHR – Barrow Hill, ELR – East Lancashire Railway, MRB – Midland Railway Butterley, RMY – Railway Museum York, SVR – Severn Valley Railway, TLW – Tyseley Locomotive Works

MAIN LINE PRESERVED CLASS 40s

The CFPS had made no secret of its desire to return 40145 to main line service, operating railtours and special workings on Network Rail metals. After a lengthy period of time preparing the locomotive for recertification it was successfully approved for operating on the main line in the summer of 2002, making its debut main line railtour in November 2002 when it hauled 'The Christmas Cracker' for Pathfinder Tours.

Since that successful return to main line action, 40145 has made numerous appearances all around the country on railtours, with the CFPS promoting most of its own railtours in recent years, with the locomotive being operated by West Coast Railway Company.

40145 was temporarily retired from the main line in 2018 to allow a bogie overhaul to take place, as its tyres had reached scrapping size. The overhauled wheelsets for the locomotive were delivered back to Barrow Hill in June 2019 and it is anticipated that it will return to main line and heritage railway use following the completion of repairs.

D213 *Andania* was recertified for main line use in summer 2018 and has been placed on a three-year hire to Locomotive Services Ltd (LSL), where it will be used to haul various railtours for LSL tour company Saphos Trains, operating out of LSL's operating base at the former Crewe Diesel Depot. The locomotive worked its first main line tours in August 2018.

At the time of writing in summer 2019, both main line certified Class 40s are out of service and are located at Barrow Hill. D213 is undergoing engine repairs before being returned to LSL at Crewe, while 40145 is out of service having new tyres fitted to its bogies and other repairs carried out. Once work has been completed, 40145 should return to its East Lancashire Railway base and will be able to return to main line use again.

MAIN LINE REGISTERED PRESERVED CLASS 40s

Loco	Owner	National Network Certification Status
D213	Privately Owned	Main Line Certified (undergoing repairs)
40145	Class 40 Preservation Society	Main Line Certified (undergoing repairs)

CLASS 41

41001 stands on display at the National Railway Museum in York. Following its withdrawal, 41001 was presented to the NRM with a sectioned Paxman Valenta power unit preventing it from operating under its own power. The 125 Group has since overhauled the locomotive and fitted a replacement overhauled engine. STEVE KEMP

While Class 41 was originally allocated for the five North British diesel-hydraulic 'Warship Class' locomotives, none of these locomotives survived long enough to receive TOPS classifications and Class 41 was reused to signify the two prototype High Speed Train power car locomotives.

The two power cars were built by BREL at Crewe Works in 1972 along with accompanying Mark 3 trailer coaches to try and introduce a new form of high speed train on to the BR network. The Class 41 locomotives were designed in a very short period of time. Fitted with a Paxman Valenta 12RP200L power unit, these were like nothing that had been seen on the railway before and their capability to regularly run at high speed would allow BR to plan for the new High Speed Trains to transform some of its more prestigious main line services.

The distinctive new train, painted in BR grey and blue livery, entered service in 1972 and the following year it achieved a speed of 143.2mph, a record speed for diesel traction at the time. After the prototype HST had entered service it was reclassified as a Class 252 multiple unit, with the two power cars 41001 and 41002 being renumbered 43000 and 43001 respectively. The production power cars that were produced later were then numbered from 43002 onwards.

In 1975 the prototype HST was reallocated to the Western Region and worked for a period on the WR before the set was withdrawn from traffic in 1976. It then saw use with the Railway Technical Centre at Derby, surviving in traffic with

LOCO	BR IDENTITIES	OWNER	LOCATION
41001	41001, 43000, ADB975812	NRM	GCRN

OWNER KEY: NRM – National Railway Museum

LOCATION KEY: GCRN – Great Central Railway (Nottingham)

the RTC until 1983, when it was taken out of use and stored pending disposal. The experiences gained with the two Class 41 locomotives proved invaluable in the development of the production built Class 43 HST power cars, which have gone on to be one of the most successful designs of locomotives to have served the UK railway network.

THE PRESERVED CLASS 41

While 41002 was scrapped in 1990, 41001 was claimed for display at the National Railway Museum following its withdrawal and it spent several years in the Great Hall at the NRM in York rubbing shoulders with the other iconic locomotives which make up the National Collection. However, at the time it was preserved, it was fitted with a sectioned engine, to show visitors to the NRM how the power unit had been built.

With interest in the High Speed Trains growing over the years among enthusiasts, the 125 Group was formed in 1994 and in 2011 agreement was reached between the 125 Group and the National Railway Museum for 41001 to be placed on long-term loan with them with a view to it being returned to serviceable condition.

41001 was moved to Neville Hill Depot in Leeds and the sectioned engine was removed and replaced with an overhauled Paxman Valenta 12RP200L engine, as well as a thorough overhaul of the locomotive and its components. It later moved to the Great Central Railway (Nottingham) and following completion of its rebuild, it hauled its first trains in

preservation over the GCRN during 2015.

Since returning to service, 41001 has been joined by a small fleet of Mark 3 coaches, some of which have been repainted in matching grey and blue livery, and the HST and its trailers have visited a number of preserved lines over the past few years.

In 2019 during a visit to the Severn Valley Railway, it was discovered that there were problems with the engine fitted to 41001 and it was immediately taken out of service. It has since moved back to Neville Hill Depot for repairs to be carried out and it is expected that it will return to the GCRN at Ruddington once work has been completed

During a working visit to the Nene Valley Railway, 41001 basks in the sun during a stop at Wansford station on April 10, 2016, during the NVR's biannual diesel weekend. The revival of the prototype HST power car locomotive is one of the recent highlights of the diesel preservation movement. ANDREW SEWELL

CLASS 41

BUILT:	BREL Crewe Works, 1972
ENGINE:	Paxman Valenta 12RP200L
NO. BUILT:	2
NO. PRESERVED:	1
OTHER SURVIVORS:	0

On May 4, 2019, 41001 hauls its train towards Haworth during a visit to the Keighley & Worth Valley Railway. Another joy of the restoration of 41001 is that the matching rake of coaches helps increase capacity at the events it attends. The Virgin Trains-liveried coaches will eventually be repainted to match the grey and blue coaches which have already been treated. KEVIN DELANEY

Both surviving Class 42 'Warships', D821 *Greyhound* and D832 *Onslaught* have been reunited on a number of occasions during their time in preservation. The most recent reunion of the pair was during the Spring Diesel Event on the Severn Valley Railway in 2018. The locomotives pass Northwood Lane in Bewdley, with a service from Bridgnorth to Kidderminster on May 19, 2018.
KEVIN DELANEY

CLASS 42

The British Railways Western Region (WR) Class 42 'Warship' diesel-hydraulic locomotives were based externally on the German V200 Class and the locomotives bore many similarities to their German counterparts. With curved cab nose ends, the locomotives were distinctive and eye-catching in their appearance.

The first three, D800-D802, were built at Swindon Works in 1958 and these differed somewhat from the production locomotives, which were built between 1959 and 1961. The production locomotives were numbered D803-D832 and D866-D870. A third batch was built by North British and were numbered D833-D865, but these had a different classification and none of them survived.

The locomotives were fitted with two Maybach MD650 power units, with the exception of D830 *Majestic*, which was fitted with Paxman Ventura power units instead of Maybach. They were a lightweight design, weighing just 78 tonnes and were fitted with Mekydro hydraulic transmission and were able to operate at speeds of up to 90mph.

Apart from the prototype locomotives, all of them were capable of working in multiple.

The locomotives gained their 'Warship' name due to all of the locomotives, with the exception of two, being named after naval vessels and all carried the wording 'Warship Class' below the chosen name on the nameplate. Pioneer D800 was named *Sir Brian Robertson* after the chairman of the British Transport Commission, while D812 was named *Royal Naval Reserve 1859-1959*.

They were delivered in dark green livery, with a grey stripe along the bodyside and yellow warning panels on the cab fronts. The WR later decided to repaint most of the fleet in maroon, before most of them were painted into the then-new BR corporate identity of blue.

They saw use hauling services out of Paddington and were also regularly found working services on the Waterloo to Exeter line. Being vacuum braked, they could not be used with newer air-braked rolling stock and the design of the locomotives meant there was no space to fit air braking to the locomotives.

The diesel-hydraulic designs had fallen out of favour with BR and the lack of space to install air brakes and electric train heating equipment were some of the reasons why they were slated for early withdrawal. Under TOPS the locomotives were classified as Class 42, but none gained a BR five-figure number identity.

The three prototype locomotives were the first to be withdrawn, with D801 *Vanguard* becoming the first to be stood down in August 1968, after just 10 years in traffic. The other two followed shortly afterwards. Withdrawals of the production locomotives began in August 1971 and was completed in December 1972.

D832 *Onslaught* was moved to Derby following withdrawal, where it was used for research purposes at the Railway Technical Centre. This locomotive remained at Derby until it was bought for preservation in 1979.

D818 *Glory* outlived its fellow locomotives by several years thanks to it being put on display at Swindon Works following withdrawal and it was restored to original BR green livery by Swindon apprentices and the locomotive was placed alongside the turntable outside the Swindon Works complex. However, in 1985, after donating many of its remaining components to the two surviving preserved 'Warships', BR decided to dispose of the remains of the locomotive and D818 was scrapped in November 1985.

LOCO	NAME	BR IDENTITIES	OWNER	LOCATION
D821	*Greyhound*	D821	DTG	SVR
D832	*Onslaught*	D832	BHG	ELR

OWNERS KEY: BHG – Bury Hydraulic Group, DTG – Diesel Traction Group

LOCATION KEY: ELR – East Lancashire Railway, SVR – Severn Valley Railway

Showing off the distinctive lines of the Class 42, D832 *Onslaught* presents an imposing image as it approaches Townsend Fold level crossing with a Rawtenstall to Heywood service on September 22, 2018. KEVIN DELANEY

In 2013, D821 *Greyhound* returned to its former home on the North Yorkshire Moors Railway for a working visit. On September 13, 2013, D821 stands at the head of its train at Grosmont prior to working a service to Pickering. As can be seen from the headboard, the 'Warship' was celebrating its 40th anniversary in preservation – the first diesel locomotive to be privately purchased. ANDREW SEWELL

THE PRESERVED CLASS 42s

As one of the early casualties for withdrawal, the Class 42 locomotives are only represented by two surviving examples, with D821 *Greyhound* based on the Severn Valley Railway (SVR) and D832 *Onslaught* at the East Lancashire Railway (ELR).

D821 will always hold a significant place in the history of preserved diesel locomotives, as it was officially the first main line diesel locomotive to be bought privately for preservation back in 1973 by the late Colin Massingham, who along with some friends went on to form the Diesel Traction Group, who still care for the locomotive along with three others.

Initially moved to Didcot Railway Centre, D821 spent spells under restoration at Reading Gas Works and Swindon Works before moving to the North Yorkshire Moors Railway in 1981. Ten years later it moved to a new home base on the SVR, which remains its

home, and after spells out of service undergoing overhaul the locomotive is once again serviceable and remains a popular member of the SVR diesel fleet.

D832 owes its survival thanks to it being used by BR's Research Department at the Railway Technical Centre at Derby, where it was used in departmental stock. It was bought for preservation in May 1979 and after being displayed at the Horwich Works Open Day in August that year it was moved to a new home on the fledgling ELR in Bury, where it was restored to service, becoming the first ex-BR diesel locomotive to haul a passenger train on

CLASS 42

BUILT: BR Swindon 1958-1961	
ENGINE: Two Maybach MD650 Engines	
NO. BUILT: 38	
NO. PRESERVED: 2	
OTHER SURVIVORS: 0	

the restored ELR when it reopened to passenger services between Bury and Ramsbottom in July 1987.

Although the locomotive, like D821, has extensively travelled around the country visiting other preserved lines, including an extended five-year loan to the West Somerset Railway, D832 has recently celebrated its 40th anniversary in preservation with a celebratory working weekend on the ELR. While privately owned, D832 is in the custodianship of the Bury Hydraulic Group.

Even though both preserved Class 42s are in working order and well maintained, it is unlikely that either will be ever recertified for main line running on Network Rail, as the DTG is already heavily committed to operating D1015 *Western Champion* on the main line. The BHG is happy to operate its locomotives at the ELR and on the heritage railway gala circuit.

D832 *Onslaught* stands at Swanage station in between duties while paying a working visit to the hugely popular annual diesel event and real ale festival on May 6, 2016. MARTIN HART

The maroon livery with small yellow warning panels certainly suits the design of the 'Warships' as shown on D821 *Greyhound*, while awaiting departure from Hampton Loade station on its home railway, the Severn Valley Railway, on May 20, 2011. MARTIN HART

CLASS 43

Following the development of the pioneer High Speed Train Class 41 locomotives, 41001 and 41002, British Rail began a programme to design and build a large fleet of High Speed Trains.

As such a new fleet of 197 locomotives were ordered from British Rail Engineering Ltd at Crewe Works. They had been designed by Kenneth Grange, who restyled the power cars from the prototypes and his suggestions were taken on board by BR. Originally it had been intended that the power cars and their trailers would be retained in set formations and as such they were classified as diesel-electric multiple units and would be given the classification under TOPS of Class 253 and Class 254. The power cars were numbered 43002 to 43198.

However, following their introduction, it was decided that the power cars should be classified as locomotives and the Class 253 and Class 254 power cars were given the classification of Class 43 (which prior to the HST had been carried by the Western Region 'Warship Class' diesel hydraulic locomotives, although all had been scrapped).

The first example was delivered to BR in 1975 and was painted in a distinctive black and yellow livery at the front, while towards the rear of the vehicle an angled change saw blue and grey livery applied, so that it matched the coaching stock that would run behind it. The locomotives also carried large InterCity 125 branding on the sides in black with a white outline to the lettering and a large BR double-arrow logo.

Subsequently, the black on the power car livery was replaced with blue to give a more uniform look to the train and since then the HST power cars have carried numerous liveries, especially since the railway network was privatised in the 1990s, with a host of different operators applying their liveries to the trains.

The Class 43 power cars were originally fitted with a Paxman Valenta 12RP200L engine and could be operated at speeds of up to 125mph, although various locomotives have been fitted with MTU 16V4000 engines or Paxman 12VP185L engines to replace the original engines. The newer designs offered improved fuel efficiency, while also helping to reduce the amount of emissions from the original engines. Some of the re-engined locomotives have received amended fleet numbers to reflect the change, but this is not the case for all operators to use them.

43002 *Sir Kenneth Grange* poses on the turntable in the National Railway Museum at York during a visit to the museum on October 2, 2016. This locomotive is due to become a permanent addition to the National Railway Museum fleet imminently and this scene will become a regular sight. JACK BOSKETT

TOP: Photographed operating at speed, the pioneer Class 43 HST power car 43002 *Sir Kenneth Grange* is captured working a Great Western Railway service through Shrivenham on May 18, 2019. JACK BOSKETT

LOCO	NAME	BR IDENTITIES	OWNER	LOCATION
43002	*Sir Kenneth Grange*	43002	NRM	RMY

OWNER KEY: NRM – National Railway Museum

LOCATION KEY: RMY – Railway Museum York

The Class 43s have seen extensive use on the high-speed services that operate around the UK and they have certainly made their mark on the history of the railways. The design has proved to be very robust and reliable and they are known for being an efficient train that is relatively straightforward to maintain. With many of the locomotives now having been in service for well over 40 years, they are still providing front line services across the country at an age where many locomotive types would have long since been retired.

Only three Class 43s have been scrapped and all of these have been as a result of serious collisions. Those scrapped so far have been 43011, 43019 and 43173. However, as new train fleets begin to replace the traditional InterCity 125 HSTs, a number of Class 43 power cars are now being stored and it is likely many of these will not be returned to use.

43002 *Sir Kenneth Grange* was one of the locomotives displayed at the Great Western Railway open day event at Old Oak Common Depot on September 2, 2017. The event was held to recognise the history of the famous depot, which has since been closed to make way for the HS2 route, which will pass through the site. KEVIN DELANEY

Following the end of its working life, 43002 *Sir Kenneth Grange* was specially moved by road from Plymouth Laira Depot to the STEAM museum in Swindon for a one-day display on July 17, 2019, as it made its way towards eventual preservation as part of the National Collection. The locomotive then moved to Ely for storage pending its acceptance at York, when it will be officially preserved. JACK BOSKETT

THE PRESERVED CLASS 43

43002 *Sir Kenneth Grange* has become the latest diesel locomotive to be preserved for the National Collection following its withdrawal by train operator Great Western Railway and it was returned to leasing company Angel Trains.

Having been earmarked for preservation following the end of front-line services, 43002 was prepared for handover to the National Railway Museum by staff at Plymouth Laira Depot on behalf of Angel Trains.

On July 17, 2019, it moved by road to Swindon for display outside the STEAM museum in what was thought to be the first part of its journey into preservation. However, following its day in the spotlight it was moved to Ely Papworth for continued storage pending it being moved north to the Railway Museum at York, which is expected to take place over the coming weeks and could well have already happened by the time this publication appears in print.

The partnership between the 125 Group and the NRM with regards to the operation of Class 41 pioneer HST power car 41001 has proved to be a very successful partnership. The Class 41 is now fully operational, having been out of service for many years before the 125 Group got involved in its reactivation and whether this sets the scene for a possible future operating role for 43002 in the future remains to be seen.

CLASS 43

BUILT: BREL Crewe Works, 1975-1982

ENGINE: Paxman Valenta 12RP200L (original engine, all since replaced)

NO. BUILT: 197

NO. PRESERVED: 1

OTHER SURVIVORS: 193

OTHER CLASS 43s

Although the iconic HST Class 43s are now reaching their twilight years, the locomotives are still very much in demand and quite a few of them have a reasonably secure medium-term future.

With 20 examples now stored out of use and three of the fleet now scrapped, the remainder are still on hire to various train operating companies where they are still in active use on a daily basis, more than 40 years after their introduction.

However, new fleets of high-speed trains are in the process of being introduced to some operators and this will mean more Class 43s can be taken out of service, with the Hull Trains and LNER fleets due to go off-lease before the end of 2019. East Midlands Trains are also due to hand back their HST power cars to their leasing company at some stage, although no target date for this to take place has yet been announced. Additionally, some of the Class 43s in use by Great Western Railway are also due to go off-lease before the end of 2019, although the operator will retain a number of its locomotives for use on Cardiff to Penzance services.

CrossCountry are also retaining their small fleet of Class 43s for the foreseeable future, while perhaps the most exciting recent development for the Class 43s and their Mark 3 trailer coaches has been the move by Scotrail for operating on services in Scotland under the Inter7City brand. The HSTs will work services between Edinburgh and Glasgow to Aberdeen and Inverness. The trains are being refurbished by Wabtec at Doncaster to give them a fresh new look and the standard of refurbishment of these trains has gained the operator many plaudits from observers who have tried the new services.

Network Rail also has three Class 43 power cars which are based at Derby for use with their Network Measurement Train, which monitors the condition of the rail network, with the train covering many of the high-speed routes. These locomotives are painted into Network Rail's vivid yellow livery.

It is clear that the programme of replacing the ageing HSTs, which helped to revolutionise high-speed rail travel in the UK, is now well under way. However, there is still very much a future for many of the power cars for several more years and the Class 43 story is far from over.

NON-PRESERVED SURVIVING CLASS 43s

CROSSCOUNTRY: 43207, 43285, 43301, 43303, 43304, 43321, 43357, 43366, 43378, 43384

EAST MIDLANDS TRAINS: 43043, 43044, 43045, 43046, 43047, 43048, 43049, 43050, 43052, 43054, 43055, 43058, 43059, 43060, 43061, 43064, 43066, 43073, 43075, 43076, 43081, 43082, 43083, 43089, 43423, 43465, 43467, 43468, 43480, 43484

GREAT WESTERN RAILWAY: 43004, 43005, 43009, 43016, 43022, 43024, 43029, 43040, 43041, 43042, 43063, 43071, 43086, 43088, 43092, 43093, 43094, 43097, 43098, 43122, 43153, 43154, 43155, 43156, 43158, 43160, 43161, 43162, 43170, 43171, 43172, 43180, 43186, 43187, 43188, 43189, 43191, 43192, 43193, 43194, 43196, 43198

HULL TRAINS: 43010, 43020, 43023, 43027

LNER: 43206, 43208, 43238, 43239, 43251, 43257, 43272, 43274, 43277, 43290, 43295, 43296, 43299, 43300, 43302, 43305, 43306, 43307, 43308, 43309, 43310, 43311, 43312, 43313, 43314, 43315, 43316, 43317, 43318, 43319, 43320, 43367

NETWORK RAIL: 43013, 43014, 43062,

SCOTRAIL: 43003, 43012, 43015, 43021, 43026, 43028, 43030, 43031, 43032, 43033, 43034, 43035, 43036, 43037, 43124, 43125, 43126, 43127, 43128, 43129, 43130, 43131, 43132, 43133, 43134, 43135, 43136, 43137, 43138, 43139, 43140, 43141, 43142, 43143, 43144, 43145, 43146, 43147, 43148, 43149, 43150, 43151, 43152, 43153, 43154, 43155, 43156, 43157, 43163, 43164, 43168, 43169, 43177, 43178, 43179, 43181, 43182, 43183

STORED: 43017, 43018, 43024, 43025, 43053, 43056, 43069, 43070, 43078, 43079, 43087, 43091, 43159, 43165, 43174, 43185, 43190, 43193, 43195, 43197

• Please note that some of these locomotives are operational, while others are stored.

D8 *Penyghent* stands at Derby Etches Park for an open day event on September 13, 2014. This event also saw D4 *Great Gable* on display and this was the first time that the two Class 44s had been reunited since entering preservation in the early 1980s. MARTIN HART

CLASS 44

In 1959 British Rail's Derby Works unveiled the first of 10 pilot scheme Type Four locomotives. Numbered D1 and carrying the name *Scafell Pike*, the locomotive cut a powerful and imposing image as it rolled off the East Midlands production line. The locomotives were fitted with a powerful Sulzer 12LDA28-A power unit and could operate at up to 75mph. They were heavy locomotives and were built on a 1Co-Co1 wheel arrangement to take account of their size and weight.

The 10 locomotives were numbered D1-D10 and were all named after mountains in England and Wales, leading to them becoming known as 'Peaks'. The initial order of locomotives was followed by two further orders for production locomotives and these were also commonly referred to as 'Peaks', even though most of them went unnamed and those that were named tended to be more closely associated with the military and regiments. The two production orders were given different classifications to separate them from the original pilot locomotives.

D1-D10 were all delivered in dark green livery with a thin grey band on the lower bodyside as a relief. As with other types, they gradually gained small yellow warning panels on the cabs and then full yellow ends. Under TOPS they became Class 44 and their BR identity saw their numbers simply change from D1-10 to 44001-44010 respectively.

All 10 locomotives were also repainted into BR blue livery with full yellow ends.

The pilot scheme 'Peaks' were quickly relegated from passenger workings, due to their lower maximum speeds than the production examples, which were better suited to passenger work. The decision to make the '44s' essentially a freight locomotive meant that they subsequently had their steam heat generators removed.

Being less useful than the Class 45s and 46s and generally not used as passenger locomotives was the main reason why the Class 44s were eventually chosen as the first 'Peaks' to be withdrawn from traffic. First to be withdrawn was 44003 *Skiddaw* in July 1976, with the final examples, 44004 *Great Gable*, 44007 *Ingleborough* and 44008 *Penyghent* withdrawn in November 1980. After a working life of around 30 years, BR ensured that the Class 44s were retired from service in style and the final three locomotives were used on various commemorative railtours before withdrawal.

LOCO	NAME	BR IDENTITIES	OWNER	LOCATION
D4	*Great Gable*	D4, 44004	PLC	MRB
D8	*Penyghent*	D8, 44008	NNLG	PKR

OWNERS KEY: NNLG – North Notts Locomotive Group, PLC – Peak Locomotive Company

LOCATION KEY: MRB – Midland Railway Butterley, PKR – Peak Rail

During a visit to the East Lancashire Railway in July 1998, D4 *Great Gable* is disguised as long-scrapped pioneer 1 *Scafell Pike*. The disguised locomotive stands at Ramsbottom during a summer diesel event. STEVE KEMP

In original BR green, D4 *Great Gable* stands at Butterley on the Midland Railway Butterley on September 26, 2009 while working a train from Swanwick Junction to Hammersmith. STEVE KEMP

THE PRESERVED CLASS 44s

Of the 10 Class 44s, two found salvation in preservation, with D4 *Great Gable* preserved on the Midland Railway Butterley (MRB) by the Peak Locomotive Company. D8 *Penyghent* is based on Peak Rail, therefore, ensuring that both preserved 'Peaks' are located in the East Midlands where they spent most of their working lives and within a short distance of where they were built in Derby.

D4 has recently undergone an overhaul at Swanwick on the MRB by its owners and has been repainted into BR blue, although retaining its D4 identity. The locomotive was due to re-enter service in spring 2019, but some teething problems with its recommissioning were experienced and it is hoped that it will return to regular use in the near future. During its time in preservation it has carried both BR blue and BR green at various times.

D8 was initially preserved in Scotland at the Strathspey Railway, but moved to Peak Rail at Matlock in 1987. Ever since it was returned to service by the North Notts Locomotive Group it has carried BR green livery.

As Peak Rail services require top-and-tail operation out of Matlock station, which is shared with East Midlands Railway services, Peak Rail trains are normally formed of a steam locomotive at one end of the train and a diesel locomotive at the other. This has meant that D8 has been regularly in use on the railway, especially as it has been the only operational main line diesel locomotive on the railway for the past

couple of years.

Other former BR diesel locomotives should be joining the Peak Rail locomotive roster over the coming months in the shape of Class 25, D7659, and Class 37, 37310, but D8 is likely to remain a regular performer on the line.

An event at Derby Etches Park in 2014 saw D4 and D8 displayed alongside each other for the first time since they were preserved and a double-headed train hauled by the pair is still on many enthusiasts' wish lists.

Hopefully at some point in the future they can be reunited on the front of a train.

While examples from Class 45 and 46 'Peaks' have operated on the main line following preservation, it is very unlikely that either of the preserved Class 44s will ever be certified for main line running and they seem destined to remain restricted to operating at heritage lines.

CLASS 44

BUILT:	BR Derby Works, 1959-1960
ENGINE:	Sulzer 12LDA28-A
NO. BUILT:	10
NO. PRESERVED:	2
OTHER SURVIVORS:	0

A Class 44 standing at Darley Dale station on the former Midland main line is very appropriate, as D8 *Penyghent* works a Peak Rail service from Matlock to Rowsley South on July 6, 2013. The locomotive has now been based at Peak Rail for longer than it was in service on British Rail. STEVE KEMP

Due to re-enter service following an overhaul, D4 *Great Gable* has recently been repainted into BR blue livery at its Midland Railway Butterley base. The locomotive is owned by the Peak Locomotive Company and the Class 44 has regularly left its Midlands base to attend diesel events at various heritage lines. Still awaiting numbers and other decals, D4 stands outside the diesel shed at Swanwick Junction on April 24, 2019. PAUL HADFIELD

CLASS 45

The Class 45 was the main production run of locomotives ordered by BR following evaluation of the 10 Type Four Sulzer 'Peak' locomotives, D1-D10, which were built as a result of the 1955 British Railways Modernisation Plan.

The order was for 127 locomotives, with construction of them shared between Derby and Crewe Works. They were numbered D11-D137 and were fitted with a Sulzer 12LDA28-B power unit, which could operate at a higher maximum speed of 90mph. Construction of this order took place between 1960 and 1962 and under TOPS these locomotives became Class 45.

Under TOPS the renumbering of these locomotives into the 45XXX series was rather more haphazard than most other types of locomotives and the Class 45s were renumbered in the order in which they visited works for attention, rather than the order in which they had been built.

As with the Class 44s, the main operating area for the Class 45s was around the Midland main line and they were regularly used on services between Manchester and London St Pancras.

When built, all the fleet were fitted with steam-heat generators, but subsequently the decision was taken to convert 50 of the locomotives, with their steam-heat boilers being removed and replaced with electric train heating equipment. These 50 locomotives were classified Class 45/1 under TOPS classification, while the remaining 77 unmodified locomotives became Class 45/0 and they retained their steam heat boilers throughout their working lives.

The Class 45/1s found use across the rail network, especially after most of their initial passenger work was displaced following the delivery of the High Speed Trains. However, it would still be more than a decade after the introduction of the HST before the final Class 45 was stood down from service.

Withdrawals of the Class 45s began in July 1977 when 45067 was officially taken out of service after suffering serious collision damage. Withdrawals of several Class 45/0s took place towards the end of 1980 and the demise of the fleet then accelerated throughout the 1980s with the final service 'Peaks' being withdrawn in August 1988.

One locomotive, 45106, was retained for railtour use and carried a variation of BR green livery, but it was withdrawn in February 1989 after suffering fire damage and consideration to reinstate one of the withdrawn Class 45/1s, but this never happened due to the selected locomotive not being suitable for reinstatement, bringing the curtain down on 'Peak' operations on British Rail.

After the withdrawal of the final Class 45/0 in 1988, a small number of Class 45/1s were retained for a few months, although the last example was withdrawn in February 1989. As with most other popular locomotive classes, the end of their time on British Rail was commemorated with a series of farewell tours, taking them back to many of the areas they had served over the previous 29 years.

A close-up profile of 45041 *Royal Tank Regiment* outside the Matthew Kirtley Museum at Swanwick Junction on the Midland Railway Butterley on September 11, 2006, with 44004 Great Gable stabled behind its younger cousin. ANDY COWARD

Entering the atmospheric surroundings of Loughborough station on the Great Central Railway, 45041 *Royal Tank Regiment* hauls a freight service on September 29, 2014. In reality this was a posed photograph at an evening photographic session for the East Midlands Railway Photographic Society, which organises many popular diesel photographic charters at heritage lines across the country. TOM MCATEE

THE PRESERVED CLASS 45s

Twelve Class 45 'Peaks' are still in existence some 30 years after the type were removed from service on British Rail. While one of these locomotives has now been sold on for commercial use with Locomotive Services Ltd and another remains in very poor condition and likely to be scrapped at some stage, the future for the other 10 preserved examples is much brighter. The majority of the survivors are from the Class 45/1 electric train heat fitted sub-class, but three Class 45/0s still remain.

Restored in original BR green livery is D123 on the Great Central Railway (GCR) at Loughborough. Following

the naming theme of some of the other Class 45s, D123 has been named *Leicestershire & Derbyshire Yeomanry* since being based on the GCR and it is a regular performer on the line. The GCR is the only heritage railway in the UK to feature a double-track formation for a long section of its line, making the appearance of a 'Peak' on a rake of stock look very authentically main line.

Two Class 45s are currently based on the East Lancashire Railway (ELR), with the Peak Locomotive Company's 45108 on long-term loan to the ELR while 45135 *3rd Carabinier* is undergoing a prolonged engine overhaul and rebuild. 45135 has now been out of service undergoing attention for more than a decade and once it returns to service on the ELR it is likely that 45108 will be returned to its Midland Railway Butterley base.

The ELR is one of just a few heritage lines to feature electric train heat-

CLASS 45

BUILT:	BR Derby Works and Crewe Works, 1960-1962
ENGINE:	Sulzer 12LDA28-B
NO. BUILT:	127
NO. PRESERVED:	11
OTHER SURVIVORS:	1

Representing the BR green era, D123 *Leicestershire & Derbyshire Yeomanry* passes Kinchley Lane on the double-track section of the Great Central Railway on November 17, 2018. At the time of writing this locomotive is the only preserved member of the Class 45 fleet carrying BR green livery. NIGEL VALENTINE

Class 45/0 45060 *Sherwood Forester* was one of the visitors to the 2015 Swanage Railway diesel event and real ale festival and departs from Harmans Cross station with a Norden to Swanage service on May 7, 2015. TOM MCATEE

After several years out of use at Crewe Heritage Centre, 45108 was purchased from its previous owner by the Peak Locomotive Company and moved to the Midland Railway Butterley, where it was reactivated. It has since moved to the East Lancashire Railway on loan and it is expected to stay at Bury until ELR-based 45135 3rd Carabinier returns to service following an engine overhaul. An immaculate 45108 passes through Burrs on the ELR on July 8, 2017 during the ELR summer diesel event. NIGEL VALENTINE

45133 is another 'Peak' that is based on the Midland Railway Butterley, but is owned by the Class 45/1 Preservation Society. It is currently undergoing an overhaul at its MRB home, but on October 2, 2009, 45133 glistens in the sun at Wansford station during a visit to the Nene Valley Railway. MARTIN HART

equipped coaches, so that the ETH capability of the Class 45/1s is useful for the railway, which operates services throughout the year.

Also usually based on the Midland Railway Butterley is 45041 *Royal Tank Regiment* and 45133. 45041 is another 'Peak' owned by the Peak Locomotive Company and it is currently on long-term loan to the Nene Valley Railway in Peterborough, while 45132 belongs to the Class 45/1 Preservation Society and is currently being overhauled at Swanwick Junction on its home railway.

45132 spent many years based on the Mid Hants Railway, but has not worked a train since 1999 and has been undergoing a prolonged rebuild over the past 20 years. It is now located on the Epping Ongar Railway and work on its restoration is now nearing completion and the locomotive made its first moves under its own power in July 2019, with its return to passenger use expected during the summer of 2019.

45149 was one of many locomotives

bought from BR by celebrity record producer and businessman Pete Waterman and it initially moved to Crewe Heritage Centre. However, following the sale of the majority of Mr Waterman's locomotive collection during the mid-1990s, it was purchased by the Cotswold Mainline Diesel Group and moved to the Gloucestershire & Warwickshire Railway (GWR), where it underwent a complete rebuild and is now in regular use on the GWR.

Barrow Hill Roundhouse is now home to 45060 *Sherwood Forester*, which was initially restored by the Pioneer Diesel Group at its former base at Matlock on Peak Rail. The locomotive was restored to BR green, regaining its D100 identity, before attending various diesel events and extended visits to heritage railways.

When Barrow Hill was purchased as a preservation base, the Pioneer Diesel Group relocated most of its collection to the new railway centre and 45060, as it had then become following a repaint into BR blue, has remained a fixture

at the Chesterfield site ever since, although it still regularly visits other heritage railways and remains a popular locomotive on the heritage railway gala circuit. There are now just two Class 45s which have yet to haul a train in preservation, although these two face very different futures.

At Barrow Hill, volunteers from the Pioneer Diesel Group are actively working on completing the long-running restoration of 45105. The locomotive is just one of several that are owned by the Pioneer Diesel Group and with the group also having taken on the contract restoration of 46010 on behalf of the D05 Preservation Company Ltd over the past 18 months, the completion of 45105 has been on the back burner for some time, although work on it recommenced in summer 2019.

At the other end of the scale, 45015 spent a number of years at Toton depot in Nottinghamshire and was used for re-railing training exercises, prior to being sold by English Welsh & Scottish

45149 has been restored to service over a number of years by the Cotswold Mainline Diesel Group on the Gloucestershire & Warwickshire Railway. The immaculate BR blue 'Peak' runs around its train at Cheltenham Racecourse station on the GWR on October 8, 2017. KEVIN DELANEY

LOCO	NAME	BR IDENTITIES	OWNER	LOCATION
45015		D14, 45015	BFL	BFL
45041	*Royal Tank Regiment*	D53, 45041	PLC	NVR
45060	*Sherwood Forester*	D100, 45060	PDG	BHR
45105		D86, 45105	PDG	BHR
45108		D120, 45108	PLC	ELR
45112	*Royal Army Ordnance Corps*	D61, 45112	Private	Nemesis
D123	*Leicestershire & Derbyshire Yeomanry*	D123, 45125	Private	GCR
45132		D22, 45132	Private	EOR
45133		D40, 45133	C45/1PS	MRB
45135	*3rd Carabinier*	D99, 45135	PDG	ELR
45149		D135, 45149	CMDG	GWR

OWNER KEY: BFL – Battlefield Railway, C45/1PS – Class 45/1 Preservation Society, CMDG – Cotswolds Mainline Diesel Group, PDG – Pioneer Diesel Group, PLC – Peak Locomotive Company

LOCATION KEY: BFL – Battlefield Railway, BHR – Barrow Hill Roundhouse, ELR – East Lancashire Railway, EOR – Epping Ongar Railway, GCR – Great Central Railway, GWR – Gloucestershire & Warwickshire Railway, MRB – Midland Railway Butterley, Nemesis – Nemesis Rail Burton upon Trent, NVR – Nene Valley Railway

In glorious sunshine a BR green 'Peak' hauling a rake of maroon Mark 1 coaches evokes many memories, as D123 *Leicestershire & Derbyshire Yeomanry* stands at Quorn & Woodhouse station on the Great Central Railway on April 17, 2010. MARTIN HART

45112 *Royal Army Ordnance Corps* stands at Derby, which was its home base for several years while it was in use with Fragonset Railways (later FM Rail). The locomotive has not worked on the main line for more than 10 years and is now based at Nemesis Rail at Burton upon Trent. NIGEL VALENTINE

Railways in 2002. It was moved to the Battlefield Railway at Shackerstone in a derelict condition, but little work was carried out on the locomotive and it has become something of a celebrity in the modern traction preservation world on the basis of just how derelict the locomotive has now become. 45015 is stored in a siding and there seems now almost no possibility of it being restored and it is likely that at some stage in the future the decaying remains of this locomotive will be broken up for scrap.

RIGHT: BR blue 45060 *Sherwood Forester* looks slightly incongruous hauling a rake of mainly LNER teak coaches on Eardington Bank during a visit to the Severn Valley Railway on May 20, 2017. KEVIN DELANEY

MAIN LINE PRESERVED CLASS 45s

While Pete Waterman's preserved Class 46, D172 *Ixion*, will always hold a special place in preservation history as being the first privately owned diesel locomotive to return to active use on the main line network, another 'Peak' also spent a long period of time hauling trains on the main line.

45112 *Royal Army Ordnance Corps* was preserved by Harry Needle from the scrap lines at March, Cambridgeshire, in summer 1991 and was moved to the East Lancashire Railway for restoration from derelict condition. It returned to service in 1995, resplendent in BR blue livery and numbered 61.

Harry Needle subsequently sold the locomotive to one of the main directors of Fragonset Railways at Derby and following its arrival at Derby, 45112 was re-certified for main line use and saw use on many main line tours and special workings for a number of years. However, it has now been more than a decade since it last hauled a train over Network Rail metals and after spells in store at Barrow Hill, it is now located at Burton upon Trent. While 45112 has now not hauled a train on either the national rail network or a heritage railway for several years, it is still operational and is used at Nemesis Rail's Burton upon Trent depot and its future appears to be safe.

MAIN LINE REGISTERED PRESERVED CLASS 45s

Loco	Owner	National Network Certification Status
45112	Private	Main Line Certification Expired

OTHER CLASS 45s

One formerly preserved 'Peak' that has now passed into commercial ownership is 45118 *The Royal Artilleryman*, which was purchased by Locomotive Services Ltd at Crewe in 2018, with a view to returning the locomotive to main line condition for hauling trains on behalf of LSL's charter company, Saphos Trains.

The locomotive was originally bought privately for preservation on the Northampton & Lamport Railway following withdrawal by BR and was returned to service on the NLR. However, in 2008 it was attacked by scrap metal thieves who robbed the locomotive of many valuable components and copper cabling, rendering it inoperable and in need of considerable repairs. Thankfully, the locomotive was insured and it moved to RVEL (now Loram) at Derby in 2009 for repairs.

Following its purchase by LSL it moved from Derby to LSL's Crewe Diesel Depot base and in 2019 it was to move again to Barrow Hill for repairs to be carried out. It is currently unknown at what stage 45118 will return to use either on heritage railways or in main line service, but its absence for more than a decade will ensure that its return will prove to be popular.

LOCO NAME	PREVIOUS NUMBERS	OWNER	LOCATION
45118 *The Royal Artilleryman*	D67, 45118	LSL	Barrow Hill

Displaying the attractive chromatic blue livery currently carried by the Peak Locomotive Company's Class 46, D182, the locomotive stands outside the Matthew Kirtley museum at Swanwick Junction on the Midland Railway Butterley on August 6, 2016. MARTIN HART

CLASS 46

O f the three locomotive orders built under the 'Peak' Type-Four design, the third and final batch of locomotives were built between 1961 and 1963 at British Railways Derby Works, also responsible for constructing the original pilot scheme 'Peaks' and who shared construction of the first production order for the 127 locomotives which went on to become the Class 45.

The final order was for 56 locomotives and these had the same Sulzer 12LDA28-B power units and structural design as the D11-D137 order, but these were fitted with Brush generators and traction motors, rather than the earlier type which had Crompton-Parkinson generators and traction motors. These locomotives were numbered D138-D193, completing the order for 'Peak' classes.

Unlike the earlier two designs, these locomotives were used mainly in the North East and around the East Coast Main Line, as well as some being based in the South West at Plymouth Laira, rather than the Midlands and the Midland main line that was the principal domain of the Class 44s and 45s. They were a mixed traffic locomotive and worked on both passenger and freight services.

Under TOPS the final order of locomotive became the Class 46 and they were numbered in build order with the prefix 460XX, i.e. D138 became 46001, D139 became 46002 etc.

The first member of the Class 46 fleet to be officially taken out of service was 46005, withdrawn in December 1977 after it suffered fire damage.

The rundown of the Class 46 fleet was much swifter than the phased withdrawals of the larger Class 45 fleet, and in November 1984 the final seven Class 46s were removed from normal traffic and withdrawn. The three locomotives that went on to be saved for preservation were all survivors in traffic until the end of normal operations.

Perhaps the most memorable moment involving the Class 46s was the deliberate destruction of 46009 by BR, when it was chosen to be used as a demonstration into the safety of the nuclear waste flasks that were being transported on the railways. At the time there were concerns about whether nuclear radiation could leak from one of the flasks if they were involved in an accident.

To demonstrate that the flasks were perfectly safe and secure for rail transport an exercise was held at the Old

Positively glistening after its recent overhaul and repaint, 46010 stands awaiting departure at Kidderminster on the Severn Valley Railway on May 16, 2019. 46010 is owned by D05 Preservation Ltd and usually based on the Great Central Railway (Nottingham) at Ruddington. STEVE KEMP

TOP: 46010 hauls a train into Bewdley on the Severn Valley Railway on May 16, 2019, passing Bewdley South signalbox. CHRIS OWEN

LOCO	NAME	BR IDENTITIES	OWNER	LOCATION
46010		D147, 46010	D05PL	GCRN
46035	Ixion	D172, 46035, 97403	Private	PKR
D182		D182, 46045, 97404	PLC	MRB

OWNERS KEY: D05PL = D05 Preservation Ltd, PLC – Peak Locomotive Company

LOCATION KEY: GCRN – Great Central Railway (Nottingham), MRB – Midland Railway Butterley, PKR – Peak Rail

Dalby Test Track, near Derby, in July 1984 where 46009 was operated remotely at high speed and deliberately crashed into a nuclear flask. The locomotive hit the flask at around 90mph and the resulting collision led to 46009 being extensively damaged and as it was assigned for withdrawal anyway, it was scrapped shortly afterwards. The nuclear flask withstood the crash remarkably well and BR was able to show that none of the contents of the flask (in this case it contained nothing more harmful than water) were not compromised and the demonstration was hailed as a great success.

Four of the locomotives were used in Departmental Use by the Railway Technical Centre following their withdrawal, with the most celebrated of these being 46035, which was painted into BR Research red and blue livery, renumbered 97403 and named Ixion. In this guise it managed to stay in service with the RTC until it was retired in 1990 and secured for preservation by Pete Waterman.

During a visit to the East Lancashire Railway in summer 1995, D172 *Ixion* stands at Rawtenstall after arriving with a service from Bury. Owned by Pete Waterman, this locomotive was the pioneer for the operation of preserved diesel locomotives under their own power on the national rail network. STEVE KEMP

Framed by the footbridge at Swanwick Junction station on the Midland Railway Butterley, D182 awaits departure on July 23, 2016. ANDREW SEWELL

THE PRESERVED CLASS 46s

Three Class 46s have survived the cutter's torch. 46010 was preserved by the Llangollen Diesel Group and restored over a period of around six years, with the locomotive first entering service on the Llangollen Railway in October 2000.

In 2009 the LDG held a review of its diesel fleet and some of its locomotives were sold, as the group sought to rationalise the size of the fleet it had to maintain and operate. As such, 46010 found itself leaving the Llangollen Railway for a new home on the Great Central Railway (Nottingham) at Ruddington. It was subsequently acquired by D05 Preservation Ltd and returned to service in spring 2019 after an extensive mechanical and bodywork overhaul and repaint into BR blue, with the work being carried out on a contract basis by the commercial arm of the Pioneer Diesel Group.

46035 *Ixion* was preserved by Pete Waterman and moved to Crewe Heritage Centre. It was restored to original BR green as D172 and became the first privately owned diesel locomotive to be recertified for use on the national rail network. Between 1995 and 2005 it saw extensive use on charter trains and other rail movements before moving to Leeds Midland Road for an overhaul which was not completed.

Now in BR blue and having not run under its own power for more than 14 years, 46035 is now located at Peak Rail and stored in the sidings at Rowsley

CLASS 46

BUILT:	BR Derby Works, 1961-1963
ENGINE:	Sulzer 12LDA28-B
NO. BUILT:	56
NO. PRESERVED:	3
OTHER SURVIVORS:	0

South. Pete Waterman's team at Rowsley have recently completed the restoration of Class 25, D7659, and it is hoped that attention will eventually turn to bringing 46035 back to life after so long on the sidelines.

D182 is owned by the Peak Locomotive Company and based along with the other PLC locomotives on the Midland Railway Butterley. The locomotive operated for a number of years in BR green, but has since been repainted into a version of BR's experimental chromatic blue livery.

It had been on loan to the Nene Valley Railway, but suffered from a generator failure and has been returned to Swanwick Junction for the necessary repairs to be carried out, with 45041 being supplied to the NVR as a replacement locomotive. It is hoped that the ever-popular D182 can be returned to active use in the near future.

MAIN LINE PRESERVED CLASS 46s

Following the preservation of 97403 *Ixion* by Pete Waterman, it was moved to Crewe, where it was repainted into BR green livery as D172 with modified small yellow ends, although it retained the name that it had received during its days with the Railway Technical Centre.

Following the lifting of British Rail's ban on preserved diesel locomotives operating under their own power on the national rail network, Mr Waterman set about preparing Ixion for a new career as a preserved main line certified locomotive for hauling charter trains on the rail network, in much the same way as had happened with scores of preserved steam locomotives. Being the first locomotive to be recertified for the main line, the process to get the locomotive back in service was lengthy and it underwent extensive works to prepare it for service, although the hard work was finally realised when D172 operated a charter from Derby to London St Pancras on October 1, 1994, returning a 'Peak' to the Midland main line for

Waiting its turn for reactivation, a forlorn-looking 46035 stands in the sidings at Rowsley South on Peak Rail on March 19, 2017. KEVIN DELANEY

the first time since the Class 45s had been withdrawn.

Ixion continued to be a regular fixture on the main line for a number of years and was repainted into BR blue in late 2001 and numbered back as 46035, but it was retired from service in 2003 and moved to Leeds Midland Road for an overhaul which was not completed. It is now located at Peak Rail where it awaits reactivation, although it seems unlikely that it will ever return to main line service in the future.

MAIN LINE REGISTERED PRESERVED CLASS 46s

Loco	Owner	National Network Certification Status
46035	Private	Main Line Certification Expired

CLASS 47

The Sulzer Type Four, or Class 47 as it became more commonly known, was the largest class of diesel locomotives built for use on the British Rail network, with 512 locomotives constructed between 1962 and 1968.

As British Rail had made the decision to rid itself of steam traction by the end of 1968, the company required a flexible locomotive design that could be used both on passenger and freight workings across the whole of the rail network.

The 20 prototype locomotives, numbered D1500-D1519, were constructed by Brush in Loughborough and were a development from the experimental locomotives Kestrel and Lion. The design was a sleek and attractive design, with roof-mounted radiators and filters, allowing the bodysides to be devoid of the grilles and louvres that were a feature of many other locomotive bodysides.

They were fitted with a powerful Sulzer 12LDA28C power unit, although five locomotives, D1702-D1706, were fitted with a Sulzer 12LVA24A power unit and classified as Class 48, but these were subsequently fitted with a standard Class 47 power unit after the trials of the alternative power unit were not deemed to have been successful.

The construction of the production locomotives was shared between Brush and BR's Crewe Works. A total of 310 locomotives were built by Brush, with BR constructing the other 202. With such a large fleet they were numbered D1500-D1999, with the final 12 numbered D1100-D1111. Most of the locomotives were painted in two-tone green livery with small yellow warning panels, although some of the later-built locomotives were outshopped in BR blue.

Under TOPS the locomotives became Class 47, but the numbering of the locomotives depended on what modifications had been carried out since the fleet had been introduced, with several different variants in use. With such a large class of locomotive there were many variations and several sub-classes were produced by BR as various modifications and pools were established for the Class 47 fleet. The original 20 prototype 'Generator' locomotives were numbered 47401-47420.

During the 1990s a number of Class 47s were used as donor locomotives for a re-engineering programme by Brush Traction to provide a new fleet of Class 57 locomotives.

The first Class 47 to be bought for preservation was Crewe Heritage Centre's D1842 (47192). The locomotive has been a regular on the heritage diesel event circuit and has visited a number of other railways as a guest. On May 20, 2017, 1842 passes Trimpley Reservoir on the Severn Valley Railway, while working a Kidderminster to Bridgnorth service during the SVR's popular annual spring diesel event. TOM MCATEE

LEFT: Second-built Class 47 'Generator' D1501 was bought from BR by Pete Waterman in 1992 and moved to the East Lancashire Railway, where it has been based ever since. After several years running in BR blue livery, it has now been restored to as-built condition and repainted into two-tone BR green colours. On September 23, 2018, D1501 heads over Roch Viaduct between Heywood and Bury, while working a Heywood to Rawtenstall service, with Class 25, D7629, at the tail end of the train. TOM MCATEE

Bringing a bright splash of colour and representing a more modern era than the traditional BR green and blue liveries is the Stratford 47 Group's 47596 *Aldeburgh Festival*, which is painted into Network SouthEast colours. On June 28, 2015, the locomotive sits outside Grosmont Shed on the North Yorkshire Moors Railway while visiting the railway for a diesel event. ANDREW SEWELL

CLASS 47

BUILT: Brush Traction, Loughborough and BR Crewe Works, 1962-1968

ENGINE: Sulzer 12LDA28C

NO. BUILT: 512

NO. PRESERVED: 30

OTHER SURVIVORS: 50

Thirty-three Class 57s were completed by Brush using Class 47 bodyshells with another couple of Class 47s scrapped when flaws were found in the donor bodyshell. While these locomotives cannot be classed as being a '47', the Class 57s are still identifiable as to their origin.

Until the mid-1980s the only withdrawals from the Class 47 fleet were as a result of serious collisions, with the first to be condemned being D1734 in March 1965 after just a year in service. It is testament to the design that only a handful of locomotives had been withdrawn until BR decided to start the gradual rundown of the fleet in the late 1980s, as newer designs of locomotives, such as the Class 56s, 58s and 60s were coming on stream.

The original 20 pioneer locomotives were the first to be withdrawn from service, as they were deemed to be non-standard. The last of the 'Generators' was withdrawn in 1992,

when D1500 and 47402 were stood down from service.

Throughout the 1990s and 2000s, more and more Class 47s were taken out of service and following privatisation the introduction of the new Class 66 proved to be the move that allowed companies such as English Welsh & Scottish Railways and Freightliner to dispense with most of their Class 47s which had been used on freight services. In the passenger sector, operators such as Virgin CrossCountry and First Great Western continued to use Class 47s on passenger services until they too were replaced with more modern trains.

Whilst there are still a number of Class 47s in use on the main line network, their days in front line service are now largely a thing of the past. However, with the locomotives all now over 50 years old, they have certainly proved their worth and it is likely that the Class 47 story still has a number of chapters still to be written.

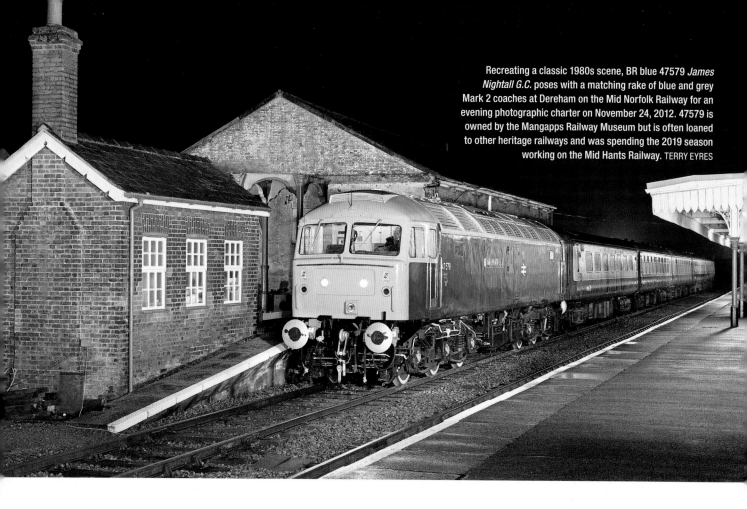

Recreating a classic 1980s scene, BR blue 47579 *James Nightall G.C.* poses with a matching rake of blue and grey Mark 2 coaches at Dereham on the Mid Norfolk Railway for an evening photographic charter on November 24, 2012. 47579 is owned by the Mangapps Railway Museum but is often loaned to other heritage railways and was spending the 2019 season working on the Mid Hants Railway. TERRY EYRES

THE PRESERVED CLASS 47s

With such a large class of locomotives, it was inevitable that a large number of Class 47s would prove to be popular with preservationists. At the time of writing this publication, there were 29 Class 47s which can be classified as being preserved, with three of these on loan to main line operators. The remainder are mainly based at preserved railways across the country.

The first Class 47 to be secured for preservation was 47192, which was bought by the Crewe Heritage Centre Trust in 1987. The locomotive has been a regular visitor to various heritage railway events and is currently

undergoing a bodywork overhaul and repaint at its home base.

Three of the initial batch of 20 locomotives have entered preservation, with pioneer 47401 (D1500) and second-built D1501 (47402) both being bought from BR in near-operational condition. 47401 is based at the Midland Railway Butterley and owned by the 47401 Project, which is also restoring sister 'Generator' D1516 to service. D1501 was bought by celebrity railway enthusiast and record producer Pete Waterman and is based on the East Lancashire Railway.

In addition to D1501, a second Class 47 is also based at the ELR since 47765

was moved to Bury in 2018 by its owner following several years based at the Great Central Railway (Nottingham). The loss of 47765 from the GCRN hasn't left it without a Class 47, as 47292 is still based on the line.

The sole-surviving member of the former Class 48 locomotives is 1705 *Sparrowhawk*, which is preserved on the Great Central Railway at Loughborough and has recently returned to service after an overhaul and repaint into BR blue. Originally preserved by Pete Waterman, the locomotive was subsequently sold to the Type 1 Locomotive Company, which also owns D8098 and D5830 on the GCR.

The Stratford 47 Group owns three locomotives, with 47367 and 47596 *Aldeburgh Festival* based on the Mid Norfolk Railway and main line-registered 47580 *County of Essex* on long-term hire to West Coast Railway Company at Carnforth, although 47580 is currently out of service undergoing repairs.

The Brush Type 4 Fund owns two Class 47s, with 47105 and 47376 *Freightliner 1995* both based on the Gloucestershire & Warwickshire Railway. 47105 has been out of service at Toddington undergoing an overhaul, while 47376 remains available for service on the railway.

The Diesel and Electric Preservation Group owns D1661 *North Star* on the West Somerset Railway. The locomotive was presented to the DEPG in 2007 by

Despite looking immaculate in a coat of EWS maroon and gold livery, 47785 is another locomotive that is still awaiting reactivation and is currently based on the Wensleydale Railway. While based at its former home at Kirkby Stephen East on the Stainmore Railway, the former *Fiona Castle* awaits its turn for attention on April 20, 2013. TERRY EYRES

former owner, Porterbrook Leasing, and has been a mainstay of the WSR diesel services ever since. It is currently out of service undergoing repairs and a repaint.

In North Wales, the Llangollen Diesel Group (LDG) owns 1566 (47449) which is painted in BR blue after running for much of its time in preservation in two-tone green. Although the LDG fleet has been reduced over recent years, 1566 remains a valuable asset of the group and regularly sees use on the LR.

Representing the Class 47s north of the border in Scotland is 47643 on the Bo'ness & Kinneil Railway. The locomotive is painted in InterCity livery and has often visited other heritage lines away from its home railway.

47205 was preserved in 2004 and moved to the Northampton & Lamport Railway where it underwent restoration to serviceable condition and it has remained on the railway ever since, now resplendent in original Railfreight Distribution grey livery.

47579 *James Nightall G.C.* was bought by James Jolly and moved to Mangapps Railway Museum, where it was restored to working order. It has since visited a number of other heritage lines, including the Mid Norfolk Railway and the ELR, but it is currently on loan to the Mid Hants Railway.

An overhaul to 47306 *The Sapper* on the Bodmin & Wenford Railway was completed in spring 2019, in time for the locomotive to make an appearance at the nearby Long Rock Depot in June. This locomotive is unique among the preserved Class 47s for carrying the later style Railfreight Distribution livery, which it has carried throughout the time it has been preserved.

Both former dedicated Royal Train Class 47s, 47798 *Prince William* and 47799 *Prince Henry* are now preserved, with 47798 part of the National Collection and on display at the Railway Museum in York and 47799 is currently stored at Warcop on the Eden Valley Railway, where it is awaiting reactivation.

Another former BR celebrity to have entered preservation has been former GW-150 locomotive 47484 *Isambard Kingdom Brunel*, which is located in a transport yard in Warwickshire. 47484 is owned by the Pioneer Diesel Group and while some restoration work has

Usually based at the Great Central Railway Nottingham, 47292 was withdrawn by Freightliner in 2003 and was one of a batch of locomotives sold to preservationists. It was quickly returned to service and was one of the visiting locomotives to the 2014 Swanage Railway Diesel Event. The locomotive is seen basking in the sunshine between duties at Swanage on May 10, 2014. MARTIN HART

been carried out on it, other restoration projects and contract commitments within the owning group mean that it is likely to be some time before the restoration of 47484 can be completed.

47524 was moved to Tyseley Locomotive Works when first preserved, before moving to the Churnet Valley Railway in 2006. However, the restoration of the '47' has not yet been completed and it has recently moved again to the Dean Forest Railway for its restoration to be finished.

Originally preserved on the Stainmore Railway at Kirkby Stephen East, 47785 is now based on the nearby Wensleydale Railway, where it awaits reactivation. The Wensleydale Railway has gained an enviable fleet of diesel locomotives in recent years and the restoration of EWS-liveried 47785 is eagerly awaited by Class 47 enthusiasts.

47771 is owned by the Class 47 Preservation Project and was based on the Colne Valley Railway for a number of years, although the locomotive suffered a major setback when it was targeted by scrap metal thieves. Undefeated,

the group has continued with work on reviving the locomotive and it has since been moved to Eastleigh Works, where work on its restoration to running order continues.

Of the preserved Class 47s, 47761 was bought by the 47401 Project at the Midland Railway Butterley as a source of spare parts for 47401 and under-restoration D1516. Although the parts taken from the locomotive have been removed carefully, it is unlikely that 47761 will ever be restored and it is likely to be scrapped, or sold on, once it has fulfilled its purpose for its current owners.

Additionally the future of D1524 is currently unclear. The locomotive has been out of service on the Embsay and Bolton Abbey Railway for a number of years in need of repairs. The locomotive is stored at Bolton Abbey station along with 31119 and D5600 (which belong to the same owner) and what the future holds for the former Old Oak Common celebrity remains to be seen.

A number of Class 47 cabs have also survived scrapping.

Network Southeast-liveried 47596 *Aldeburgh Festival* is posed at the head of a rake of Mark 2 coaches at Dereham on the Mid Norfolk Railway during an evening photographic charter on November 24, 2012. TERRY EYRES

LOCO	NAME	BR IDENTITIES	OWNER	LOCATION
D1524		D1524, 47004	Private	EBAR
47105		D1693, 47105	BT4F	GWR
1705	*Sparrowhawk*	D1705, 47117	T1LC	GCR
47192		D1842, 47192	CHCT	CHC
47205		D1855, 47205, 47395	Private	NLR
47292		D1994, 47292	Private	GCRN
47306	*The Sapper*	D1787, 47306	B&WMLDG	BWR
47367		D1886, 47367	S47G	MNR
47376	*Freightliner 1995*	D1895, 47376	BT4F	GWR
47401	*North Eastern*	D1500, 47401	47401P	MRB
D1501		D1501, 47402	Private	ELR
D1516		D1516, 47417	47401P	MRB
1566		D1566, 47449	LDG	LR
47484	*Isambard Kingdom Brunel*	D1662, 47484	PDG	Private
47524		D1107, 47524	Private	DFR
47579	*James Nightall G.C.*	D1778, 47183, 47579, 47793	MRM	MHR
47580	*County of Essex*	D1762, 47167, 47580, 47732	S47G	Carnforth
47596	*Aldeburgh Festival*	D1933, 47233, 47596	S47G	MNR
47635	*Jimmy Milne*	D1606, 47029, 47635	Private	EOR
47643		D1970, 47269, 47643	SRPSDG	BKR
47712	*Lady Diana Spencer*	D1948, 47505, 47712	CDPG	Crewe
47761		D1619, 47038, 47564, 47761	47401P	MRB
47765		D1643, 47059, 47631, 47765	Private	ELR
47771		D1946, 47503, 47771	C47PP	Eastleigh
D1755		D1755, 47541, 47773	Private	TLW
47785		D1909, 47232, 47820, 47785	Private	WR
47798	*Prince William*	D1656, 47072, 47609, 47834, 47798	NRM	RMY
47799	*Prince Henry*	D1654, 47070, 47620, 47835, 47799	Private	EDVR
47828		D1966, 47266, 47629, 47828	D05PL	Carnforth
D1661	*North Star*	D1661, 47077, 47613, 47840	DEPG	WSR

OWNERS KEY: 47401P – 47401 Project, BT4F – Brush Type 4 Fund, B&WMLDG – Bodmin & Wenford Main Line Diesel Group, C47PP – Class 47 Preservation Project, CDPG – Crewe Diesel Preservation Group, CHC – Crewe Heritage Centre Trust, D05PC – D05 Preservation Company, DEPG – Diesel & Electric Preservation Group, LDG – Llangollen Diesel Group, MRM – Mangapps Railway Museum, NRM – National Railway Museum, PDG – Pioneer Diesel Group, S47G – Stratford 47 Group, SRPSDG – Scottish Railway Preservation Society Diesel Group, T1LC – Type 1 Locomotive Company

LOCATION KEY: BKR – Bo'ness & Kinneil Railway, BWR – Bodmin & Wenford Railway, Carnforth – Carnforth West Coast Railway Company, CHC – Crewe Heritage Centre, Crewe – Locomotive Services Crewe Diesel Depot, DFR – Dean Forest Railway, Eastleigh – Eastleigh Works, EBAR – Embsay & Bolton Abbey Railway, ELR – East Lancashire Railway, EOR – Epping Ongar Railway, EDVR – Eden Valley Railway, GCR – Great Central Railway, GCRN – Great Central Railway Nottingham, GWR – Gloucestershire Warwickshire Railway, LR – Llangollen Railway, MHR – Mid Hants Railway, MNR – Mid Norfolk Railway, MRB – Midland Railway Butterley, NLR – Northampton & Lamport Railway, RMY – Railway Museum York, WR – Wensleydale Railway, WSR – West Somerset Railway

Representing the Railfreight Distribution era is 47306 *The Sapper*, which has spent its entire time in preservation based on the Bodmin & Wenford Railway. The locomotive has recently undergone an overhaul by its owning group and was one of the exhibits at the GWR Long Rock Depot Open Day on June 10, 2019. CHRIS MORGAN

Upon withdrawal by English Welsh and Scottish Railways, both former 'Royal' Class 47s were preserved, with 47798 *Prince William* claimed by the National Railway Museum and 47799 *Prince Henry* moving to the Eden Valley Railway at Warcop. 47798 was preserved in main line condition and saw some use on the main line moving locomotives for the NRM. It also worked some trains for West Coast Railway Company and made a couple of visits to heritage lines. In rather grubby condition, 47798 pauses at Glaisdale while working a North Yorkshire Moors Railway Whitby service on September 16, 2012. ANDREW SEWELL

After spending a number of years based on the Great Central Railway Nottingham, 47765 joined the fleet of diesel locomotives at the East Lancashire Railway in 2018. The ScotRail-liveried locomotive runs through Heap Bridge between Heywood and Bury on August 25, 2018. NIGEL VALENTINE

LEFT: 47643 is preserved on the Bo'ness and Kinneil Railway in Scotland and is appropriately painted in InterCity red stripe livery. On January 2, 2016, the locomotive works a service towards Birkhill station during a winter diesel event. KEVIN DELANEY

BELOW: The pioneer member of the Class 47 fleet, D1500 (now 47401 *North Eastern*) was preserved in 1992 by the 47401 Project on the Midland Railway Butterley. On July 23, 2016, the locomotive run around its train at Swanwick Junction. ANDREW SEWELL

Another Class 47 to carry a more modern colour scheme is the Brush Type 4 Funds 47376 *Freightliner 1995* on the Gloucestershire and Warwickshire Railway. The locomotive presents an imposing image as it heads through Gotherington with a service to Winchcombe on October 8, 2017. KEVIN DELANEY

MAIN LINE PRESERVED CLASS 47s

As with many other types of preserved locomotives, some of the preserved examples have been registered for main line running over Network Rail metals, with the most prolific of these being 47580 *County of Essex*, which has been in use with West Coast Railway Company for a number of years. 47580 is currently out of service undergoing repairs and is expected to return to main line use once the necessary repairs have been carried out.

In 2018 Tyseley Locomotive Works gained a train operating licence for its Vintage Trains charter operation. The company has the use of privately owned D1755/47773 and this locomotive is used by Vintage Trains alongside its fleet of former Great Western Railway steam locomotives. The locomotive is preserved, but has only seen use by Vintage Trains and it has not yet worked at any other heritage railway away from Tyseley or on the main line.

Former 'Royal' locomotive 47798 *Prince William* was donated to the National Railway Museum by English Welsh and Scottish Railways. It arrived at the NRM in operational condition and it retained its main line certification to allow it to be used for moving locomotives whenever it was required. It also saw use on a number of services for WCRC, but has since been retired to York, where it has been repainted into its former Rail Express Systems royal grey and claret colours.

However, the NRM has recently held a comprehensive review of its locomotive fleet and the decision has been taken that the museum's operational main line diesel locomotives will no longer be used on the main line and 47798 is currently destined to spend the foreseeable future on static display at the NRM in York.

In 2019, two preserved Class 47s are being prepared for a return to main line use, with 47712 *Lady Diana Spencer* currently at Crewe Diesel Depot in readiness for a return to action with Locomotive Services, while D05 Preservation's 47828 has recently joined the operational fleet of locomotives in use by WCRC in a similar arrangement to the long-term hire of 47580.

MAIN LINE REGISTERED PRESERVED CLASS 47s

Loco	Owner	National Network Certification Status
47580	Stratford 47 Group	Main Line Certified (undergoing repair)
47712	Crewe Diesel Preservation Group	Awaiting Main Line Certification
47773	Private	Main Line Certified
47798	National Railway Museum	Main Line Certification Expired
47828	D05 Preservation Ltd	Main Line Certified

One locomotive still waiting to return to traffic is D1516 at the Midland Railway Butterley. The 'Generator' is owned by the 47401 Project, which owns the pioneer Class 47, which is also based at the MRB along with spares donor locomotive 47761. The restoration of D1516 is a long-term project and there is no target date in place for its return to action. The locomotive is seen at Swanwick on July 21, 2013. MARTIN HART

What does the future hold for the former Old Oak Common celebrity locomotive 47004 (D1524), which has lain out of use at Bolton Abbey on the Embsay and Bolton Abbey Railway for a number of years? On May 4, 2015, D1524 awaits its turn for attention. ANDREW SEWELL

Located on the Midland Railway Butterley, 47761 was purchased as a source of spares by the 47401 Project for its two other locomotives, 47401 and D1516. Once its owners have recovered all the parts they need from the locomotive it is likely to be scrapped. KEVIN DELANEY

As the largest type of diesel locomotives ordered by British Railways, there are still a number of Class 47s in main line service across the UK. While the main passenger operators and freight operators DB Cargo, Direct Rail Services and Colas have dispensed with all their remaining Class 47s, a number of spot hire and charter operators still regularly use the locomotives on the main line.

The largest current operator of Class 47s is Carnforth-based charter operator West Coast Railway Company. The company has a number of operational '47s', as well as a large number of stored locomotives, which are either waiting resurrection or used for spare parts to keep the operational fleet in service.

Locomotive Services Ltd, which is based at the former Crewe Diesel Depot, currently has eight Class 47s on its books, with six of these locomotives in use or being prepared for services, while 47811 and 47816 are being used as spares donor locomotives. Rail Operations Group bought six Class 47s from Riviera Trains and its operational locomotives are now used for spot hire, based at Leicester Depot.

Harry Needle Railroad Company owns four Class 47s, with two, 47703 and 47714 in industrial use, while 47769 is undergoing an overhaul at Barrow Hill and 47715 has been in use on the Wensleydale Railway in recent years, but has now moved to the new HNRC storage facility at Worksop.

GB Railfreight acquired three Class 47s, 47727, 47739 and 47749, from Colas Rail and these locomotives are being used to bolster GBRf growing fleet.

Nemesis Rail owns four Class 47s, with three, 47488, 47701 and 47744 based at Burton upon Trent, although none of these are registered for main line use. 47640 also belongs to the company, but this is based on the Battlefield Line at Shackerstone and has been used to haul services on the heritage line.

Freightliner and Arlington Fleet Services each have one Class 47 available to them. Additionally, one locomotive, 47375, has been exported to Hungary for Continental Rail Services, with work on its conversion carried out by Nemesis Rail at Burton upon Trent.

NON-PRESERVED SURVIVING CLASS 47s

ARLINGTON FLEET SERVICES, EASTLEIGH WORKS: 47818

FREIGHTLINER: 47830

GB RAILFREIGHT: 47727, 47739, 47749

HARRY NEEDLE RAILROAD COMPANY: 47703, 47714, 47715, 47769

LOCOMOTIVE SERVICES LTD: D1924, D1935, D1944, 47593, 47614, 47811, 47816, 47841

NEMESIS RAIL: 47488, 47640, 47701, 47744

RAIL OPERATIONS GROUP: 47812, 47813, 47815, 47843, 47847, 47848

WEST COAST RAILWAY COMPANY: 47194, 47237, 47245, 47270, 47355, 47368, 47492, 47500, 47526, 47746, 47760, 47768, 47772, 47776, 47786, 47787, 47802, 47804, 47826, 47832, 47851, 47854

EXPORTED TO HUNGARY: 47375

• Please note that some of these locomotives are operational, while others are stored or being used as spares donor locomotives.

A preserved Class 47 that regularly sees main line use is D1755/47773 which is privately owned but used by charter operator Vintage Trains from its base at Tyseley Locomotive Works. On May 4, 2018, the locomotive stands on the turntable at Tyseley awaiting its next duties. RICHARD THOMPSON

The first Class 50 to haul a train in preservation was 50002 *Superb*, which was based at the Paignton and Dartmouth Steam Railway. However, a planned main line return for 50002 failed to materialise and the locomotive has spent more than 20 years out of use. Now based at the South Devon Railway, the Devon Diesel Society is working to return *Superb* to operational condition, with the locomotive being returned cosmetically to as-built condition as D402. On November 7, 2009, D402 stands at Buckfastleigh while work on its bodywork overhaul was reaching an advanced stage. MARTIN HART

CLASS 50

The 50 mixed-traffic English Electric Type Four locomotives, numbered D400-D449, which became Class 50 under the British Rail TOPS classification system (50001-50050), were built at Vulcan Foundry in Newton-le-Willows in 1967 and 1968. They were the final mixed-traffic diesel locomotive design constructed for British Rail.

Initially they were used on the West Coast Main Line before being transferred to the Western Region in the early 1970s following the electrification of the WCML. A refurbishment programme for the type saw BR undertake a number of modifications designed to make the locomotives more reliable and remove some of the obsolete equipment which had been fitted when they were built.

The first withdrawals from the Class 50 fleet came in February 1987 when 50011 Centurion was taken out of service to enable it to become a test-bed locomotive for overhauled Class 50 English Electric 16CSVT power units at Crewe Works. This was followed five months later by 50006 *Neptune*, which was used as a spares donor locomotive before being scrapped.

A trial of 50049 by the Railfreight sector of BR to see if the Class 50s could be modified for use on heavier freight services saw the locomotive receive a pair of re-geared bogies, along with its power unit being de-rated to 2400 brake-horsepower. The modified locomotive was renumbered 50149 and painted into Railfreight grey livery, although the trials proved to be unsuccessful and it was converted back into a standard Class 50 just 18 months later with no further locomotives given a similar treatment.

The rundown of the class was gradual at first, but accelerated considerably during 1990 and 1991, until the majority of the fleet had been stood down by spring 1992, with the exception of three locomotives – 50007 *Sir Edward Elgar*, 50033 *Glorious* and fleet pioneer D400 (50050 *Fearless*) – which were retained as dedicated railtour locomotives for a further two years, working a series of tours.

The enthusiastic following of the type during their rundown

The first member of the Class 50 fleet to be officially bought for preservation was 50035 *Ark Royal*, which was purchased by the Fifty Fund in 1991. As with many other preserved locomotives, 50035 has now been in preservation for longer than it was in BR service. Now restored to BR blue livery with its cab front headlight removed, 50035 arrives at Swanage, with the 11:30 Norden to Swanage service on May 9, 2015, during the Swanage Railway's annual diesel and real ale event. TOM MCATEE

was fully endorsed by BR, through Plymouth Laira Depot, with a number of the locomotives receiving celebrity repaints during the final years.

Indeed, celebrity mock-GWR green liveried 50007 was withdrawn following major engine failure, only to be repaired, repainted and reinstated back into traffic to allow it to stay in service until the end of Class 50 operations on BR.

In March 1994, 50033 was admitted into the National Railway Museum as part of the National Collection, while 50007 and 50050 worked the '50 Terminator' railtour on March 26, 1994, bringing down the curtain on Class 50 operations on British Rail.

The Old Oak Common Depot Farewell Open Weekend in September 2017 saw seven of the surviving Class 50s reunited together, including a line-up of six of the survivors. On September 2, 2017, 50050 *Fearless*, 50049 *Defiance*, 50044 *Exeter*, 50026 *Indomitable*, 50017 *Royal Oak* and 50007 *Hercules* pose together for the assembled crowds. 50035 *Ark Royal* was also in attendance at the event, but was displayed elsewhere. MARTIN HART

CLASS 50

BUILT: Vulcan Foundry, Newton-le-Willows, 1967-68
ENGINE: English Electric 16CSVT Power Unit
NO. BUILT: 50
NO. PRESERVED: 16
OTHER SURVIVORS: 2

THE PRESERVED CLASS 50s

Of the 18 surviving Class 50s, 16 can be classed as being preserved, with the remaining two in regular main line use on the national rail network for commercial workings on a spot-hire basis and these are essentially commercial assets of their owners.

Such was the popularity of the Class 50s at the time of their withdrawal, it was inevitable that the type would be well represented in preservation, although few could have envisaged more than one-third of the type surviving the cutter's torch.

The first Class 50s to be bought for preservation were 50035 *Ark Royal* and 50019 *Ramillies*, which were bought in summer 1991 by The Fifty Fund and the Class 50 Locomotive Association respectively.

50035 was officially handed over to its new owners by Network SouthEast managing director Chris Green at the Old Oak Common Depot Open Day in August 1991 and moved to a new base at St Leonards depot shortly afterwards, while 50019 moved to the fledgling Tunbridge Wells and Eridge Railway (now the Spa Valley Railway). 50019 is now located at the Mid Norfolk Railway, where it is currently out of service awaiting a major overhaul.

Throughout the next three years a steady stream of other '50s' were secured for the preservation section, with many of those examples bought being complete and in generally good condition and capable of being returned to use relatively quickly.

The first Class 50 to haul a train in preservation was the Devon Diesel Society's 50002 *Superb*, which worked its first services on the Paignton and Dartmouth Railway in April 1992 just a few weeks after it had arrived on the private line. 50002 is now located at the South Devon Railway undergoing a comprehensive restoration and overhaul, and has not hauled a train for more than two decades.

Other early Class 50s to enter service on preserved lines were 50031 *Hood* on

Class 50 pioneer locomotive D400 (50050 *Fearless*) was originally preserved by Dutch preservationist Harry Schneider, but was sold in 2015 to Boden Rail Engineering Ltd and was re-registered for main line running, where it sees occasional use on a spot-hire basis, often working for Colas Rail. On April 1, 2016, the doyen of the class stands at Thuxton station on the Mid Norfolk Railway during a short working visit to the line. MARTIN HART

50031 *Hood* was the first Class 50 to be re-registered for use on the main line in November 1997, some three-and-a-half years after the final Class 50 had been withdrawn by British Rail. After many years flying the flag for the Class 50 Alliance, 50031 is no longer working on the main line and is based on the Severn Valley Railway, where it is painted into InterCity livery. Class 50s were never allocated to the InterCity sector, although it is possible that this could have happened had they survived in service much longer. 50031 provides a flavour of what might have been when it was paired with matching stock for the SVR diesel gala on May 20, 2017. KEVIN DELANEY

50015 *Valiant* is located on the East Lancashire Railway, where it has been based since being originally preserved in October 1992. The locomotive is owned by a consortium of ELR volunteers under the Bury Valiant Group banner. Restored to the popular Large Logo blue livery, 50015 passes through Pilsworth with a train of blue and grey coaches, while working a Heywood to Rawtenstall service on November 23, 2013. TOM MCATEE

50027 *Lion* was bought by preservationist Mike Fuller in 1992 and moved to the Mid Hants Railway, where it became one of the first Class 50s to return to operational use in preservation. After spending several years at the North Yorkshire Moors Railway, it returned to the Mid Hants in 2012. 50027 has carried revised Network SouthEast livery throughout its time in preservation and is pictured at Alresford on October 20, 2017. Sadly, Mr Fuller passed away in August 2019. MARTIN HART

the Severn Valley Railway (starting a long association between the railway and Class 50s), 50027 *Lion* on the Mid Hants Railway, along with 50008 *Thunderer* and 50015 *Valiant* on the East Lancashire Railway.

The Class 50 Alliance is responsible for the preservation and maintenance of six of the locomotives (four owned directly, with another two under its custodianship).

The organisation is based on the Severn Valley Railway and was formed following a merger between The Fifty Fund (owners of 50035 *Ark Royal* and 50044 *Exeter* and custodians of 50031 *Hood*) and Project Defiance (the owner of 50049 *Defiance*).

Since the merger the group has acquired 50007 *Hercules* (the former *Sir Edward Elgar*) and is also now working hard on the restoration of former National Railway Museum-owned 50033 *Glorious* after a number of years stored out of use at Tyseley Locomotive Works. The Class 50 Alliance maintains its fleet of locomotives at the excellent diesel depot facility that was built at Kidderminster on the Severn Valley Railway.

Another Class 50 due to return to service in the near future after almost two decades out of use is 50021 *Rodney*, which is now nearing the end of an extensive rebuild by its owning group, spearheaded by respected Class 50 preservationist Paul Spracklen, who also restored 50026 *Indomitable* to service from scrap condition.

Two preserved Class 50s have not yet worked a train in preservation, with 50029 *Renown* and 50030 *Repulse* based on Peak Rail and undergoing restoration from near-scrap condition by their owner, the Renown Repulse Restoration Group.

While 50030's overhaul and restoration is now reaching an advanced stage, 50029 is still in a largely unrestored condition and it is likely to be a number of years before this locomotive returns to use.

50042 *Triumph* is based on the Bodmin & Wenford Railway in Cornwall, making it the most southerly based Class 50 in preservation. The locomotive is regularly in service on the railway and remains a popular member of the railways diesel fleet. 50042 runs around its train at Bodmin Parkway on November 3, 2018. MARTIN HART

The construction of a dedicated diesel depot at Kidderminster on the Severn Valley Railway has provided the various locomotive groups on the railway with enviable facilities for the maintenance of the many diesel locomotives based on the railway. During the Class 50 50th anniversary celebration event, visiting 50017 *Royal Oak* and 50026 *Indomitable* stand inside the facility during a photographic charter on October 3, 2018. TERRY EYRES

After being removed from the National Collection, former railtour favourite 50033 *Glorious* has spent a number of years out of use with an increasingly uncertain future. However, in early 2018 agreement was reached with owners Tyseley Locomotive Works for 50033 to be placed on loan to the Class 50 Alliance, with the experienced Class 50 preservationists working to return the locomotive to service. After much effort 50033 was restored to use in time for the ground-breaking 50th anniversary event organised by the Class 50 Alliance at the Severn Valley Railway in October 2018. Time did not allow for 50033 to be repainted prior to the event, with it turned out in green primer and enthusiasts encouraged to 'tag' the Class 50 as a fundraising initiative towards its eventual repaint into Large Logo blue livery. 50033 runs light engine into Bewdley on October 4, 2018. MARTIN HART

LEFT: In January 2019, main line registered 50017 *Royal Oak* was put up for sale by its former owner, Boden Rail Engineering, with the possibility that the locomotive would be broken up for spares should a buyer not be forthcoming. It was subsequently purchased by a member of the Great Central Railway and moved to Loughborough the following month. Now with its mandatory main line operating equipment removed, 50017 worked its first services at the GCR during their diesel event in April 2019. On April 13, 2019, 50017 runs around its train at Loughborough, prior to working a service to Leicester Central. MARTIN HART

LOCO	NAME	PREVIOUS IDENTITIES	OWNER	LOCATION
D402	*Superb*	D402, 50002	DDS	SDR
50007	*Hercules*	D407, 50007	C50A	SVR
50015	*Valiant*	D415, 50015	BVG	ELR
50017	*Royal Oak*	D417, 50017	Private	GCR
50019	*Ramillies*	D419, 50019	C50LA	MNR
50021	*Rodney*	D421, 50021	Private	Eastleigh
50026	*Indomitable*	D426, 50026	Private	Eastleigh
50027	*Lion*	D427, 50027	Private	MHR
50029	*Renown*	D429, 50029	RRRG	PKR
50030	*Repulse*	D430, 50030	RRRG	PKR
50031	*Hood*	D431, 50031	Private/C50A	SVR
50033	*Glorious*	D433, 50033	TLW/C50A	SVR
50035	*Ark Royal*	D435, 50035	C50A	SVR
50042	*Triumph*	D442, 50042	B&WMLDG	BWR
50044	*Exeter*	D444, 50044	C50A	SVR
50049	*Defiance*	D449, 50049, 50149	C50A	SVR

OWNERS KEY: B&WMLDG – Bodmin & Wenford Main Line Diesel Group, BVG – Bury Valiant Group, C50A – Class 50 Alliance, C50LA – Class 50 Locomotive Association, DDS – Devon Diesel Society, RRRG – Renown Repulse Restoration Group, TLW – Tyseley Locomotive Works

LOCATION KEY: BWR – Bodmin & Wenford Railway, Eastleigh – Eastleigh Works, ELR – East Lancashire Railway, GCR – Great Central Railway, MHR – Mid Hants Railway, MNR- Mid Norfolk Railway, PKR – Peak Rail Rowsley South, SVR – Severn Valley Railway

In 2019 agreement was reached between the Class 50 Alliance and freight operator GB Railfreight for preserved main line registered locomotives 50007 *Hercules* and 50049 *Defiance* to be repainted into GBRf's distinctive orange and blue livery, with the locomotives being employed by GBRf for various spot hire workings. A few days after the pair had been unveiled at Eastleigh Works, they worked a railtour 'the 50 Terminator Phoenixed' for Pathfinder Tours to mark the 25th anniversary of the final BR Class 50 railtour on March 26, 1994. 50049 and 50007 stand at Plymouth on March 23, 2019, with 50049 carrying both a headboard from the original 1994 tour alongside its modern-day tour headboard. MARTIN HART

RIGHT: Now nearing the end of a comprehensive overhaul at Eastleigh Works is 50021 *Rodney*, which is owned by a consortium of shareholders led by the owner of 50026 *Indomitable*, Paul Spracklen. The locomotive has been completely rebuilt following almost 20 years out of use and is expected to be completed over the next few months. 50021 is pictured inside Eastleigh Works on June 30, 2018. MARTIN HART

MAIN LINE PRESERVED CLASS 50s

There have been several Class 50s which have been returned to operate trains on the national network by their owners, with seven Class 50s having returned to main line use since being bought from BR, while at least one more locomotive is waiting in the wings for a main line return over the coming months.

With several of the preserved Class 50s being in good condition when they were bought for preservation, the lifting of restrictions of privately owned diesel locomotives running on the national railway network heralded a return to the main line for preserved Class 50s, with The Fifty Fund deciding to register 50031 *Hood* for main line running in 1997.

The first main line trip to be worked by a privately owned Class 50 was the 'Pilgrim Hoover' railtour from Birmingham International to Plymouth in November 1997, just over three-and-a-half years after the type had finally been dispensed with by BR.

50031 remains in operational condition on the Severn Valley Railway and is now painted into InterCity livery. The locomotive is no longer registered for main line running, as it requires new tyres fitting, with the Class 50 Alliance currently raising funds to fit new tyres to both 50031 and 50035 *Ark Royal*.

50044 *Exeter* was another regular performer on the main line under the auspices of the Class 50 Alliance, prior to it suffering a serious failure of its power unit in 2012. The locomotive has now received a replacement power unit recovered from one of the similar Portuguese 1800 Class locomotives and it was returned to use on the Severn Valley Railway in September 2018. 50044 has not yet been recertified for use on the national network.

Currently flying the flag for the Class 50 Alliance on the main line are 50007 *Hercules* and 50049 *Defiance*, both of which were repainted into GB Railfreight livery in March 2019 to mark a successful working relationship between the national freight operator and the owners of the locomotives. Both locomotives are regularly used for spot hire main line duties, as well as occasional charters, heritage railway visits and other workings. Although now painted in the livery of GB Railfreight, they are not exclusively used by the freight company and remain based at Kidderminster Depot on the Severn Valley Railway when not working on the national network.

The owner of 50026 *Indomitable*, Paul Spracklen, has stated his intention to register his locomotive to main line use and this is expected to take place over the next couple of years.

The mandatory safety equipment required for locomotives to operate over Network Rail infrastructure has recently been acquired by Mr Spracklen for use on 50026, following the decision by Boden Rail Engineering Ltd to sell its main line-registered 50017 *Royal Oak* to a member of the Great Central Railway for preservation. With its main line running equipment removed prior to its sale, 50017's main line career has now effectively come to an end.

It is likely to be a number of years before 50029 *Renown* returns to use, as its owners concentrate on completing the restoration of 50030 *Repulse* at their Peak Rail base. Although 50029 was repainted in 2004 it is in a largely unrestored condition and will require a complete overhaul to bring it back into service, although the restoration of 50030 by the Renown Repulse Restoration Group is now reaching an advanced stage. 50029 stands awaiting its turn for attention at Rowsley South on April 3, 2007. MARTIN HART

OTHER CLASS 50s

Two main line-registered Class 50s are regarded as commercial assets of their respective owners and not strictly classed as preserved locomotives, although both have appeared at various heritage railway events, courtesy of their owners.

50008 *Thunderer* is owned by Garcia Hanson and is regularly in use on spot-hire work for his Hanson & Hall Rail Services business. The locomotive was originally preserved by Pete Waterman prior to being sold to Sea Containers and prepared for export to be used in Peru. However, this proposal never materialised and the locomotive was subsequently sold to Mr Hanson.

During its abortive preparation for use in Peru, the vacuum braking equipment on the locomotive was removed and, therefore, it is now capable of working air-braked trains only. 50008 was re-registered for main line use in early 2017 and has also regularly attended various heritage railways as a guest locomotive at diesel events.

50050 *Fearless*, is owned by Boden Rail Engineering Ltd and is based at the company's Nottingham Eastcroft depot base. 50050 was originally bought from BR by Dutch railwayman Harry Schneider and worked on the main line for a brief period in the late 1990s before undergoing a programme of restoration and repairs by the D400 Fund at Yeovil Railway Centre, prior to being sold to Neil Boden's company in January 2015.

Boden Rail Engineering also formerly owned 50007 *Hercules* and 50017 *Royal Oak*, but both of these locomotives have since been sold on, with 50007 now owned by the Class 50 Alliance and 50017 has entered preservation on the Great Central Railway.

MAIN LINE REGISTERED PRESERVED CLASS 50s

Loco	Owner	National Network Certification Status
50007	Class 50 Alliance	Main Line Certified
50017	Privately Owned	Main Line Certification Expired
50026	Privately Owned	Awaiting Main Line Certification
50031	Private, under care of Class 50 Alliance	Main Line Certification Expired
50044	Class 50 Alliance	Main Line Certification Expired
50049	Class 50 Alliance	Main Line Certified

LOCO	NAME	PREVIOUS IDENTITIES	OWNER	LOCATION
50008	*Thunderer*	D408, 50008	GH	Leicester TMD
50050	*Fearless*	D400, 50050	BREL	Nottingham Eastcroft

OWNER KEY: BREL – Boden Rail Engineering Ltd, GH – Garcia Hanson (operated by Hanson & Hall Rail Services)

The classic lines of the 'Westerns' are shown to good effect during the 2013 50th anniversary celebrations for D1062 *Western Courier* entering service with BR in 1963. The locomotive is lined up against the Western Locomotive Association's other Class 52, D1013 *Western Ranger*, which is currently out of service undergoing a major overhaul. KEVIN DELANEY

CLASS 52

The policy of the Western Region to develop fleets of diesel-hydraulic designs saw a fleet of highly distinctive and powerful locomotives emerge from Swindon and Crewe Works. The 'Westerns' were another product of the 1955 British Railways Modernisation Plan.

The 'Westerns' were fitted with two Maybach MD655 power units with hydraulic-transmission and could be operated using one or both engines, although the performance of the locomotives was more efficient when they were running on both engines. They were capable of speeds of up to 90mph and were vacuum braked (although many of the locomotives were subsequently also fitted with air brakes).

The order was for 74 locomotives and they would be known as the 'Western' class, with each locomotive named, with each name being prefixed with the 'Western' name and a number of themes were contained within the locomotive names.

The first locomotive, D1000 *Western Enterprise*, emerged in a striking Desert Sand livery, complete with cast fleet numbers beneath the driver's side cab window and cast nameplates midway along the bodyside. Another of the locomotives, D1015 *Western Champion*, was also outshopped in an experimental orange-based golden-ochre livery, with an experimental yellow warning panel at the A end of the locomotive.

The remainder of the fleet mainly emerged in maroon livery, with yellow buffer beams, although a few examples did make their service debut painted in an attractive dark green livery also. Small yellow warning panels were later added and then the majority had standard BR blue applied with full yellow ends.

The locomotives were generally used on the longer and faster routes radiating from the Western Region, where their performance allowed them to maintain schedules, as the other main line diesel-hydraulic 'Warships' and 'Hymeks' were not considered to be powerful enough for some of the more top-link services.

Under TOPS the 'Westerns' were given the classification of Class 52, but none of the locomotives had BR five-figure identification numbers applied and they retained their cast names and number plates until they were withdrawn from service.

With BR deciding to phase out its Western Region diesel-hydraulic fleet, the writing was on the wall for the 'Westerns' after just over a decade in traffic and with plenty of life left in them. However, they were now deemed non-standard and the first two locomotives were removed from service in May 1973 with the withdrawal of D1019 *Western Challenger* and D1032 *Western Marksman*.

Over the course of the next four years the rest of the fleet was gradually taken out of service, with the final five examples, D1010 *Western Campaigner*, D1013 *Western Ranger*, D1023 *Western Fusilier*, D1041 *Western Prince* and D1048 *Western Lady* being withdrawn in February 1977 – all five went on to find salvation in preservation.

The type bowed out on February 26, 1977 when D1013 and D1023 hauled the 'Western Tribute' farewell tour from London Paddington, taking in many of the routes that had closely been associated with the locomotives while they had reigned the Western Region.

Operating on one engine, following the failure of one of its Maybach MD655 engines during a main line tour in 2016, D1015 *Western Champion* departs from Bewdley with a train for Bridgnorth on the Severn Valley Railway during a diesel event on May 19, 2018. The locomotive has since been taken out of service to allow both its engines to be rebuilt and it has been repainted into early BR blue livery. KEVIN DELANEY

THE PRESERVED CLASS 52s

Seven 'Westerns' passed into preservation following withdrawal and all are considered to have long-term futures on heritage lines and, in the case of D1015 *Western Champion*, also on the main line. However, as at summer 2019, there is currently only one of the surviving locomotives actively in service.

D1010 *Western Campaigner* remains based in the West Country, where the locomotives spent all of their working lives on BR. It is owned by the Diesel & Electric Preservation Group on the West Somerset Railway. The locomotive was originally preserved by the Foster Yeoman company and was disguised as long-scrapped D1035 *Western Yeoman* and was displayed at the company's Merehead Quarry for several years.

Following its purchase by the DEPG it moved to the Didcot Railway Centre and was returned to service in 1989, although it retained its D1035 identity for a while and moved to the West Somerset Railway in 1991, where it made its debut in the distinctive Desert Sand livery that had been originally carried by fleet

pioneer D1000 *Western Enterprise*. It has remained at the WSR ever since and has been a regular performer on the line, although it is currently out of service after suffering a major failure of the locomotive's transmission in 2018.

D1013 *Western Ranger* and D1062 *Western Courier* are both owned by the Western Locomotive Association (WLA) and based on the Severn Valley Railway (SVR), where they have been based since 1978 after a short period working on the Paignton & Dartmouth Steam Railway following preservation.

D1013 was originally owned by a supporter of the WLA but was subsequently sold to the association. D1062 was extensively overhauled at the turn of the century and returned

CLASS 52

BUILT: BR Swindon Works and Crewe Works, 1961-1963

ENGINE: Two Maybach MD655 Power Units

NO. BUILT: 74

NO. PRESERVED: 7

OTHER SURVIVORS: 0

to use in 2006, with D1013 coming out of service in 2009 for an overhaul, which has yet to be completed. D1062 is currently the only serviceable 'Western' and has regular running days at the SVR.

D1015 *Western Champion* is the Class 52 which flies the flag for the design on the main line network following its return to main line use in 2002. The locomotive is nominally based at the SVR when not in main line use but, in December 2016, D1015 suffered an engine failure that requires specialist repairs.

Subsequently the owning Diesel Traction Group has taken the decision to take it out of service to rebuild both of its engines and it is expected to return to main line use once the necessary repairs have been completed. It has also been repainted into early BR blue livery with small yellow warning panels, although it has yet to make its debut in traffic in these colours due to its ongoing engine repairs at Kidderminster.

D1023 *Western Fusilier* was one of the locomotives chosen to work the final Class 52 hauled trains on BR and was

On June 13, 1989, D1010 *Western Campaigner*, disguised as scrapped D1035 *Western Yeoman*, makes its first moves under its own power at Didcot Railway Centre, following restoration to working order. The locomotive moved to the West Somerset Railway shortly afterwards and remains at the WSR, where it is currently awaiting repairs to a failed transmission. RICHARD THOMPSON

Now on display in the Railway Museum at York is D1023 *Western Fusilier*, which was one of the final two locomotives to haul a 'Western'-hauled train on BR on February 26, 1977, the 'Western Tribute' along with D1013 *Western Ranger*. On November 22, 2014, D1023 is on display in the Great Hall at York alongside pioneer Class 31, 31018. TOM MCATEE

The Severn Valley Railway is now home to three Class 52s, with D1013, D1015 and D1062 all based on the line. D1062 *Western Courier* is currently the only serviceable preserved 'Western' and is photographed passing through Foley Park with a Kidderminster to Bridgnorth service on October 6, 2012. This locomotive has since been painted into BR blue after spending much of its time in preservation carrying maroon livery. TOM MCATEE

Prior to being taken out of service for static display at the Railway Museum in York, D1023 *Western Fusilier* departs from Goathland on the North Yorkshire Moors Railway during a visit to the line on September 19, 2009. KEVIN DELANEY

subsequently claimed by the National Railway Museum. After making several visits to various heritage lines, the locomotive is now a static exhibit at the Railway Museum in York and there are no plans for the 'Western' to return to action at this stage.

At the East Lancashire Railway, D1041 *Western Prince* was one of the first main line locomotives to be based on the railway, with it arriving at Bury alongside D832 *Onslaught* in 1980. In 1988 the locomotive was given an extensive bodywork overhaul at Crewe and was returned to original BR maroon

livery before returning to service on the ELR and at other heritage railway events to which it was invited. D1041 continued to give regular service to the ELR for many years, but it was taken out of service in 2005 and has been undergoing an extensive rebuild and overhaul at Bury, which is now reaching an advanced stage, although there is still no target for its return to use.

The final preserved Class 52 is D1048 *Western Lady*, which is undergoing a comprehensive rebuild at the Midland Railway Butterley. The locomotive is owned by a small consortium of

friends, who have been working on its restoration since buying it in 1997.

D1048 was originally preserved on the North Yorkshire Moors Railway where it briefly saw use on passenger trains, but it has not worked a train since 1980 and its return to service is eagerly awaited by many enthusiasts. In the intervening years, the locomotive has spent time stored or undergoing attention at Horwich Works, the now-closed Steamport Museum in Southport, the Bodmin & Wenford Railway and Crewe Heritage Centre, before its move to Butterley.

LEFT: A suitably grubby D1010 *Western Campaigner* hauls a goods train through Crowcombe Heathfield station on the West Somerset Railway in this undated view. The locomotive had been deliberately weathered to provide a more authentic recreation of the final years of the 'Westerns' on BR. RICHARD HOLMES

MAIN LINE PRESERVED CLASS 52s

The Diesel Traction Group had originally intended to preserve D821 *Greyhound* as a main line registered locomotive, but subsequently decided to return its 'Western', D1015 *Western Champion*, to main line use, with the locomotive undergoing an extensive rebuild over many years before it was re-certified for main line use in 2002.

It made its first main line test runs in January 2002 painted in an attractive Golden Ochre livery before its first main line passenger tour in more than 25 years, operated the following month. Since then it has worked a number of tours across the country.

It was repainted into maroon livery in 2006 and continued to work on the main line regularly until it suffered an engine failure in 2016, with the locomotive currently undergoing repairs before it is expected to return to service both on the SVR and the main line when the necessary engine repairs on the locomotive have been completed.

While D1015 has been widely travelled and has remained a popular locomotive on the main line, it is unlikely any of the other six survivors will also be registered for main line running at any point in the future.

LOCO	NAME	BR IDENTITIES	OWNER	LOCATION
D1010	*Western Campaigner*	D1010	DEPG	WSR
D1013	*Western Ranger*	D1013	WLA	SVR
D1015	*Western Champion*	D1015	DTG	SVR
D1023	*Western Fusilier*	D1023	NRM	RMY
D1041	*Western Prince*	D1041	BHG	ELR
D1048	*Western Lady*	D1048	Private	MRB
D1062	*Western Courier*	D1062	WLA	SVR

OWNERS KEY: BHG – Bury Hydraulic Group, DEPG – Diesel & Electric Preservation Group, DTG – Diesel Traction Group, NRM – National Railway Museum, WLA – Western Locomotive Association

LOCATION KEY: ELR – East Lancashire Railway, MRB – Midland Railway Butterley, RMY – Railway Museum York, SVR – Severn Valley Railway, WSR – West Somerset Railway

MAIN LINE REGISTERED PRESERVED CLASS 52s

Loco	Owner	National Network Certification Status
D1015	Diesel Traction Group	Main Line Certified (undergoing repairs)

Covered in a layer of dirt, D1010 *Western Campaigner* departs from Williton on the West Somerset Railway in this undated view of the locomotive. Williton is the maintenance base of the Diesel & Electric Preservation Group, which owns, maintains and operates most of the diesel locomotives that are based on the WSR. RICHARD HOLMES

D1041 *Western Prince* has been undergoing a comprehensive rebuild at Bury on the East Lancashire Railway for the past few years, although its rebuild is now reaching an advanced stage. Shortly before being taken out of service, the 'Western' clears its throat as it makes a smoky departure from Irwell Vale with a Bury to Rawtenstall service. NIGEL VALENTINE

Pausing at Arley, while awaiting the arrival of a Kidderminster-bound service from Bridgnorth, D1013 *Western Ranger* provides an imposing image during the October 2004 Severn Valley Railway autumn diesel event. ANDY COWARD

D1015 *Western Champion* pokes its nose out of the shed at Didcot Railway Centre on June 25, 2011, as it undergoes maintenance. NIGEL VALENTINE

D1048 *Western Lady* is undergoing an extensive overhaul by its owners at the Midland Railway Butterley, which has been progressing over the past 20 years. Having now not hauled a passenger train for almost 40 years, its return to service at some point in the future will prove to be extremely popular with enthusiasts. D1048 stands outside the Matthew Kirtley Museum at Swanwick Junction on June 15, 2019. KEVIN DELANEY

CLASS 55

The first production 'Deltic' entered service on the East Coast Main Line (ECML) between London Kings Cross and Edinburgh in 1961, starting another legendary chapter in the history of ECML traction, which would last for just 21 years before the final example was withdrawn from service.

The 22 locomotives, numbered D9000-D9021, were constructed by Vulcan Foundry at Newton-le-Willows, near Preston, to an English Electric design. Like the original DELTIC prototype which had been built in 1955, the production locomotives were fitted with two 18-cylinder Napier Deltic engines and could be operated on one or both engines.

They were delivered in two-tone green livery, with the bodysides painted dark green, with a lighter green applied at solebar height. Yellow warning panels were added shortly after they entered service.

They were the first diesel locomotives designed with component exchange in mind. Due to the size of the fleet and the high availability required by BR, 13 spare engines were ordered in addition to those delivered with the locomotives. The float of spare engines was ordered to allow defective engines to be quickly exchanged, with spare engines fitted to allow the locomotives to re-enter service as quickly as possible, thereby minimising downtime for the locomotive undergoing engine repairs. Faulty engines were then repaired and held as spares until required.

The 'Deltics' were originally allocated to three BR depots: Finsbury Park, Gateshead and Haymarket, with major repairs

carried out at Doncaster Works.

Shortly after entering service the locomotives were named, with the Gateshead and Haymarket examples being named after British Army regiments, while the Finsbury Park machines were named after famous racehorses, carrying on a tradition started by the London North Eastern Railway.

Under the TOPS numbering system, the 'Deltics' became Class 55, numbered 55001-55022, with pioneer D9000 taking the highest number 55022. The new corporate image of BR launched in the late 1960s saw the two-tone green livery make way for BR blue, with full yellow ends, although the Finsbury Park allocated examples often sported white window surrounds.

Despite the purchase of spare engines when the fleet was delivered to BR, the intensive nature of the ECML timetable and the relatively small size of the fleet saw BR struggle with spare parts and when the High Speed Trains were launched in the late 1970s this spelt the beginning of the end for the 'Deltics'.

The first locomotives to be withdrawn were 55001 *St Paddy* and 55020 *Nimbus* in January 1980, although both had been out of service for several months and were used to donate vital spares to the remaining examples. The next withdrawal would be 55003 *Meld* in December 1980, but BR planned that 1981 would be the last year of the 'Deltics' on the ECML.

With the locomotives nearing the end of their working lives on BR, it was recognised that the fleet had gained a popular following among enthusiasts and BR acknowledged this by

55019 *Royal Highland Fusilier* is another locomotive owned by the Deltic Preservation Society and based at Barrow Hill. While this locomotive was formerly the DPS main line-registered 'Deltic', 55019 is now just used on heritage lines. On May 19, 2018, 55019 hauls a train through Northwood Lane, near Bewdley, while working a Severn Valley Railway service from Kidderminster to Bridgnorth. KEVIN DELANEY

LEFT: The decision by the Bluebell Railway to host diesel events took many enthusiasts by surprise, as the railway is predominantly steam, but the railway has hosted some very popular diesel events over the past few years, including a 'Deltic' themed event featuring the NRM's D9002 and the DPS owned D9009 and 55019. On October 6, 2017, D9009, 55019 and D9002 stand at Horsted Keynes. KEVIN DELANEY

BELOW: D9009 *Alycidon* hauls a train along the Swanage Railway during a visit to the line on May 8, 2011. The locomotive is main line registered and has worked extensively on the main line and at heritage railways, but is currently out of service following a serious failure in spring 2019. The loss of the NRM's D9002 from main line service means that D9009 is currently the only main line registered 'Deltic'. KEVIN DELANEY

painting 55002 *Kings Own Yorkshire Light Infantry* into BR two-tone green livery with full yellow ends. This locomotive quickly became popular for railtours as the fleet was being run down throughout 1981.

The end came on January 2, 1982, when the 'Deltic Farewell' tour operated, hauled by 55015 *Tulyar* from London Kings Cross to Edinburgh, while 55022 *Royal Scots Grey* worked the return leg. The return of the train to the Capital saw unprecedented scenes as thousands of people descended on the station to witness the arrival of the last Deltic-hauled train, with the event being covered by ITN's News at Ten.

The withdrawn locomotives were stored at Doncaster and an impromptu open day was held on February 27, 1982, attended by thousands of enthusiasts who came to say goodbye to their favourite locomotives. Thankfully, six Class 55s would escape the attention of the scrapman.

The Settle-Carlisle line is quite far removed from the East Coast Main Line where the 'Deltics' spent their working lives. However, D9009 *Alycidon* makes light work of its train as it passes Birketts Common on the S&C as it works a Carlisle to Willington charter on September 29, 2018. KEVIN DELANEY

THE PRESERVED CLASS 55s

Six 'Deltics' survived the cutter's torch, although two of these are now owned by Locomotive Services Ltd (LSL) at Crewe Diesel Depot. Of the other four, three are owned by the Deltic Preservation Society (DPS) and one by the National Railway Museum (NRM).

55002 *Kings Own Yorkshire Light Infantry* gained fame during the rundown of the 'Deltics' on BR, as it was repainted into green livery with full yellow ends for its final few months in traffic. It was subsequently claimed by the National Railway Museum and arrived at York in 1982 after withdrawal.

55002 spent many years on display at York, making occasional appearances at heritage railway events before spending a number of years on static display at the NRM. It went on loan to the East Lancashire Railway (ELR) from 1996, with volunteers quickly returning the locomotive to operation for use alongside the DPS's D9019 *Royal Highland Fusilier*, which was also based on the ELR at the time.

The NRM then entered into an agreement with Deltic 9000 Locomotives (DNLL) for 55002 to be returned to the main line and be operated by DNLL and the locomotive was moved to Brush Traction in Loughborough for work to begin on main line certification. However, DNLL got into financial difficulties while work was under way and it was left incomplete at Loughborough and in a state of limbo.

A supporters' group, the KOYLI Group, was set up to work with the NRM on reviving 55002 and it was subsequently moved to Barrow Hill and

repainted in BR blue. Over the next few years it was returned to serviceable condition by the KOYLI Group and was subsequently re-registered for the main line. It was repainted into BR green in 2016, regaining its original D9002 identity.

However, the NRM has recently held a review of its diesel fleet and in spring 2019 it announced that D9002 would no longer be maintained in an operational condition and it would now remain a static exhibit. As a result of this, the supporting volunteer-led KOYLI Group has disbanded, with many of the former KOYLI volunteers now assisting the DPS with their three locomotives.

The DPS was successful in purchasing 55009 *Alycidon* and 55019 following their withdrawal by BR. The two 'Deltics' then saw use on the North Yorkshire Moors Railway (NYMR) for a number of years.

While 55009 was subsequently given a prolonged major overhaul to allow it to be returned to the main line, 55019 became the DPS roving 'Deltic', spending extended loan periods at the Great Central Railway and ELR.

When the DPS was approached by luxury train operator Venice Simplon Orient Express to use the society's locomotives in conjunction with VSOE

trains, agreement was reached to certify both D9009 and 55019 for main line use and in 1999 both locomotives were recertified, although the VSOE hire deal was terminated somewhat earlier than had been envisaged. However, the funds generated from the main line operating contract allowed the DPS to fund the construction of a dedicated depot for its locomotives and spare parts at Barrow Hill Roundhouse, which is now considered to be the home base of the DPS.

These days, D9009 is still certified for main line running and has regularly run on the main line and at heritage railway events, although it is currently out of service following traction motor damage incurred during a main line tour in spring 2019, while 55019 is no longer main line certified but is regularly hired out to heritage railways as the DPS's roving ambassador.

55015 *Tulyar* was originally privately owned, but was subsequently acquired by the DPS and was based on the Midland Railway Butterley. It was taken out of service for a major overhaul in 1997 and moved to the new DPS Depot at Barrow Hill in 2004 where it has remained under overhaul ever since. The locomotive has been completely rebuilt from end to end and the inner and outer bodywork skin has also been replaced. The overhaul is now nearing completion, but no date has yet been announced for its return to use.

While pioneer D9000 *Royal Scots Grey* (55022) and D9016 *Gordon Highlander* (55016) are no longer owned by preservationists, their story

CLASS 55

BUILT:	Vulcan Foundry, 1961-1962
ENGINE:	Napier Deltic D18-25B power units
NO. BUILT:	22
NO. PRESERVED:	4
OTHER SURVIVORS:	2

Five 'Deltics' consisting of 55022, 55019, 55002, D9016 and D9009 stand in the yard at Buckley Wells at a special photographic evening on the East Lancashire Railway during a 'Deltic' event held by the railway in September 2012. At the time D9016 and 55022 were both based on the line while owned by Martin Walker. TOM MCATEE

is also worth inclusion. D9000 was purchased from BR by DNLL and moved to the Nene Valley Railway (NVR). The locomotive was quickly returned to use and saw use on heritage railways across the country. 55016 was also bought by DNLL, initially as a source of spare parts for D9000, but was found to be in generally good condition and the decision was then taken to also return D9016 to service.

D9000 will go down in history as the first 'Deltic' to return to the main line when it worked the 'Deltic Deliverance' railtour on November 30, 1996 – albeit a tour which ended in disappointment when the locomotive suffered a collector drum fire.

However, it was quickly back in service and continued in service, including use on some service trains for Virgin CrossCountry, until DNLL went into liquidation in 2003. By the time of DNLL's demise D9000 had fallen into disrepair and was stored at Hornsey Depot pending its disposal. D9000 was sold to Martin Walker in late 2004 and, after an extensive overhaul carried out by the commercial engineering division of the DPS at Barrow Hill, it moved to a new home on the ELR.

When not in main line use the locomotive was based on the ELR, but in more recent years it moved home base to the NYMR and also spent periods on loan to the NVR and Severn Valley Railway.

D9016 *Gordon Highlander* has also had a very chequered history since the demise of DNLL. When the company got into financial difficulties the locomotive was claimed by Porterbrook in lieu of payments for the main line overhaul

that it had financed. It was subsequently sold to a private individual who moved it to Tyseley Locomotive Works before it moved to Peak Rail in 2007 for a three-year loan, which was subsequently ended when the locomotive was sold to Harry Needle Railroad Company in autumn 2008.

Mr Needle stated D9016 had been bought as a source of spares and he intended to scrap the locomotive once parts had been recovered. He then offered D9016 for sale and it was bought by national freight operator Direct Rail Services, which intended to use it on

charter services – although this work never materialised and it was sold on again in December 2009 to Martin Walker. The purchase by Mr Walker brought the two former DNLL 'Deltics' back together again and based on the ELR.

Two 'Deltic' cabs have also survived, with one cab from 55008 *The Green Howards* in the ownership of the DPS and which was used for a period as a driving simulator. The other surviving cab comes from 55021 *Argyll and Sutherland Highlander* and is located at The Cab Yard in South Wales.

Pioneer 'Deltic' 55022 *Royal Scots Grey* was originally preserved by Deltic 9000 Locomotives, but was subsequently bought by Martin Walker after the original owners got into financial difficulties. Mr Walker had the locomotive rebuilt and overhauled by the commercial arm of the Deltic Preservation Society, before it re-entered service in 2006. The locomotive is seen approaching Bury on the East Lancashire Railway on June 8, 2008. This locomotive is now owned by Locomotive Services Ltd at Crewe. NIGEL VALENTINE

LEFT: The interesting preservation history of D9016 has had more twists and turns than virtually every other preserved locomotive, including several different owners and a threat of scrapping. On April 29, 2007, D9016 stands at Rowsley South on Peak Rail during one of its final appearances on the railway prior to it moving to Barrow Hill and an uncertain future. Thankfully it survived and is now one of two 'Deltics' owned by Locomotive Services Ltd. STEVE KEMP

LOCO	NAME	BR IDENTITIES	OWNER	LOCATION
D9002	Kings Own Yorkshire Light Infantry	D9002, 55002	NRM	RMY
D9009	Alycidon	D9009, 55009	DPS	Nemesis
D9015	Tulyar	D9015, 55015	DPS	BHR
55019	Royal Highland Fusilier	D9019, 55019	DPS	BHR

OWNER KEY: DPS – Deltic Preservation Society, Nemesis – Nemesis Rail Burton upon Trent Depot, NRM – National Railway Museum

LOCATION KEY: BHR – Barrow Hill Roundhouse, RMY – Railway Museum York

An interesting development in the history of formerly preserved D9016 *Gordon Highlander* was its repaint into Porterbrook purple livery, following the leasing company funding a main line overhaul for the locomotive on behalf of its owners, Deltic 9000 Locomotives. The purple Deltic stands outside the National Railway Museum on November 22, 2002. RICHARD THOMPSON

55019 *Royal Highland Fusilier* arrives at Horsted Keynes on the Bluebell Railway on October 6, 2017. The appearance of these locomotives in sleepy Sussex was far removed from their time working express services on the East Coast Main Line. KEVIN DELANEY

LEFT: On October 7, 2017, D9002 *Kings Own Yorkshire Light Infantry* arrives at Horsted Keynes on the Bluebell Railway during their autumn diesel weekend. This locomotive was restored to main line condition by the KOYLI Group at the National Railway Museum. However, the museum has recently announced a change in strategy which means the locomotive is now destined to remain a static exhibit at York for the foreseeable future. KEVIN DELANEY

MAIN LINE PRESERVED CLASS 55s

Out of the six 'Deltics' to originally enter preservation, five of them have been returned to main line use. The summarised details of the preserved 'Deltics' operating on the main line are given earlier in this section, but differing fortunes in the history of those five locomotives have now seen the number of main line-registered 'Deltics' reduced to just one.

With the sale of 55022 to Locomotive Services Ltd in November 2017 and the decision by the NRM to retire D9002 from operational use, it has left D9009 *Alycidon* flying the flag for the type on the main line.

However, in spring 2019 the locomotive suffered a serious failure caused by a power surge to its traction motors while hauling a charter on the main line and it is now in need of major repairs to its traction motors. It is currently located at Nemesis Rail at Burton upon Trent where it has been undergoing assessment pending the necessary repairs being carried out. However, the DPS has stated that the repairs to D9009 are likely to be costly.

The only preserved 'Deltic' which has not yet worked on the main line is D9015 *Tulyar*, which has been undergoing an overhaul at Barrow Hill over the past two decades.

The locomotive is being overhauled to main line standards and the DPS has extensive experience of operating these locomotives on the main line through its experiences with 55009 and 55019.

MAIN LINE REGISTERED PRESERVED CLASS 55s

Loco	Owner	National Network Certification Status
55002	National Railway Museum	Main Line Certification Expired
55009	Deltic Preservation Society	Main Line Certified (undergoing repairs)
55019	Deltic Preservation Society	Main Line Certification Expired

OTHER CLASS 55s

In November 2017, preserved 'Deltics' D9016 *Gordon Highlander* and 55022 *Royal Scots Grey* were sold by Martin Walker to Locomotive Services Ltd at Crewe. Both locomotives were in need of repairs before they could be used again. Both have previously been main line registered, although it is now a number of years since D9016 last worked a train over Network Rail metals under its own power. 55022 was a regular main line performer until 2017, although had not worked a passenger service for some time due to only having one operational engine.

55022 had been operating for some time on one power unit, following problems experienced with leaking seals on a replacement Napier Marine power unit which had been fitted following a serious engine failure to one of the original Napier Deltic locomotive power units in November 2006. The complicated nature of the Napier Deltic power units means that overhauling and repairing them is a specialist and expensive job, but the locomotives were sold by Mr Walker along with an extensive collection of spare parts, including power unit components and spares.

At the present time it is unconfirmed what plans are in place for either locomotive, although it is thought that 55022 will receive the necessary repairs to allow it to return to main line service, hauling trains for LSL's operating company Saphos Trains.

It is planned that D9016 will move to the former Hornby factory in Margate, Kent, which has been acquired by LSL and is to be used as a museum facility for housing and displaying some of their locomotives which are not currently active on the main line. The advantages of this site are that it will provide covered accommodation to prevent further deterioration of out-of-service locomotives, while also making them available for viewing by the general public and enthusiasts. It is likely that D9016 will have a bodywork overhaul completed and a repaint before its planned move to Kent.

Although neither of these locomotives is thought to be at risk of scrapping at any stage in the future, their acquisition by LSL means that they are no longer classed as preserved locomotives and are now commercial assets of their owner.

NON-PRESERVED SURVIVING CLASS 55s
LOCOMOTIVE SERVICES LTD: D9016, 55022

At Barrow Hill, 56006's engine is started up in front of assembled photographers during a photographic charter on July 23, 2004. At this stage the locomotive was still owned by English Welsh & Scottish Railways, but was stored at the heritage site and it was subsequently purchased by the Class 56 Group. NIGEL VALENTINE

CLASS 56

During the 1970s, BR decided to order a new fleet of heavy freight locomotives and 135 new type-five locomotives were constructed and given the classification of Class 56. The first 30 examples were built in Romania, while the remainder were assembled by BREL at either Doncaster or Crewe Works.

The locomotives had a smart, if functional, appearance and were delivered mainly in BR blue livery with TOPS numbering of 56001-56135. They were fitted with powerful Ruston Paxman 16RK3CT engines and were the first design of locomotive in the UK to be fitted with air brakes only, which was by that stage becoming the standard form of braking for UK rolling stock, as vacuum-braked stock was being phased out.

The first locomotives, 56001 and 56002, arrived in the UK in August 1976, but it would be eight years before the last member of the fleet entered service in 1984.

While the locomotives were strong performers when they were working trains, the fleet often suffered from reliability issues and the Class 56s were expensive to maintain. In the run-up to the privatisation of British Rail in the 1990s, the Class 56s were split between the three freight businesses, Mainline Freight, Trainsrail and LoadHaul, but when the three companies were all bought by English Welsh & Scottish Railways (EWS) the surviving Class 56 locomotives passed to the new company.

The first withdrawal from the Class 56 fleet came in September 1991 when 56042 was withdrawn. A number of other Class 56s were withdrawn during the early 1990s, with those chosen coming mainly from the first 30 locomotives which had been built in Romania and were considered to be of a poorer build quality than those manufactured in Doncaster or Crewe.

EWS subsequently decided to dispense with the Class 56 fleet in its entirety following the delivery of a new fleet of Class

66s and in 2004 the final examples were withdrawn. Following their removal from traffic in the UK, a number of the stored locomotives were reactivated along with a number of Class 58s for use on the construction of a new railway line in France and these were repainted into the Fertis grey livery. Following the end of their use in France, the locomotives were returned to the UK. In recent years, a number of Class 56s have been reactivated for the main line under a number of new operators, returning these locomotives to service on Network Rail metals once again.

LOCO	PREVIOUS IDENTITIES	OWNER	LOCATION
56006	56006	C56G	ELR
56097	56097	Private	GCRN
56301	56045, 56301	C56G	On Hire

OWNER KEY: C56G – Class 56 Group

LOCATION KEY: ELR – East Lancashire Railway, GCRN – Great Central Railway (Nottingham)

MAIN LINE PRESERVED CLASS 56s

There is just one preserved Class 56 certified for use on Network Rail and that is the Class 56 Group's 56301. The former Fastline Freight Class 56 was bought by the preservationists following its former owner going out of business and it is usually on hire to UK Rail Leasing at Leicester. For most of 2019, the locomotive has been hired to assist with shunting duties at Peak Forest in Derbyshire.

MAIN LINE REGISTERED PRESERVED CLASS 56s

Loco	Owner	National Network Certification Status
56301	Class 56 Group	Main Line Certified

The Class 56 Group also owns former Fastline Freight-liveried 56301, which is main line registered. As well as spending time on the main line network, 56301 has also occasionally visited heritage railway events and on May 8, 2011, the locomotive departs from Harmons Cross on the Swanage Railway. KEVIN DELANEY

While essentially a freight locomotive, the BR blue livery of 56006 is well suited on a passenger train, especially when paired with blue and grey-liveried coaches. On July 8, 2017, 56006 departs from Ramsbottom with a Bury to Rawtenstall service on the East Lancashire Railway, which is its current home base. TOM MCATEE

THE PRESERVED CLASS 56s

As with the Class 37s, the number of Class 56s in the railway preservation sector is now considerably lower than it used to be, as various locomotives have been purchased by main line operators for reactivation, or export. These developments have seen the number of preserved Class 56s reduced to just three examples, and one of these, 56301, is mainly used on hire to commercial companies for main line operations.

The Class 56 Group own 56006 and 56301. 56006 became something of a celebrity in 1999 when it was repainted into original BR blue livery for its final months in service with English Welsh & Scottish Railways. It has since passed into preservation and retains the same colours. It is currently based at the East Lancashire Railway where it is used alongside the rest of the ELR's diesel fleet, although during 2019 it has been out of traffic undergoing repairs. The second Class 56 Group locomotive is 56301, which is main line registered and is usually on hire to UK Rail Leasing. When not in main line use, 56301 has also visited various heritage railway diesel events. 56097 is preserved on the Great Central Railway (Nottingham) where it has been restored to working order and is painted in Trainload Freight Coal Sector colours, representing the class as many were during the early 1990s.

Restored to Trainload Freight grey livery, with Coal sector decals, 56097 is based on the Great Central Railway (Nottingham) where it is now operational following an extensive restoration and rebuild by volunteers. The locomotive is pictured at Ruddington on June 7, 2013. MARTIN HART

CLASS 56

BUILT: Romania, BREL Crewe and Doncaster Works, 1976-1984

ENGINE: Ruston Paxman 16RK3CT

NO. BUILT: 135

NO. PRESERVED: 3

OTHER SURVIVORS: 34

RIGHT: Currently in use for shunting duties around Peak Forest is the Class 56 Group's main line registered 56301, which is pictured shunting wagons on February 11, 2019. The former 56045 was bought following the collapse of Fastline Freight, but still retains its former operator's colours. TERRY EYRES

OTHER CLASS 56s

In recent years the Class 56 locomotive has enjoyed something of a renaissance, with the locomotives being given a second lease of life doing what they were designed to do, hauling freight services around the UK rail network. The biggest current operator to make use of Class 56s is Colas Rail, which owns 10 Class 56s, which see use on a variety of workings, with many of these locomotives maintained by Boden Rail Engineering at its Nottingham Eastcroft depot facility.

Perhaps the most exciting development concerning the Class 56s was the decision by GB Railfreight (GBRf) to buy the locomotives which had been purchased by UK Rail Leasing and based at Leicester Depot, pending reactivation.

Although a couple of the GBRf Class 56s are in serviceable condition and have recently been employed on shunting duties around Peak Forest in Derbyshire, the majority have been stored out of use for several years.

Many of these locomotives have now been moved to EMD at Longport and GBRf has begun a programme of reactivating many of the locomotives, although they will not be reactivated as Class 56s and will receive replacement EMD 12-710 engines as part of their rebuild. Upon completion of the project, the locomotives are due to be classified as Class 69, in much the same way that the Class 57 locomotives were re-engineered from former Class 47s.

DC Rail has two operational main line certified Class 56s in the shape of 56091 and 56103, with the company also owning 56303, which is currently out of traffic awaiting repairs.

Three Class 56s have been exported to Hungary for use with open access operator Floyd. Two locomotives, formerly preserved 56101 and stored 56115, were prepared for their new roles by Europhoenix, who also worked on the preparation of a number of Class 86s for export to Floyd, while 56117 was also exported to Hungary for use as a spares donor.

NON-PRESERVED SURVIVING CLASS 56s

COLAS RAIL:	56049, 56051, 56078, 56087, 56090, 56094, 56096, 56105, 56113, 56302
DC RAIL:	56091, 56103, 56303
GB RAILFREIGHT:	56007, 56009, 56018, 56031, 56032, 56037, 56038, 56060, 56065, 56069, 56077, 56081, 56098, 56104, 56106, 56128, 56311, 56312
EXPORTED TO FLOYD HUNGARY:	56101, 56115, 56117

• Please note that some of these locomotives are operational, while others are stored or being used as spares donor locomotives.

The only truly preserved Class 58 is 58016, which has been undergoing restoration since 2010 at Barrow Hill and, more recently, Leicester Depot. The locomotive is seen on August 2, 2015, inside the roundhouse at Barrow Hill, with its bodyside doors removed to show the power unit. PAUL HADFIELD

CLASS 58

When the first Class 58 emerged from the production line of BREL's Doncaster Works in 1983, its striking appearance certainly made it stand out from other designs that had come before.

The locomotive was created to address concerns that BR had about the predicted growth in railfreight traffic throughout the 1980s. BR also had an increasingly ageing fleet of locomotives, some of which would soon need to be replaced with more modern technology.

The railway company felt it needed a heavy freight locomotive that could be built at a relatively low cost with ease of maintenance in mind and component exchange a straightforward exercise and an order for 50 Class 58s, to be numbered 58001-58050, was placed. The locomotives were built by BREL at Doncaster Works between 1983 and 1987.

The body of the locomotives was a modular design with a load-bearing underframe, with cabs at each end of a thinner bodyside between them. External walkways were featured along the length of the bodyside and access to the power units and other ancillary equipment was through doors along the length of the body, rather than accessed through the cab, as in most in other UK designs. They were powered by a Ruston Paxman 12RK3ACT engine and weighed in at a hefty 130 tonnes.

Their distinctive appearance led to them being nicknamed 'Bones' by enthusiasts. The new locomotives also looked striking, with them all emerging from Doncaster painted in the then-new Railfreight red-stripe grey livery. The final locomotive, 58050, was accepted into traffic in March 1987 and

had become the last locomotive to be constructed at Doncaster Works. When delivered into traffic, all 50 locomotives were allocated to Toton Depot in Nottinghamshire and they were employed hauling 'merry-go-round' coal trains around the Midlands. Although they weren't solely used for hauling coal traffic, it was certainly their main work during their early years while the coal industry was still strong in the UK.

The Class 58s were rarely used in passenger traffic, being predominantly a freight design, but they did occasionally get allocated to hauling railtours and special workings. The first passenger working was a railtour from London Paddington to Matlock in September 1983, which had 58002 in charge.

In 1994, as BR was preparing for privatisation, the Trainload Freight business was split into three sectors, with the Class 58s all becoming the responsibility of the newly created Mainline Freight business.

This saw several of the locomotives being painted into the company's attractive aircraft blue and silver livery and those examples that weren't repainted received Mainline Freight branding.

Following privatisation, the three freight sector businesses, including Mainline Freight, were acquired by English Welsh & Scottish Railways (EWS). Officials from EWS initially praised the design, but the decision by EWS to order 250 Class 66 heavy freight locomotives spelt the beginning of the end for the Class 58s in the UK and the first locomotive, 58017, was stored in May 1999 and destined to never work again. Over the next three years the fleet were all taken out of traffic, with a final railtour operating in September 2002.

Not long for this world in its present format, 58022 stands at Peak Rail's Rowsley South yard on March 19, 2017, following its purchase by the Ivatt Diesel Recreation Group, who will be using the chassis of the Class 58 as the frame for their planned recreation of LMS diesel locomotive 10000. KEVIN DELANEY

LOCO	NAME	PREVIOUS IDENTITIES	OWNER	LOCATION
58016		58016	C58LG	Leicester
58022		58022 (to be basis of recreated LMS 10000)	IDRG	PKR

Undergoing restoration at the Battlefield Railway in Shackerstone, 58023 is now nearing the end of its rebuilding and has moved under its own power over the last few months. This locomotive is not strictly preserved and is destined to re-enter commercial use at some stage in the future. 58023 is partially repainted into Mainline blue livery on May 10, 2018. RICHARD THOMPSON

THE PRESERVED CLASS 58s

At the time of writing there are two Class 58s officially in preservation, with 58016 belonging to the Class 58 Locomotive Group and undergoing restoration at UK Rail Leasing's Leicester Depot and 58022 at Peak Rail. However, these two locomotives face very different futures.

58016 entered preservation in 2010 and was moved to Barrow Hill, which was to become its restoration home, returning one of the locomotives to a depot that had once played host to the Class 58s on a regular basis. Restoration work got under way almost immediately, but the locomotive has still not yet returned to service and in December 2015 it moved to Leicester Depot, where restoration work continues. The Class 58 Locomotive Group also bought 58045, but this was used as a source of spares for 58016 and has since been scrapped.

The second Class 58 in preservation is 58022, which has been purchased by the Ivatt Diesel Recreation Group, but the locomotive is not intended to be restored in its current guise, with the frame of the Class 58 destined to be used for the construction of LMS 10000, recreating a locomotive that was scrapped back in 1968.

While it is not intended that 10000 will be an exact recreation of the original locomotive, it is hoped that it will look almost identical to the pioneer LMS diesel locomotive, using an

CLASS 58

BUILT:	BREL Doncaster Works, 1983-1987
ENGINE:	Ruston Paxman 12RK3ACT
NO. BUILT:	50
NO. PRESERVED:	2
OTHER SURVIVORS:	40

English Electric 16SVT power unit and other English Electric parts, with any remaining parts being manufactured from new. It is an ambitious project, but the purchase of 58022 was seen as being crucial to its viability. At some stage the upper part of the locomotive will be stripped down, to allow the frames to be prepared for their new role.

The final Class 58, 58050, was designated by the Railway Heritage Committee for preservation as part of the National Collection on the strength of it being the final BR locomotive built at Doncaster Works. The locomotive is one of those exported to Spain for use by Continental Railways and it has now been in store for a number of years. It is not known at this stage whether 58050 will be returned to the UK or if it will ever take up its designated place as part of the National Collection.

OTHER SURVIVING CLASS 58s

Perhaps one of the most surprising parts of the Class 58 history was the widespread export of most of the fleet to Europe for further work, although this work has now ended and the surviving locomotives are now all in store awaiting either a return to the UK, or scrapping abroad.

In 2003 three Class 58s, 58038, 58039 and 58044, were exported to the Netherlands for use by railfreight operator ACTS. Spanish operator GIF also gained 58041 and 58043 for use on infrastructure trains in connection with the construction of a new railway line between Madrid and the French border. Further contracts for freight locomotives in Spain were also won by EWS and more Class 58s were soon heading over to Spain in May 2014.

A large number of Class 58s were also exported to France for use on construction trains for Fertis on the building of a new railway line between Paris and Strasbourg. Further locomotive supply contracts saw French operators Seco and TSO hire Class 58s and while some of the Fertis locomotives were returned to the UK following the end of the contract, the remainder have remained in France awaiting a decision on their future.

In addition to preserved 58016, there are also three Class

58s currently located on the Battlefield Railway at Shackerstone, in Leicestershire. 58012, 58023 and 58048 were purchased by private individuals with it being intended that 58023 and 58048 will be returned to service and 58012 will be used as a parts donor for the other two. 58023 and 58048 are being returned to use by Shackerstone-based Heritage Transport Restorations and 58023 is now nearing the end of its restoration, having undertaken some test runs along the Battlefield Railway during spring 2019.

Neither 58023 nor 58048 are believed to be preserved locomotives and it is thought that these locomotives may be used for commercial work when they are complete, although it is possible they may see some use at their host railway before moving away to resume a main line running career.

NON-PRESERVED SURVIVING CLASS 58s

STORED IN FRANCE: 58001, 58004, 58005, 58006, 58007, 58009, 58010, 58011, 58013, 58018, 58021, 58026, 58032, 58033, 58034, 58035, 58036, 58038, 58039, 58040, 58042, 58044, 58046, 58049

STORED IN SPAIN: 58015, 58020, 58024, 58025, 58027, 58029, 58030, 58031, 58041, 58043, 58047, 58050

SHACKERSTONE: 58012, 58023, 58048

The sole-surviving Class 71, E5001 stands in the yard at Barrow Hill along with a couple of stored Brighton Belle Pullman cars on September 22, 2012. The locomotive is now usually found on display at the Railway Museum in Shildon. ANDREW SEWELL

On September 12, 1992, E5001 and 73132 stand at London Waterloo. At the time the preserved Class 71 was permitted to operate a number of passenger charters over BR metals and it saw use for a number of years on passenger workings, although it has not operated under its own power for many years now. STEVE KEMP

CLASS 71

The Class 71 locomotive, or Southern Region HA as it was originally known, was a class of 24 electric locomotives that were built by British Railways at Doncaster Works between 1958 and 1960. They were another product to emerge as a result of the 1955 British Railways Modernisation Plan. They were painted in dark green with a lined thin red band along the bodyside and were numbered E5000-E5023.

They were designed to operate over the extensive electrified third-rail network of the Southern Region of BR, with them able to operate over both the 650v or 750v DC third rail routes. They were built primarily to serve the Kent Coast main lines and while they operated over the third rail network, they were also fitted with a pantograph which could be used for shunting the locomotives in depot yards that were not equipped with electrified third rails, but were fitted with overhead catenary. The pantographs eventually became largely redundant.

The locomotives had impressive rates of acceleration and were strong performers on the trains they hauled. Although they had been intended to be primarily freight locomotives, they did find employment on some of the Southern Region's most high-profile services, such as the 'Golden Arrow' Pullman trains and the 'Night Ferry' overnight services.

Ten of the locomotives were subsequently taken out of traffic and were converted to become diesel-electric locomotives under the Class 74 classification. These modified locomotives proved not to be successful and all of them were subsequently scrapped.

Under TOPS, the locomotives became Class 71. The 14 remaining locomotives were numbered 71001-71014 and all were repainted into BR blue livery with full yellow ends.

The introduction of various electric multiple units and diesel locomotive designs, along with the electro-diesel locomotives, saw the Class 71s fall out of favour and the need for them to operate on solely electrified lines made their operation somewhat restrictive. Unusually, the whole unmodified Class 71 fleet was withdrawn en-masse in November 1977 and all but one were scrapped.

LOCO	PREVIOUS IDENTITIES	OWNER	LOCATION
E5001	E5001, 71001	NRM	RMS

OWNER KEY: NRM – National Railway Museum

LOCATION KEY: RMS – Railway Museum Shildon

THE PRESERVED CLASS 71

Following withdrawal, 71001 was claimed by the National Railway Museum and was repainted into original BR green livery as E5001. The locomotive spent many years on display at York. In the early 1990s the locomotive was returned to main line use for a series of charters along its former Southern Region haunts, but it was subsequently retired from these duties and returned to York for display. Apart from steam locomotives, the use of preserved locomotives was very much frowned on by British Rail at the time, so the use of this locomotive for a

limited period certainly created a lot of interest, especially for those who had not witnessed the Class 71s in action prior to their withdrawal by BR.

E5001 also visited a number of open day events and spent several years on display at Barrow Hill Roundhouse in Derbyshire. By the time it left Barrow

CLASS 71

BUILT:	British Railways Doncaster Works, 1958-1960.
NO. BUILT:	24
NO. PRESERVED:	1
OTHER SURVIVORS:	0

Hill and was moved to Locomotion, the National Railway Museum at Shildon, the locomotive was presenting a rather sorry sight. This was due to the length of time since the Class 71 had last been painted and a period of time where it had been stored outside at Barrow Hill.

Upon arrival at Shildon in 2017, it was moved into their conservation workshop for a bodywork overhaul and repaint. The locomotive has undergone a lot of bodywork repairs and once these have been completed, the application of paint should give the locomotive its prestigious look once again.

Class 73/0 E6003 *Sir Herbert Walker* gained an enthusiastic following during its final years on British Rail following a repaint into BR green. Following its withdrawal, the locomotive spent a number of years based on the Great Central Railway before moving to the Swindon & Cricklade Railway, where it remains. On May 12, 2019, E6003 stands at Hayes Knoll station. AARON CRYAN

CLASS 73

The electro-diesel Class 73 was introduced because of the need for a versatile locomotive that could work on both the electrified 750v DC third-rail network and by a diesel engine on non-electrified lines across the Southern Region (SR) of British Rail.

The first six, E6001-E6006, were built by BR at Eastleigh Works, entered service in 1962 and were given a classification of 'JA'. They could be operated on electrified lines using eight collector shoes attached to their bogies and when operating on diesel power they used an English Electric 600hp 4SRKT power unit. They could run at a maximum speed of 80mph.

The success of the initial design saw a further order for 43 locomotives made by BR but these, which would be classified 'JB', were built by English Electric at Vulcan Foundry in Newton-le-Willows and entered service between 1965 and 1967. The main differences between the 'JA' and 'JB' locomotives were the newer examples were fitted with different bogies and traction motors. The 'JBs' were able to operate at a maximum of 90mph, as opposed to the 80mph attained by the earlier locomotives.

Under TOPS, the 'JA' locomotives became Class 73/0, while the 'JB' became Class 73/1. When the Class 73s were chosen as the locomotives to be used for the Gatwick Express services from London Victoria, 12 of the locomotives were re-classified as '73/2' and had their vacuum-braking equipment removed. These 12 '73/2' locomotives were later joined by 73112, which became 73213, and 73135, which became 73235.

The Class 73 fleet remained largely intact until the 1990s and there was only one example withdrawn relatively early in its career when E6027 was withdrawn in July 1972 following a serious collision six months earlier, making it the only member of the fleet to not receive TOPS numbers. One example, 73115, was withdrawn in 1982, while a number were stood down during the 1990s, including several that were subsequently preserved.

Four of the Class 73/0 locomotives eked out their days working on the Merseyrail network, where they were used on engineering and sandite services, before they were withdrawn. A fifth 'JA', 73003, had earlier been repainted into BR green livery, renumbered E6003 and named Sir Herbert Walker. With the exception of 73004, all of the 'JAs' survive.

English Welsh and Scottish Railways inherited many of the remaining Class 73/1s following privatisation of the rail network, but following a traction review their remaining examples were withdrawn in 2003 and sold for scrap by CF Booth in Rotherham. Many of these locomotives were in excellent condition and a large number were bought for preservation.

The Class 73/2s were replaced on Gatwick Express services by new trains in 2005. GB Railfreight acquired a number of them for working infrastructure trains. The company has since gone on to purchase a large number of the other remaining Class 73s from various places and is now by far the largest operator of the fleet.

A number of other operators also made use of Class 73s following privatisation, such as Eurostar, FM Rail, Network Rail (originally Railtrack), Southern and South West Trains. The Eurostar locomotives, 73118 and 73130, were both fitted with Scharfenberg couplers on their cab front, making them easily identifiable from the other members of the fleet and both of these locomotives also survive following their disposal by Eurostar.

For a relatively small fleet of locomotives it is somewhat surprising that so many survive in front line service, but that is testament to the design and versatility of these useful machines.

73129 was one of the Class 73/1 locomotives sold to CF Booth for scrap following withdrawal by EWS and it was subsequently bought for preservation on the Gloucestershire & Warwickshire Railway. It has since been restored to early BR blue as E6036 and is pictured at Winchcombe on July 26, 2013. MARTIN HART

73140 was preserved on the Spa Valley Railway and restored to early BR blue as E6047. It is pictured at the rear of a train consisting of a Class 08 shunter and a Thumper DEMU on October 19, 2013. 73140 has since been repainted into Network SouthEast livery. KEVIN DELANEY

THE PRESERVED CLASS 73s

There are now six Class 73s in preservation, which is now considerably fewer than was in preservation a decade ago. Following the disposal of the Class 73 fleet by EWS at the end of 2003, several locomotives were sold to CF Booth's scrapyard in Rotherham for scrapping. Many of these '73s' were in excellent condition and were either still operational, or only needing minor repairs to return them to service. As such, a number of preservationists seized on the opportunity to purchase these locomotives from the scrapman and they were moved to various lines for reactivation.

One of the most prolific collectors of Class 73s was the Dean Forest Diesel Association on the Dean Forest Railway, who purchased four of the original 'JA' locomotives when they were withdrawn by Merseyrail.

Following the sale of previously preserved 73001, 73002, E6005 and E6006 from the Dean Forest Railway, E6003 *Sir Herbert Walker* is now the only remaining member of the former 'JA' examples to be classified as a preserved

locomotive. Following preservation, it initially moved to The Lavender Line, before spending a number of years at the Great Central Railway. It then moved to the Swindon & Cricklade Railway, where it has undergone an overhaul and is now back in regular service on the railway.

The two former Eurostar locomotives are now classed as preserved, with 73118 based on the Barry Tourist Railway in South Wales and 73130 located at Finmere Station, where it is being restored.

E6036 represents the Class 73 design on the Gloucestershire & Warwickshire Railway and has spent its entire time in preservation based on the GWR, where it is restored to early BR blue livery.

73140 is now preserved on the Spa Valley Railway in Kent. After spending many years operating in BR blue as E6047, the locomotive was repainted into the comparatively modern Network SouthEast livery, which is becoming increasingly popular with the owners of preserved locomotives.

The only Class 73/2 now in preservation is 73210 *Selhurst* on the Ecclesbourne Valley Railway, after spending a number of years based at the Mid Norfolk Railway.

The preservation sector has offered rich pickings for main line operators who have realised the potential of re-using these locomotives on main line services and a large number of formerly preserved Class 73s have been purchased by main line operators for reactivation on Network Rail metals, including a number that were purchased by GB Railfreight for conversion into Class 73/9s for use on the Caledonian Sleeper contract. Network Rail has also benefited from formerly preserved Class 73s, with 73138 once owned by the AC Locomotive Group.

CLASS 73

BUILT:	British Rail, Eastleigh Works, 1962 (E6001-E6006) Vulcan Foundry, 1965-1967 (E6007-E6049)
ENGINE:	English Electric 4SRKT
NO. BUILT:	49
NO. PRESERVED:	6
OTHER SURVIVORS:	0

The sole preserved Class 73/2 is 73210 *Selhurst*, which was originally preserved on the Mid Norfolk Railway, but has since moved to the Ecclesbourne Valley Railway in Derbyshire, some distance from the Gatwick Express route where it once was one of the pool of dedicated locomotives. During a working visit to the East Lancashire Railway 73210 departs from Rawtenstall on July 7, 2013. ANDREW SEWELL

Class 73/0 E6003 *Sir Herbert Walker* stands at Hayes Knoll station on the Swindon & Cricklade Railway awaiting departure on June 8, 2019. AARON CRYAN

The first 'JA' Class 73/0 was E6001 which became 73001 and following withdrawal it was preserved on the Dean Forest Railway. 73001 has recently been purchased by Locomotive Services Ltd and it is thought that the locomotive will be returned to main line running under LSL. While still preserved, 73001 spent a spell on hire to the East Lancashire Railway and is pictured passing through Burrs while working a Rawtenstall to Heywood service on April 18, 2015. TERRY EYRES

Following restoration at the Dean Forest Railway, Class 73/0 locomotives E6005 and E6006 spent several years on loan to the Severn Valley Railway, where they proved to be useful for working engineering trains, along with the occasional passenger service and gala appearances. E6006 stands at Highley in October 2004. Both E6005 and E6006 were subsequently sold to GB Railfreight and converted to Class 73/9 locomotives for use on the Caledonian Sleeper contract. ANDY COWARD

LOCO	NAME	BR IDENTITIES	OWNER	LOCATION
E6003	*Sir Herbert Walker*	E6003, 73003	Private	SCR
73118		E6024, 73118	Private	BTR
E6036		E6036, 73129	Private	GWR
73130		E6037, 73130	Private	FMS
73140		E6047, 73140	Private	SPVA
73210	*Selhurst*	E6022, 73116, 73210	Private	EVR

LOCATION KEY: BTR – Barry Tourist Railway, EVR – Ecclesbourne Valley Railway, FMS – Finmere Station, GWR – Gloucestershire & Warwickshire Railway, SCR – Swindon & Cricklade Railway, SPVA – Spa Valley Railway

73114 is owned by Nemesis Rail, but has spent many years based on the Battlefield Railway at Shackerstone, where a number of its locomotives have been located and used by the railway alongside its fleet of preserved diesel locomotives. On May 15, 2010, 73114 stands in the sidings at Shackerstone alongside 56040, 56098 and 56086. KEVIN DELANEY

OTHER CLASS 73s

The largest operator of Class 73s on the main line now is GB Railfreight, which has acquired a large number of locomotives from various places, including the purchase of a number of previously preserved Class 73s.

A project to modify a number of Class 73s for operating on the Caledonian Sleeper contract saw the chosen locomotives re-engined for hauling the sleeper trains over the non-electrified portions of the sleeper route in Scotland. Previously preserved 'JA' locomotives E6005 and E6006 were two of the locomotives chosen for this project and they are now 73966 and 73967 respectively. Network Rail also owns three Class 73s, including two Class 73/9s that were re-engined and modified by Loram at Derby. The company also owns formerly preserved 73138, which is also based at Derby.

While not strictly a preserved locomotive, 73114 is owned by Nemesis Rail and is based on the Battlefield Railway at Shackerstone. The locomotive has previously been regularly used by the railway alongside its fleet of preserved diesels, but is currently out of service.

Transmart Trains, Southern and South Western Railway each own one Class 73 and these are all registered for use on Network Rail metals. The most recent locomotives to leave

preservation are 'JA' locomotives 73001 and 73002, which moved in spring 2019 from their previous home on the Dean Forest Railway to Locomotive Services at Crewe.

While operational 73001 was quickly moved from Lydney to Crewe Diesel Depot, spares donor locomotive 73002 has been sent to Eastleigh Works, where it is due to be cosmetically restored prior to moving to the LSL's storage facility and planned museum site at the former Hornby factory in Margate, Kent. No details have yet been released by LSL as to its plans for the locomotives but it is anticipated that 73001 will be re-registered for main line use.

NON-PRESERVED SURVIVING CLASS 73s

GB RAILFREIGHT: 73101, 73107, 73109, 73110, 73119, 73128, 73134, 73136, 73139, 73141, 73201, 73212, 73213, 73961, 73962, 73963, 73964, 73965, 73966, 73967, 73968, 73969, 73970, 73971

LOCOMOTIVE SERVICES: 73001, 73002

NEMESIS RAIL: 73114

NETWORK RAIL: 73138, 73951, 73952

SOUTHERN: 73202

SOUTH WESTERN RAILWAY: 73235

TRANSMART TRAINS: 73133

CLASS 76

The Class 76 locomotives were one of two electric locomotive designs that were built for the Manchester to Sheffield 'Woodhead' line when the route was electrified for 1500v DC operation.

Plans had been put in place by the LNER to electrify the Woodhead route from the mid-1930s but the project was put on hold following the outbreak of the Second World War. Electrification of the route started in 1952 and the LNER produced a prototype locomotive intended for the line at Doncaster Works in 1941. Numbered 6701, the prototype was tested on various lines that featured 1500v DC overhead electrification. With the project to electrify the line put on hold due to the war, the prototype was exported to the Dutch State Railway in 1947, where it saw use for five years before being returned to the UK.

During its time in the Netherlands the prototype, by this stage numbered 6000, was nicknamed 'Tommy' and when it returned to the UK it was overhauled, renumbered E26000 and was officially named *Tommy*.

The production order for the Woodhead line locomotives was for 57 locomotives, to be known as 'EM1'. They were built at Doncaster Works and at Gorton Works in Manchester. They were designed predominantly as freight locomotives and featured a Bo-Bo wheel arrangement, four MV186 traction motors, vacuum brakes (a number were later equipped with air brakes) and regenerative braking. A dozen locomotives were also fitted with steam heat boilers to allow them to be used on passenger services.

When delivered, the locomotives were painted in lined black livery, before later being painted into dark green with small yellow cab warning panels. As with most other designs, they went on to receive BR blue livery with full yellow ends as the BR corporate image spread across the rail network.

Electric services on the line began in February 1952, although it would be three years before the whole 41-mile route had been electrified. The locomotives had a distinctive appearance with twin pantographs and a box-like construction typical of the age when they were built.

Under TOPS, the 'EM1' became Class 76 and the E26XXX numbers were replaced with 76XXX identification. Not all locomotives survived long enough to receive TOPS numbers, but a large number of the fleet did.

The first withdrawals of the fleet came in March 1970 when pioneer E26000 and four of the production locomotives were taken out of use, with another three withdrawn the following year, mainly as a result of the removal of passenger traffic from the Woodhead line. It would be another six years before more Class 76s were withdrawn, but the decision by British Rail to close the Woodhead line meant that the remaining examples were on borrowed time and the final examples were withdrawn upon closure of the line in the early hours of July

Former Woodhead Route Class 76 electric locomotive, 26020, stands on display in the Great Hall at the National Railway Museum in York on July 13, 2013.
STEVE KEMP

LOCO	PREVIOUS IDENTITIES	OWNER	LOCATION
26020	26020, 76020	NRM	RMY

OWNER KEY: NRM – National Railway Museum

LOCATION KEY: RMY – Railway Museum, York

18, 1981, when 76010 and 76016 hauled a train of ferry wagons along the line as the last train to operate on the Woodhead route before closure. The only trains that would now operate were the demolition trains.

THE PRESERVED CLASS 76

Only one locomotive from the Class 76 fleet survived into preservation, with 76020 being selected as the example to be preserved as part of the National Collection at the National Railway Museum. Now restored to original condition and painted in lined black livery as 26020, the locomotive is displayed in the Great Hall at the Railway Museum in York.

The historical importance of the locomotive and the changes to overhead

electrification mean that 26020 is destined to spend the rest of its days as a static exhibit, but its presence in York is a physical reminder of the important part the Woodhead route played in the

CLASS 76

BUILT:	BR Doncaster Works & Gorton Works, 1950-1953 (E26000 built in 1941)
NO. BUILT:	58
NO. PRESERVED:	1
OTHER SURVIVORS:	0

history of our railways.

Additionally, one of the cabs from 76039 is preserved and displayed at the Museum of Science & Industry in Manchester, with a glazed full-width panel at the back of the cab, giving museum visitors the chance to view the locomotive's controls and cab layout without needing to go inside the cab. The cab has been preserved in BR blue livery to represent how the locomotives appeared at the end of their careers.

CLASS 77

The locomotives which went on to become Class 77 were the second electric locomotive design built for use on the Manchester to Sheffield 'Woodhead' railway line. The much smaller fleet of passenger locomotives would only see a relatively short working career on the line for which they were built, but they were later exported by BR and enjoyed a successful second working life overseas.

The original intention had been to have a fleet of 27 Co-Co electric express passenger locomotives capable of operating at speeds of up to 90mph. Designated 'EM2', they were designed to be larger and more powerful than the 'EM1' (Class 76) locomotives and featured six traction motors on two six-wheel bogies.

However, reviews of the services using the Woodhead route saw the order significantly reduced and in the end only seven 'EM2s' were built. The locomotives were delivered between 1953 and 1954 and were numbered 27000-27006. They were all subsequently named after Greek goddesses, with the exception of 27000 *Electra*, which was named after the emblem of electrical supplier Metropolitan-Vickers.

Under TOPS, the 'EM2s' were classified as Class 77, but they were all withdrawn before they gained the five-figure BR numbering identities.

BR decided that it did not wish to have two passenger routes between Manchester and Sheffield and the Woodhead line would be retained mainly for freight traffic and, as such, in anticipation of the withdrawal of passenger services the 'EM2s' were taken out of traffic. The seven 'EM2' locomotives were all withdrawn in September 1968 and were moved to Bury for storage shortly afterwards, where they remained until they were sold for use in the Netherlands, with all seven locomotives being shipped out of the UK, although E27005 was never returned to service and was used as a spares donor.

27000 stands on display in the yard at Swanwick Junction on the Midland Railway Butterley on May 31, 2009, where it has been based for most of the time since returning to the UK in 1989. While it has been displayed at a number of open day events, it hasn't now ventured away from Swanwick for a number of years. MARTIN HART

LOCO	NAME	PREVIOUS IDENTITIES	OWNER	LOCATION
27000	*Electra*	27000, (Also Netherlands 1502)	EM2LS	MRB
1505	*Ariadne*	27001, Netherlands 1505	MOSI	MOSI

OWNER KEY: EM2LS – EM2 Locomotive Society, MOSI – Museum of Science & Industry Manchester

LOCATION KEY: MOSI – Museum of Science & Industry Manchester, MRB – Midland Railway Butterley

The exported locomotives continued to give good service in their new home until 1986, when they were withdrawn from service, although the pioneer locomotive E27000 *Electra* was restored to original BR green livery with small yellow warning panels for a series of railtours in 1989 as part of the NS150 commemorations.

While two of the former Woodhead locomotives were returned to the UK, a third survived to be preserved in the Netherlands, where it remains.

THE PRESERVED CLASS 77s

In the UK there are two surviving Class 77s, with 27000 *Electra* on display inside the Matthew Kirtley Museum at the Midland Railway Butterley and representing the Netherlands Railway connection is 1505 *Ariadne* at the Museum of Science & Industry in Manchester. Both of these locomotives were repatriated to the UK following the end of their working life in the Netherlands. 27000 was returned to the UK in 1989 and is owned by the EM2 Locomotive Society and after a spell in lined green livery, it is now painted in original black with red lining, in the same style as preserved 'EM1', 26020, at the National Railway Museum.

1505 retains the yellow and grey livery that was applied to it when it was working in the Netherlands and it is on permanent display in the Power Hall at MOSI.

Both the preserved UK-based locomotives are believed to be complete, but it is unlikely either will ever work again and they are preserved as examples of the passenger locomotives that worked on the Manchester to Sheffield 'Woodhead' route.

Additionally, 27003 *Diana* is preserved in the Netherlands by Werkgroep 1501, where it was operated on main line specials after preservation.

CLASS 77

BUILT: Gorton Works, 1953-1954

NO. BUILT: 7

NO. PRESERVED: 3

OTHER SURVIVORS: 0

A varied lineup of traction is displayed in the yard at the Museum of Science & Industry in Manchester, with the contrasting old and new architecture providing an interesting backdrop. 1505's yellow and grey livery provides a splash of colour next to the museum's *Planet* steam locomotive and visiting Beattie Well Tank locomotive No. 30587 on July 2, 2017. TERRY EYRES

CLASS 81

The 1955 British Railways Modernisation Plan resulted in the construction of many different types of locomotives and many of the classes of locomotives that have been featured in this publication were built as a direct result of that significant report.

Another aspect of the Modernisation Plan was the electrification of the West Coast Main Line (WCML). The first section of the route to be electrified would be the section from London Euston to Birmingham, Liverpool and Manchester, but unlike the then-standard 1500v DC overhead electrification system that was in use on other parts of the BR network, the WCML would be electrified to 25,000v AC.

This decision required the construction of a new fleet of locomotives to haul services on the electrified sections of the WCML. As with many of the diesel designs, it was decided to order 100 locomotives for the WCML services, with the order divided between five locomotive builders, allowing BR to evaluate the various designs while trying to find the best possible locomotives for the route.

The five different designs would be classified 'AL1' to 'AL5' and the first 25 locomotives would be the 'AL1'. They were ordered from British Thomson-Houston, who subcontracted the construction to Birmingham Railway Carriage & Wagon Company. It was originally planned that there would be two different types of locomotives within the 'AL1' fleet, with 23 Type A locomotives, numbered E3001-E3023, for mixed-traffic workings and two Type B locomotives, E3301 and E3302, which were to be geared for heavy freight traffic use. The first member of the fleet, E3001, entered service in November 1959.

The two locomotives designed to be Type B examples were delivered later than the original 23 Type As, but these two were geared for passenger working and were instead numbered E3096 and E3097.

When introduced, the locomotives were painted in a striking and attractive light blue livery, which became known as electric blue, and the locomotive fleet numbers were raised alloy numbers attached to the cab sides, with a cast BR cycling lion emblem carried on the mid-bodyside, giving the locomotive a smart and distinctive look. As the new BR corporate look spread during the late 1960s, the locomotives were painted into the darker rail blue livery with full yellow cab fronts.

They were used on passenger, freight and parcel traffic along the WCML, but did not venture away from the route during their working lives.

The first withdrawal of an 'AL1' came in August 1968 when E3009 was officially condemned after sustaining serious damage in a level crossing collision a few months earlier.

On April 28, 2019, 81002 stands on display in the yard at Barrow Hill, alongside 85006. The locomotive has had three owners since purchase for preservation in 1991, but the AC Locomotive Group has carried out a huge amount of restoration work on the Class 81 and it is now in excellent mechanical and electrical condition. PAUL HADFIELD

LOCO	PREVIOUS IDENTITIES	OWNER	LOCATION
81002	E3003, 81002	ACLG	BHR

OWNER KEY: ACLG – AC Locomotive Group

LOCATION KEY: BHR – Barrow Hill Roundhouse

Another two withdrawals took place before the locomotives gained their TOPS Class 81 identifications, with E3002 and E3019 withdrawn following fire damage – something of an Achilles heel for the locomotives, with several meeting the same fate during the lifetime of the design.

Under TOPS the 'AL1' became Class 81, but as three of the fleet had already been withdrawn when the five-figure identification numbers were introduced, the locomotives were numbered 81001-81022 in the order they were built, rather than the normal practice of the E30XX assuming the corresponding 810XX number (i.e. E3003 became 81002, as E3002 had already been withdrawn). The two planned Type B locomotives, E3096 and E3097, took the final two TOPS numbers of 81021 and 81022. The Class 81 fleet was run down gradually during the 1980s and by 1990 just seven locomotives remained in service. The final two Class 81s to survive in traffic, 81012 and 81017, were withdrawn in July 1991.

THE PRESERVED CLASS 81

One example of the Class 81 was preserved following the end of their reign on the West Coast Main Line and 81002 was purchased by a private individual and moved to Crewe Heritage Centre in 1991, within sight of its former stomping ground, where it was quickly repainted into electric blue livery as E3003. It made a visit away from its home base to the East Lancashire Railway, where it was hauled along the Bury to Rawtenstall line to recreate a WCML electric 'drag'.

It was purchased by Pete Waterman the following year, who had also

purchased examples of the Class 82, 83 and 85 locomotive fleets, with the collection remaining at Crewe.

However, when Mr Waterman's locomotive collection was largely disposed of during the mid-1990s, 81002 was purchased by the newly formed AC

CLASS 81

BUILT: Birmingham Railway Carriage & Wagon Company, 1959-1964

NO. BUILT: 25

NO. PRESERVED: 1

OTHER SURVIVORS: 0

Locomotive Group in 1997, which set up home at the then-new Barrow Hill Roundhouse.

The locomotive has since been repainted into BR blue livery after a spell in Large Logo blue and a lot of restoration and conservation work has taken place on the locomotive, with the Class 81 now being essentially complete.

In theory, the locomotive is in a condition whereby it could easily be prepared for testing under its own power, but the chances of 81002 returning to main line use in the future seems unlikely.

Still looking presentable six years after its repaint into InterCity Executive livery, 82008 stands alongside the platform at Barrow Hill Halt on February 5, 2011. MARTIN HART

CLASS 82

Designated 'AL2', these locomotives were part of another order for electric traction for the West Coast Main Line (WCML). British Railways ordered 10 AC electric locomotives from the Associated Electrical Industries (AEI) division of Metropolitan Vickers, but construction of the locomotives was subcontracted to Beyer, Peacock at Gorton Works in Manchester.

The new 'AL2s' were able to operate at speeds of up to 100mph and were also considered to be the best of the five designs in terms of their ride quality, possibly aided by their sturdy construction. As with the other earlier AC electric locomotives, the 'AL2s' were delivered in electric blue livery with cast alloy numbers on their cabsides.

LOCO	PREVIOUS IDENTITIES	OWNER	LOCATION
82008	E3054, 82008	ACLG	BHR

OWNER KEY: ACLG – AC Locomotive Group

LOCATION KEY: BHR – Barrow Hill Roundhouse

Unlike the other designs, they were built with a separate underframe and body, making them the heaviest of the early AC designs, but they were also considered the most powerful of the five different early types. They were allocated to Manchester Longsight depot, which remained their home depot for the majority of their working lives. With two locomotives withdrawn before the introduction of TOPS Class 82 numbering, the TOPS identities of the surviving examples saw E3047 to E3054 becoming 82001 to 82008 respectively.

First-built E3046 was condemned in September 1969 and last-built E3055 in January 1971, both being withdrawn as a result of catching fire. When the decision was taken to retire the Class 82s from passenger workings in July 1983, five members of the fleet were withdrawn with two others, 82005 and 82008, taking up empty coaching stock duties between Willesden and London Euston. 82003 was also moved to Willesden, where it was retained as a spare parts donor for the other two.

The final surviving member of the fleet, 82008, was officially withdrawn from traffic in December 1987.

THE PRESERVED CLASS 82

The survival of last-withdrawn 82008 is again thanks to the foresight of celebrity record producer and renowned railway enthusiast Pete Waterman, who bought 82008 from BR in 1993. At the time it was one of three Class 82s to survive, but was in better condition than the other surviving withdrawn examples, 82003 and 82005, which were both then scrapped in September 1993.

As with the other AC electric

CLASS 82

BUILT:	Beyer, Peacock Gorton Works, 1960-1962
NO. BUILT:	10
NO. PRESERVED:	1
OTHER SURVIVORS:	0

locomotives purchased by Mr Waterman, 82008 was sold in 1997 to the AC Locomotive Group and it subsequently moved to Barrow Hill, where it was repainted into BR Large Logo livery, which it retained until it received a bodywork overhaul and repaint into InterCity Executive livery in 2005.

Some electrical restoration work has been carried out on the locomotive and the ACLG aims to continue with the electrical restoration of the locomotive in the future, although this is a long-term project for the group, which is committed to maintaining its operational fleet of locomotives and the ongoing restoration to main line condition of 89001.

82008 stands in the yard at Barrow Hill on June 1, 2019. The ACLG has carried out some electrical restoration on this locomotive, but completion of works is very much a long-term project for the group, due to its other commitments. ANDY COWARD

On April 28, 2018, E3035 stands at Barrow Hill on display alongside 85006. The vintage electric locomotive represents how the design looked at the time they were delivered to BR, carrying electric blue livery and cast numbers and BR cycling lion embellishments on the bodywork. PAUL HADFIELD

CLASS 83

The third order of AC electric locomotives for the West Coast Main Line was for 15 'AL3' locomotives. The order for these was placed with English Electric and the locomotives were delivered to BR in the same light electric blue livery that had been applied to the other designs, with them also having cast fleet numbers attached to their cabsides.

The 'AL3' featured two different types, with it originally planned that there would be 12 Type A mixed traffic locomotives, numbered E3024-E3035 and three Type B heavy freight locomotives which had a different type of gearing, E3098-E3100. In the end only two Type B locomotives were required and E3100 emerged as a standard Type A locomotive, although it was fitted with experimental silicon rectifiers.

The 'AL3s' suffered from major problems with their Mercury-Arc rectifiers, which had been fitted to 14 of the 15 locomotives, during their early operating days and this resulted in the whole fleet being taken out of service pending a solution being found to the problems, with the locomotives

spending a considerable period of time in store.

With the electrification of the West Coast Main Line advancing, BR decided that it needed to get the 'AL3s' back into service and efforts were concentrated on getting the stored locomotives back in use. The answer lay in the replacement of the original rectifiers with silicon rectifiers and the locomotives were also refurbished before they were returned to traffic. They were also equipped with dual-braking before re-entering service.

Under the TOPS numbering scheme, the 'AL3' became Class 83 and they were renumbered in the 830XX series in the order in which they were built, with E3024-E3035 becoming 83001-83012 and E3098-E3100 becoming 83013-83015. All 15 received rail blue paintwork under the new BR corporate identity.

The first Class 83 to be withdrawn from traffic was 83003, which was stood down in May 1975 and 83004 succumbed in January 1978. However, the majority of the fleet was withdrawn in July 1983.

The surviving three locomotives, 83009, 83012 and 83015 saw further use, with 83012 and 83015 being used for hauling empty coaching stock workings between London Euston and Willesden Depot, while 83009 was converted for use as a static current converter to assist with the maintenance of Class 506 EMUs. All three of the survivors were withdrawn in the first few months of 1989.

LOCO	PREVIOUS IDENTITIES	OWNER	LOCATION
E3035	E3035, 83012	ACLG	BHR

OWNER KEY: ACLG – AC Locomotive Group

LOCATION KEY: BHR – Barrow Hill Roundhouse

THE PRESERVED CLASS 83

As with 82008, the survival of a Class 83 is thanks to the efforts of Pete Waterman, who sought to secure one example of each of the early designs that was not already earmarked for preservation. As one of the final two examples to be withdrawn in March 1989, 83012 was the locomotive selected for preservation and it was bought from BR in the early 1990s and moved to Crewe Heritage Centre (then known as The Railway Age).

It remained at Crewe until it was sold to the AC Locomotive Group in 1997 and moved to Barrow Hill along with the other locomotives the group

had purchased from the former Waterman collection.

The new owners decided to restore the Class 83 into original as-delivered condition and the locomotive was repainted into electric blue, regaining its previous E3035 identity and making its debut in its new old colours in 2000. The

CLASS 83

BUILT: Vulcan Foundry, Newton-le-Willows, 1960-1962.

NO. BUILT: 15

NO. PRESERVED: 1

OTHER SURVIVORS: 0

locomotive has retained this choice of livery ever since and is representative of how the early AC designs looked when they first entered service on BR.

The locomotive has also undergone some mechanical and electrical restoration by its owning group and its electrical systems have been powered up using a generator car on a number of occasions.

As with the other early AC electric locomotives, it is unlikely that E3035 will ever haul a train under its own power, but it remains an important part of UK railway history, along with the other surviving designs.

CLASS 84

The small fleet of 10 'AL4' locomotives was awarded by BR to GEC, which in turn subcontracted the design and construction to the North British Locomotive Company at Springburn Works in Glasgow.

The locomotives had a similar physical appearance to the other early AC electric locomotive designs and they were also painted into the attractive electric blue livery upon completion, with cast numbers on the cabsides and British Railways embellishments on the bodysides. They had a top speed of up to 100mph but like the 'AL3s', the 'AL4s' were also found to be suffering problems with their Mercury-Arc rectifiers and this fleet of locomotives also required a programme of modifications to address the problems. There were also regular complaints from train crews about poor ride quality on the locomotives when they were travelling at speed.

As with the 'AL3s' they were taken out of service pending a resolution and were eventually authorised repairs by BR, who needed the locomotives back in service due to the expansion of the electrification on the West Coast Main Line. They were all given similar treatment to the 'AL3s' with the Mercury-Arc rectifiers replaced with silicon rectifiers. They were also fitted with dual-brakes and were brought back into service in 1972. Under TOPS the 'AL4' locomotives became Class 84 and E3036-E3045 were numbered 84001-84010 respectively.

However, the Class 84s were still not immune from problems and, yet again, the locomotives suffered from repeated traction motor and tap changer failures, which seriously affected the reliability and availability of the fleet.

In 1976 BR decided that it would no longer spend large amounts of money on the Class 84s, which could never be described as being a successful design.

As a result of the ongoing failures and reliability issues, the Class 84s were relatively early casualties, with the first

84001 stands in the yard at Barrow Hill on April 19, 2015, while in store following the end of its loan period between the NRM and the AC Locomotive Group. It moved to Bo'ness in 2016 for display in the Museum of Scottish Railways on the Bo'ness & Kinneil Railway. STEVE KEMP

LOCO	PREVIOUS IDENTITIES	OWNER	LOCATION
84001	E3036, 84001	NRM	BKR

OWNER KEY: NRM – National Railway Museum

LOCATION KEY: BKR – Bo'ness & Kinneil Railway

two locomotives, 84005 and 84007, withdrawn from service in April 1977. Over the next three-and-a-half years the other eight followed, with the final two, 84003 and 84010, withdrawn in November 1980. 84009 saw use in departmental service as a mobile load bank locomotive following its withdrawal from normal service and it was repainted into the distinctive Research Department red and blue livery and numbered ADB968021.

Following the end of this work, the locomotive was scrapped in 1995, but one of the cabs from this locomotive was saved by a member of the AC Locomotive Group.

THE PRESERVED CLASS 84

The preserved Class 84 owes its survival to it being loaned to the National Railway Museum (NRM) in 1979 for an exhibition. 84001 had been withdrawn from service in January 1979 and after a repaint it was delivered to York in May 1979 for display and remained on loan for the next 15 years, until it was claimed by the NRM for the National Collection and it officially became a preserved locomotive in 1994.

When not on display in the Great Hall, 84001 spent long periods of time stored outside, where its bodywork suffered from corrosion and the paintwork became faded and in need of restoration. However, a solution to the problem that would suit both the locomotive itself and the NRM came from a trusted preservation group with a specialism for electric locomotive preservation.

With a collection of WCML early

electric locomotives based at Barrow Hill Roundhouse in Derbyshire, the addition of the only missing design from the original fleets made perfect sense and in 2000 the Class 84 was moved to Barrow Hill on a loan basis from the NRM to join those other classic electric locomotives on display which belonged to the AC Locomotive Group (ACLG).

Shortly after it arrived at Barrow Hill, 84001 underwent bodywork repairs and was repainted into a new coat of BR blue for display at various open day events, as well as being displayed with the other AC electric locomotives on display at Barrow Hill. The loan arrangement for 84001 between the NRM and the ACLG expired in 2012 and it remained based at Barrow Hill while the NRM decided what to do with it.

In 2016 the preserved Class 84 was on the move again. Following the end of the loan deal between the ACLG and the NRM, agreement was reached between the NRM and the Scottish Railway Preservation Society for 84001 to move to the society's Museum of Scottish Railways on the Bo'ness & Kinneil Railway, where it would be displayed under cover in the museum, which

On July 26, 2003, 84001 was one of the locomotives displayed at the Doncaster Works Open Day. The locomotive had recently been repainted by the AC Locomotive Group and at the time was on loan to the ACLG from the National Railway Museum. The locomotive is now displayed in the Museum of Scottish Railways on the Bo'ness & Kinneil Railway. NIGEL VALENTINE

contains rolling stock and artefacts related to the railways of Scotland. Naturally, a North British-built electric locomotive built in Glasgow for use on the WCML between Scotland and England certainly fits the bill for this collection and 84001 remains on display inside this fascinating museum.

CLASS 84

BUILT: North British, Springburn Works, Glasgow, 1960-1961

NO. BUILT: 10

NO. PRESERVED: 1

OTHER SURVIVORS: 0

85006's BR blue paintwork glistens in the sun in the yard at Barrow Hill Roundhouse on April 28, 2019. The salvation of the Class 85 completed the collection of early AC electric locomotive designs, with examples from all five original types now preserved. PAUL HADFIELD

Immaculately presented in BR blue with its 85006 identity, the Class 85 stands on display around the roundhouse turntable at Barrow Hill on June 1, 2019. This was the last of the early AC electric locomotives to be withdrawn from passenger service in November 1992. ANDY COWARD

CLASS 85

The 'AL5' electric locomotive design was the largest of the original AC classes, with 40 locomotives constructed by British Railways at Doncaster Works, with the fleet numbered E3056-E3095. As with the other designs, they were painted in electric blue livery. The first of the fleet were handed over to BR for service in 1961 and it would be three years before all 40 of the locomotives were in service.

Unlike the other designs, very few problems were experienced with the 'AL5' design, which was considered to be a good locomotive. The locomotives shared many components with the similar 'AL1' and 'AL2' designs.

Under TOPS classifications the 'AL5' became Class 85 and the locomotives were numbered 85001-85040. Subsequently

the decision was taken to convert 14 members of the fleet into freight-only locomotives as Class 85/1 and these were numbered 85101-85114. The Class 85/1 locomotives had their train heat equipment removed and a maximum running speed of 80mph applied, while the unmodified passenger Class 85/0 locomotives could operate at up to 100mph.

Of the five AC designs, the Class 81s and Class 85s were certainly the most successful and the Class 85s remained intact until the first example was withdrawn in July 1983. Despite there being a handful of other casualties during the 1980s, the design was still largely intact at the start of 1990.

However, the writing was definitely on the wall by the start of 1990 and over the next two years the majority of the remaining locomotives had been stood down from service. By the start of 1992 just one locomotive, 85101, remained in service and by the time it was withdrawn from service in November 1992 it had outlived the rest of its classmates by a year. The withdrawal of 85101 was also the final example of the 100 early AC electric locomotive designs to be stood down from service.

LOCO	PREVIOUS IDENTITIES	OWNER	LOCATION
85006	E3061, 85006, 85101	ACLG	BHR

OWNER KEY: ACLG – AC Locomotive Group

LOCATION KEY: BHR – Barrow Hill Roundhouse

THE PRESERVED CLASS 85

Having survived in traffic until the end of 1992, when 85101 was bought for preservation in 1993 by Pete Waterman, it was hoped that it would become the first AC electric locomotive to be returned to main line operation in private ownership. However, work on its reactivation never took place.

Following its sale to the AC Locomotive Group in 1997, the locomotive moved to Barrow Hill Roundhouse and in 2002 it was restored into triple grey livery with Railfreight Distribution red and yellow decals applied. The following year it was named *Doncaster Plant 150 1853-2003* at the Doncaster Works Open Weekend to celebrate the 150th anniversary of the works that had been responsible for the

construction of the locomotive 42 years earlier. 85101 remained in grey for a further decade before being returned to a more traditional livery, although the nameplates were subsequently removed.

In 2013 the locomotive was moved to Boden Rail Engineering's then-base at Washwood Heath where it was repainted into BR blue livery as 85006, before returning to Barrow Hill for display in its new colours.

CLASS 85

BUILT: British Railways, Doncaster Works, 1961-1964

NO. BUILT: 40

NO. PRESERVED: 1

OTHER SURVIVORS: 0

In addition to keeping the locomotive looking good for visitors to Barrow Hill, the AC Locomotive Group has done a lot of mechanical and electrical restoration work on the Class 85. The owning group has always intended to try and progress the restoration to the stage where the locomotive could be made operational again. The passage of time, and the requirements now necessary to re-certify a locomotive for main line running, mean that it is unlikely any of the early AC electric locomotives would be brought back to main line running condition, although with 85006 being essentially complete and in very good condition it would probably be the natural choice out of the four ACLG early locomotives for a main line revival.

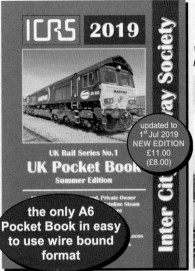

LEFT: Immaculately restored in electric blue livery, 86259/E3137 *Les Ross/Peter Pan* hauls a 'Cumbrian Mountain Express' tour from London Euston to Carlisle on July 12, 2014, seen heading through Red Bank. The Class 86's colour scheme was never carried by Class 86s from new, but suits the locomotive design well and was carried by some of the earlier West Coast Main Line electric locomotives. TOM MCATEE

BELOW: During a rare trip away at a heritage railway gala, 86101 *Sir William A Stanier FRS* is hauled by 31438 on the Mid Norfolk Railway, recreating a WCML 'drag' of the 1980s on May 14, 2011. KEVIN DELANEY

CLASS 86

The Class 86 has gone down as one of the most versatile electric locomotive designs to have been built for the British Railway network. The 100 locomotives, originally known as 'AL6', were built by BR at Doncaster Works and also Vulcan Foundry at Newton-le-Willows. Numbered E3101-E3200 they were delivered to BR between 1965 and 1966 and were delivered in an early style of BR rail blue livery, with small yellow warning panels on the cab fronts.

Following TOPS, the AL6s became Class 86 and they were divided into two sub-classes. The Class 86/0s were essentially as-built with a maximum speed of 80mph, while the Class 86/2s were fitted with improved suspension and bogies, allowing for a higher maximum speed of 100mph. These classifications meant that the Class 86/2s were used mainly on higher-speed passenger workings, with the unmodified Class 86/0s restricted to non-passenger freight workings.

When the Class 87 locomotive design was being developed, three Class 86s, 86201-86203, were fitted with new bogies and transformers and these three were renumbered as 86101-86103 respectively. These locomotives were subsequently able to operate at a maximum speed of 110mph.

Further sub-classes emerged as, following wheel modifications, some of the Class 86/0s were reclassified as Class 86/3. In the late 1980s all the remaining unmodified Class 86/0s and Class 86/3s were all fitted with improved suspension and, in turn, these locomotives became Class 86/4.

Some of the Class 86/4 locomotives were subsequently employed on freight services and these locomotives had their electric train heating equipment isolated and their maximum speed was reduced to 75mph. These were classified Class 86/6 and a number of these locomotives remain in service with Freightliner to the present day.

A number of Class 86/2 locomotives were then dedicated to freight traffic, becoming Class 86/5, although this was relatively short-lived and they reverted to their original Class 86/2 identities.

The first Class 86 withdrawals came in 1986 when 86211 and 86429 were taken out of traffic. A steady flow of withdrawals followed, but the vast majority of the fleet was still in traffic at the turn of the century.

On July 19, 2014, 86259/E3137 *Les Ross/Peter Pan* hauls a 'Cumbrian Mountain Express' tour through Lower Walton on the West Coast Main Line. The locomotive hauled a service from London Euston to Preston, where a steam locomotive took over to continue the tour to Carlisle, with the Class 86 picking up the tour on its return to Preston later in the day. TERRY EYRES

Following privatisation the surviving Class 86/2s were employed by Virgin Trains on its West Coast and CrossCountry franchises, and with Anglia Railways. Virgin Trains dispensed with its final Class 86/2s in September 2003 following the introduction of the new 'Voyager' and 'Super Voyager' fleets. Anglia retained its Class 86/2s for a further two years, with the final examples being stood down in September 2005.

On the freight side, English Welsh & Scottish Railways inherited 15 Class 86s, which were mainly used on postal services and the occasional charter operation, although these were all gone by the end of 2004.

Freightliner gained a fleet of 30 Class 86/6s and these locomotives have still proved to be successful for the company, despite their advancing years. The company still has 16 of the locomotives and they continue to be an important part of its fleet.

Network Rail had two Class 86/2 locomotives converted to mobile load bank locomotives and these were classified as Class 86/9, although both have subsequently been withdrawn. The company also owned 86424 but this was never operated by Network Rail. It has since been sold on and is now one of the locomotives exported to Hungary.

LOCO	NAME	BR IDENTITIES	OWNER	LOCATION
86101	*Sir William A Stanier FRS*	E3191, 86201, 86101	ETL	On Hire
86259	*Les Ross/Peter Pan*	E3137, 86045, 86259	Private	Rugby
86401	*Mons Meg*	E3111, 86001, 86401	ETL	On Hire

OWNER KEY: ETL – Electric Traction Ltd (AC Locomotive Group)

LOCATION KEY: Rugby – Network Rail, Rugby

THE PRESERVED CLASS 86s

There are three Class 86s in the UK which can be currently considered as preserved, although two of these, 86101 *Sir William A Stanier FRS* and 86401 *Mons Meg*, are operated by Electric Traction Ltd and the company essentially operates the locomotives commercially to support the heritage activities of the ACLG Class 81, 82, 83 and 85 locomotives at Barrow Hill. The operation of 86101 and 86401 is also currently supporting ETL's restoration of unique 89001 to main line running condition.

86101 was originally preserved by the AC Loco Group in 2005 and was recertified for the main line in March 2007.

This was the first preserved Class 86 to be recertified for main line use and it then saw use on a number of charter trains.

86401 was also preserved by the AC Loco Group and was repainted into its unique Network SouthEast livery as *Northampton Town*, but it was not returned to operational condition and spent a long period in store at Long Marston. The locomotive was subsequently returned to main line condition in 2015.

86259/E3137 *Les Ross/Peter Pan* is owned by former West Midlands Radio presenter Les Ross MBE, who bought the locomotive following its withdrawal by Virgin West Coast. In September 2002

CLASS 86

BUILT: BR Doncaster Works and Vulcan Foundry, Newton-le-Willows, 1965-1966

NO. BUILT: 100

NO. PRESERVED: 3

OTHER SURVIVORS: 33

the locomotive had been named after Mr Ross upon his retirement from hosting the BRMB Radio Breakfast Show after 26 years on the station.

After the locomotive was moved to Tyseley Locomotive Works for storage and, following the intervention by TLW's Bob Meanley, the locomotive was sold by its leasing company to Mr Ross in 2005. It was subsequently recertified for main line running in March 2008 and while it ran with Tyseley-based Vintage Trains for a few years, it subsequently moved to Willesden Depot, where it was based until 2017, when it moved again to its current home at Rugby.

Les Ross has stated that he intends to keep 86259 running on the main line as long as he can and as long as the locomotive remains in good order, it is likely to remain a regular on the main line for many years to come.

On March 3, 2008, 86259 *Les Ross* makes its debut on the main line in preservation as it hauls the 'Les Ross Daytripper' charter between Birmingham New Street and Preston. The locomotive has since gone on to be a regular performer on charters on the main line, mainly operating on its former West Coast Main Line stomping ground. TERRY EYRES

Since 2015, 86101 *Sir William A Stanier FRS* and 86401 *Mons Meg* have been on hire to GB Railfreight for hauling Caledonian Sleeper rolling stock. On April 17, 2015, 86101 stands at London Euston, having arrived with a rake of stock. STEVE KEMP

On May 9, 2019, 86101 *William A Stanier FRS* hauls a rake of Caledonian Sleeper stock from Polmadie to Wembley, photographed south of Preston. Both 86101 and 86401 are expected to come off hire for the Caledonian Sleeper contract over the coming months. KEVIN DELANEY

MAIN LINE REGISTERED PRESERVED CLASS 86s

Loco	Owner	National Network Certification Status
86101	Electric Traction Ltd	Main Line Certified
86259	Peter Pan Locomotive Ltd	Main Line Certified
86401	Electric Traction Ltd	Main Line Certified

OTHER CLASS 86s

In addition to the preserved examples, there are currently 33 other Class 86s still in existence, although 15 of these are no longer plying their trade in the UK.

The main operator still to make use of the Class 86 design is Freightliner, which currently has 18 of the locomotives on its books.

While not all of these locomotives are still operational – indeed, 86229 and 86251 have been purchased from Europhoenix as spares donor locomotives – the company still uses the locomotives on a daily basis to haul container trains and they are often used in pairs due to the steep gradients and the heavy trains they haul. Freightliner has no immediate plans to replace its Class 86 locomotives and it would seem that this small fleet will remain in service for some time to come.

After Virgin Trains and Anglia Railways dispensed with its Class 86/2s, many of them were moved to Long Marston for storage pending possible reuse. However, they were subsequently sold to Europhoenix, which had successfully begun a project to convert Class 87s for use in Bulgaria for the Bulgarian Railway Company.

Europhoenix subsequently began a project to do a similar conversion programme on a number of Class 86s for Hungarian open access operator, Floyd. In total, eight Class 86s were exported to Hungary for Floyd.

The company also found a market for the Class 86s in Bulgaria with Bulmarket, which also purchased some former UK Class 87s. There are now seven Class 86s in Bulgaria, although 86233 is only a spares donor and has not been reactivated.

NON-PRESERVED SURVIVING CLASS 86s

FREIGHTLINER: 86229, 86251, 86604, 86605, 86607, 86608, 86609, 86610, 86612, 86613, 86614, 86622, 86627, 86628, 86632, 86637, 86638, 86639, 86901

EXPORTED TO BULGARIA: 86213, 86231, 86233, 86234, 86235, 86701, 86702

EXPORTED TO HUNGARY: 86215, 86217, 86218, 86228, 86232, 86242, 86248, 86250, 86424

87001 *Stephenson* stands on display in the Great Hall at the National Railway Museum in York on May 31, 2008. This locomotive was claimed for the National Collection following its withdrawal by Virgin West Coast. MARTIN HART

CLASS 87

The story of the Class 87 began with the decision by British Rail to electrify the northern section of the West Coast Main Line (WCML). BR realised that it would need a powerful electric locomotive to haul services on some of the steep gradients on the route. Prior to electrification, the services had been handled mainly by Class 50s working in pairs. The introduction of the electric fleet would render the relatively young Class 50s redundant and they would go on to be transferred through to the Western Region.

While BR was planning for the new fleet it was arranged for three Class 86s to be fitted with new bogies and transformers to give them a higher rate of performance of 5000hp and an increased maximum speed of 110mph. The three locomotives, 86101-86103, became the testbeds for what would become the Class 87.

The new fleet was built by BREL at Crewe Works between 1973 and 1975. Visually the locomotives were similar to the Class 86s, although they featured two large cab windscreens, rather than the three windows on the '86s'. The Class 87s also didn't feature headcode boxes, which were included on the Class 86, as headcodes were no longer required to be displayed on locomotives by the time the Class 87s were introduced. When complete, they were finished in BR blue livery, with full yellow ends and TOPS five-figure 87XXX numbers.

The order was for 36 locomotives, although the final member of the fleet was fitted with experimental thyristor power control equipment instead of the tap-changer transformers and rectifiers fitted to the other 35 locomotives. This meant that this locomotive was classified as Class 87/1, numbered 87101, with the remainder classified as Class 87/0, numbered 87001-87035.

All of the Class 87s went on to be named, with 87001 the first to be named when it became *Stephenson* in January 1976. This name was eventually transferred to 87101 and a BR policy saw the '87/0s' named after cities along the WCML as well as various Anglo-Scottish themes. Some of these names were changed during the lives of the locomotives.

Following privatisation of BR, the Class 87/0 fleet transferred to the Virgin West Coast and were quickly repainted into the operator's distinctive red and grey livery. However, the days of the Class 87s on Virgin duties were numbered as the operator had committed to supplying a brand new fleet of 'Pendolino' high-speed electric trains for use on the WCML.

Although not preserved, 87006 is one of the former West Coast Main Line Class 87s that has found a new home in Bulgaria working for the Bulgarian Railway Company. The locomotive still carries a variation of the GB Railfreight livery it carried for a brief while in the UK when being trialled by the freight operator. The locomotive rests outside Sofia Depot in Bulgaria on May 24, 2009, clearly showing the modifications carried out to the locomotives for their new use. KEVIN DELANEY

87101 was subsequently inherited by Railfreight Distribution but was stored in 2001 and scrapped the following year.

The first Class 87/0 to be withdrawn was 87005 *City of London* in September 2003. The rundown of the '87s' was marked by Virgin West Coast with the repainting of 87001 into original BR blue and renaming as *Stephenson*, while 87002 was repainted into the distinctive purple and silver colours of Porterbrook Leasing and named *AC Locomotive Group* in tribute to the widely respected preservation society which had preserved examples of the early WCML electric locomotive fleet.

In 2004 two further 'celebrity' repaints took place with 87012 being painted into a variation of Network SouthEast livery and named *The Olympian* to promote the awarding of the 2012 Olympic Games to London, while 87019 was painted into LNWR lined black livery and named *Association of Community Rail Partnerships*. The last timetabled Virgin Class 87-hauled service took place in June 2005, but the following year a Pendolino modification programme saw Class 87s reinstated on to a peak-hour WCML passenger working which carried on until the end of 2006.

Following their withdrawal from Virgin West Coast, most of the Class 87/0 fleet were put into store, but Direct Rail Services, Cotswold Rail and GB Railfreight all trialled the locomotives on freight and other non-passenger workings. GB Railfreight was the last UK operator to use Class 87s in regular service, with 87022 *Cock o' The North* and 87028 *Lord President* used on parcels services until the end of 2007.

87002 *Royal Sovereign* stands at Glasgow Central while working a Spitfire Railtours 'Electric Scot' tour from Birmingham New Street to Glasgow Central on July 11, 2009. KEVIN DELANEY

During the past few years 87002 *Royal Sovereign* has earned its corn hauling Caledonian Sleeper stock while on hire to traction provider GB Railfreight. The locomotive was painted into Caledonian Sleeper's teal livery, but the arrival of a new fleet of coaching stock for the sleeper trains means that the hire deal to use 87002 is due to end shortly and the future of the locomotive is currently unconfirmed. 87002 heads through Warrington Bank Quay on October 24, 2015. TERRY EYRES

THE PRESERVED CLASS 87s

There are three Class 87s in preservation, with pioneer locomotive 87001 *Stephenson* claimed by the National Railway Museum where it is on display at York. With the recent review of the modern traction exhibits at the NRM, the likelihood of 87001 ever running again under its own power is highly unlikely.

87002 *Royal Sovereign* was bought by Electric Traction Ltd, the operational arm of the AC Locomotive Group, and it was revived at Long Marston

primarily for main line use.

After recertification works and a repaint into BR blue, 87002 returned to main line action when it hauled its first trains over Network Rail metals in July 2008.

CLASS 87

BUILT:	BREL Crewe, 1973-1975
NO. BUILT:	36
NO. PRESERVED:	3
OTHER SURVIVORS:	21

The final Class 87 to be preserved is 87035 *Robert Burns*, which was acquired by the Crewe Heritage Centre Trust and is now on display at Crewe Heritage Centre.

A group of volunteers has been working hard on its restoration and conservation and while there are no plans for the locomotive to be returned to main line action, it is being maintained to a high standard within sight of the West Coast Main Line, where it spent so long in active service.

MAIN LINE PRESERVED CLASS 87s

Flying the flag for the Class 87 design on the main line has been 87002 *Royal Sovereign*, which returned to main line use in 2008. Originally, 87002 had been one of the locomotives earmarked for export to Bulgaria, but thanks to Porterbrook Leasing and with the blessing of the Bulgarian Railway Company, it was agreed that 87002 could remain in the UK and be removed from the export programme.

It has worked a number of railtours during its time in preservation and has spent the past few years on hire to GB Railfreight for use on Caledonian Sleeper stock movements.

However, the introduction of new Mk 5 sleeper rolling stock during 2019 means that the hire of 87002, along with 86101 *Sir William A Stanier FRS* and 86401 *Mons Meg*, is due to end shortly and ETL has indicated that it is possible the locomotives will be offered for sale to another operator or for possible export.

LOCO	NAME	BR IDENTITIES	OWNER	LOCATION
87001	*Stephenson*	87001	NRM	RMY
87002	*Royal Sovereign*	87002	ACLG	On Hire
87035	*Robert Burns*	87035	CHCT	CHC

OWNER KEY: ACLG – AC Locomotive Group, CHCT – Crewe Heritage Centre Trust, NRM – National Railway Museum

LOCATION KEY: CHC – Crewe Heritage Centre, RMY – Railway Museum York

OTHER CLASS 87s

Following their withdrawal by Virgin West Coast, the Class 87s were moved to Long Marston by their leasing company Porterbrook and were subsequently purchased by Electric Traction Services (now Europhoenix). Following enquiries from the Bulgarian Railway Company two locomotives, 87012 and 87019, were exported for trials of the design in Bulgaria.

ETS and Romic UK prepared the locomotives for export and they were exported to Bulgaria for use on freight services between Sofia and Varna. These trials proved to be successful and over a three-year period the majority of the remaining stored Class 87s were prepared at Long Marston for a second career working overseas in Bulgaria.

Various modifications were carried out to the locomotives in preparation for their new roles, but they are still identifiable as the former West Coast stalwarts. The most visible signs of change are the roof-mounted horns and high-intensity headlights, external cab wing mirrors and imposing obstacle deflectors beneath the cab fronts. The success of the project with the Bulgarian Railway Company saw another Bulgarian operator, Bulmarket, also acquire some of the redundant 87s and these too were reactivated.

Despite being unlikely to operate under its own power again, volunteers at Crewe Heritage Centre are busily restoring 87035 *Robert Burns* to a very high standard. The locomotive was repainted into BR blue livery during 2018 and is pictured during a special event at its home base on August 4, 2018. KEVIN DELANEY

NON-PRESERVED SURVIVING CLASS 87s

BULGARIAN RAILWAY COMPANY: 87003, 87004, 87006, 87007, 87008, 87010, 87012, 87013, 87014, 87019, 87020, 87022, 87026, 87028, 87029, 87033, 87034

BULMARKET: 87009 87017, 87023, 87025

Under a dark and threatening sky, 89001 stands at Barrow Hill on September 18, 2011. The unique locomotive has been based at the Derbyshire railway centre since 2004 and volunteers from the AC Locomotive Group are now actively working on its restoration to working order, with a main line return expected over the coming months. TOM MCATEE

On June 1, 2019, 89001 sits in the yard at Barrow Hill following bodywork repairs and a coat of yellow undercoat, pending final repainting. The locomotive had been extensively overhauled in preparation for a return to main line use over the next few months. ANDY COWARD

CLASS 89

Not only is 89001 a unique survivor in preservation, it has also had an interesting history since emerging from Brush Traction in 1986 and as Electric Traction Ltd, the commercial arm of the AC Locomotive Group (ACLG), works to reactivate the 'Badger' (nicknamed, due to its distinctive sloping cab fronts) for main line use once again, it is clear that the story of this East Coast Main Line (ECML) pioneer is far from over.

89001 was built by Brush as the company sought to produce a locomotive that could be used to revolutionise travel on BR's ECML, which was electrified during the mid-1980s. It was built to a Co-Co wheel arrangement and powered by six Brush TM2201A traction motors.

However, BR's decision to use fixed-formation trains and Class 91 locomotives, which would be built by BREL at Crewe Works and could operate at a higher maximum speed of 140mph, meant that follow-on orders from BR to Brush for more Class 89 locomotives were not forthcoming and 89001 would remain a one-off.

However, it would still be used by BR on ECML services. It was fitted with Time Division Multiplex equipment in 1988, allowing it to be used in push-pull mode, with a Driving Van Trailer (DVT) at the other end of the train. It then became a regular performer on the ECML between London Kings Cross and Leeds.

When delivered, 89001 was painted in InterCity colours. It was subsequently repainted into InterCity Executive livery. In 1989 it was named *Avocet* by then-Prime Minister Margaret Thatcher and followed the Brush tradition of naming prototype locomotives after birds.

In 1990, 89001 was taken out of service by BR following problems with reliability of the unique locomotive and availability of spare parts.

After a period in store it was purchased for preservation and moved to the Midland Railway Butterley. It was displayed at Swanwick Junction on the MRB, but licensing restrictions on the use of the InterCity brand meant that the InterCity branding on the locomotive had to be painted over.

However, its retirement in Derbyshire was destined to be short-lived and following privatisation of BR, 89001 was purchased by ECML franchisee GNER for another spell of passenger operation on the prestige route. The locomotive was moved back to Brush at Loughborough for an overhaul and repairs, returning to use in 1997.

Despite being given a second lease of life, 89001 proved problematical again and spent several lengthy periods of time out of use between 1997 and 2000. After a rather brief reprieve, 89001 was stored by GNER in 2000 and spent time at Bounds Green as a carriage heater, before moving to Doncaster Works for storage.

Many of the problems associated with the Class 89 would probably have been solved had the locomotive become the standard locomotive design for use on the ECML and a full fleet of '89s' had been built, but its unique nature meant that repairs would often be expensive and time consuming.

In 2004, the locomotive was placed on long-term loan to the ACLG and moved to Barrow Hill for static display.

LOCO	PREVIOUS IDENTITIES	OWNER	LOCATION
89001	89001	ACLG	BHR

OWNER KEY: ACLG – AC Locomotive Group

LOCATION KEY: BHR – Barrow Hill

THE PRESERVED CLASS 89

As a one-off prototype locomotive, 89001 is also unique in that it has now been preserved twice and its current owners, the AC Locomotive Group, are now nearing the end of a comprehensive overhaul of the locomotive, which should hopefully see it return to main line service in the near future under the auspices of the ACLG's Electric Traction Ltd subsidiary company.

In 2006 GNER announced that 89001 was to be sold to the highest bidder and the ACLG launched a high-profile appeal to secure the locomotive for preservation, leading to its purchase in

November 2006. It was quickly repainted out of its GNER dark blue and orange livery into InterCity Executive colours, emerging in June 2007.

The owning group has made no secret of its desire to return 89001 to main line use at some stage in the future and a project is now under way at Barrow Hill

CLASS 89

BUILT: Brush Traction, Loughborough, 1986	
NO. BUILT: 1	
NO. PRESERVED: 1	
OTHER SURVIVORS: 0	

to bring the 'Badger' back to life.

The locomotive's bogies have been overhauled and damaged traction motors have been overhauled and repaired. A whole host of electronic and electrical components have been repaired and tested and bodywork repairs have been carried out.

It is currently being prepared for testing and in early 2019 the locomotive was given a coat of yellow undercoat, prior to final repainting into an as-yet-unspecified livery. The owners hope to return 89001 to main line use over the coming months.

18000 was a gas-turbine electric locomotive built for British Railways in 1949 after being developed by the Great Western Railway and it was used for hauling express passenger trains out of Paddington station. 18000 could operate at speeds of up to 90mph and also had a diesel engine which could move the locomotive at slow speed. Reliability issues saw the locomotive withdrawn by BR in 1960 and it was moved abroad for further use, where it was heavily modified internally and it then spent many years on display in Vienna. The locomotive was subsequently returned to the UK in the early 1990s and was initially displayed at Crewe Heritage Centre, before moving to Barrow Hill Roundhouse and then Didcot Railway Centre. The chances of this locomotive ever being restored to operational condition appear to be remote. On June 9, 2019, 18000 stands on display in the yard at Didcot Railway Centre. STEVE KEMP

Unclassified Prototype Locomotives

As well as the main locomotive types that have seen salvation in preservation, there are also two locomotives which hold a special place in preservation, as they are prototype locomotives which have survived. Many of the prototype locomotives that were devised during the advent of diesel locomotive design were either exported, scrapped or destroyed in accidents.

The English Electric DP1 locomotive, more commonly known as *DELTIC*, was built as a demonstrator by English Electric in 1955 and was used to demonstrate the Napier Deltic engines that would eventually be used in the order for 22 production 'Deltic' locomotives for the East Coast Main Line. It was withdrawn from service in 1961 after suffering a serious failure and was subsequently preserved as part of the National Collection in 1963 and it is now preserved at Locomotion, the National Railway Museum at Shildon. It is clear where the production 'Deltics' got their distinctive looks, with the attractive light blue livery and cream embellishments of *DELTIC*. It is pictured while it was on loan to the Ribble Steam Railway at Preston Docks on October 5, 2013. STEVE KEMP

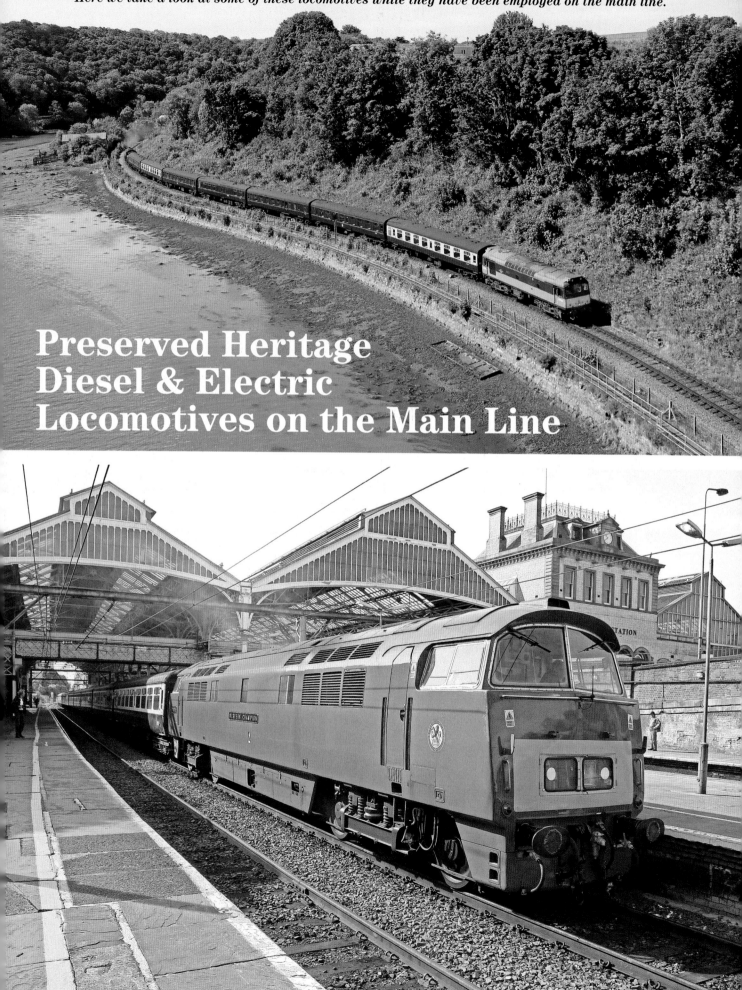

The return to the main line of Pete Waterman's Class 46 'Peak' D172 Ixion in 1994 heralded the relaxation of the ban on privately owned diesel locomotives on the main line. Since that historic day, there have been many preserved diesel and electric locomotives that have been returned to main line operating condition. Here we take a look at some of these locomotives while they have been employed on the main line.

Preserved Heritage Diesel & Electric Locomotives on the Main Line

The second 'Peak' to operate on the main line in preservation was from the Class 45 type, with 45112 *Royal Army Ordnance Corps* operating on the main line between 2001 and 2008. On a dull January 21, 2007, 45112 hauls 'The Tubular Belle' railtour through Penmaenmawr. The locomotive is now stored at Nemesis Rail at Burton upon Trent. TOM MCATEE

There are now two Class 40s registered for the main line. On November 30, 2002, D345, belonging to the Class 40 Preservation Society, stands at Crewe while working its inaugural railtour 'The Christmas Cracker IV' railtour. In 2018, D213 *Andania* became the second Class 40 to return to the main line. KEVIN DELANEY

TOP LEFT: D7628 *Sybilla* is the only Class 25 currently registered for operating on Network Rail metals and it is registered by the North Yorkshire Moors Railway for use on its services between Grosmont and Whitby. On July 2, 2018, D7628 skirts the River Esk while working a service to Whitby. TOM MCATEE

LEFT: D1015 *Western Champion* is the only Class 52 'Western' to be registered for the main line. Owned by the Diesel Traction Group, the locomotive returned to main line use in 2002 and on September 3, 2005, D1015 stands at Preston while working the 'Western Heights' railtour from Bristol Temple Meads to Carlisle. NIGEL VALENTINE

20205 is one of two locomotives belonging to the Class 20 Locomotive Society which have been returned to main line use and hired to 20189 Ltd. On February 7, 2015, 20205 leads 20189 into Peak Forest while hauling a rake of freight wagons. KEVIN DELANEY

Owned by the Scottish Railway Preservation Society, 37403 *Isle of Mull* returned to the main line in 2016 and has spent much of its time since then on hire to Direct Rail Services, where it is used alongside its own fleet of Class 37/4 locomotives. On June 7, 2018, 37403 departs from Ravenglass while working a Barrow to Carlisle service. TERRY EYRES

LEFT: The Stratford 47 Group's 47580 *County of Essex* has seen extensive use on the main line, while hired to West Coast Railway Company for use on its charter services, based from Carlisle. On June 8, 2013, 47580 passes Daresbury while working a Carnforth to Bristol empty coaching stock train. TERRY EYRES

Between 1999 and 2000, preserved 50017 was returned to the main line and hired to haul the prestigious Northern Belle luxury dining tour services. The locomotive was painted into a distinctive maroon and gold livery and on August 19, 2000, 50017 stands at Bath Spa station after arriving with a Northern Belle service from Manchester Victoria. TERRY EYRES

Preserved in electric blue livery, 86259/E3137 *Les Ross/Peter Pan* certainly adds a bright splash of colour whenever it works. Returned to the main line in 2008 under the auspices of Tyseley Locomotive Works, 86259 hauls a Vintage Trains tour through Moore on the West Coast Main Line on May 30, 2009. TERRY EYRES

Pioneer 'Deltic' 55022 *Royal Scots Grey* had two periods of main line operation under two different owners. While its first period on the main line was as D9000, the second was as BR blue-liveried 55022 from 2006. On May 9, 2015, 55022 hauls the luxurious Royal Scotsman train through Kinloid, disguised as long-scrapped 55003 *Meld*. 55022 is now owned by Locomotive Services Ltd and is expected to return to the main line at some stage in the future, although it is no longer classed as a preserved locomotive. TERRY EYRES

MAIN LINE REGISTERED PRESERVED
DIESEL AND ELECTRIC LOCOMOTIVES

CLASS	IDENTITY	NAME	PERIOD ACTIVE
20	20205		2015-Present
20	20227		2007-Present
25	D7628	Sybilla	2007-Present
31	31106	Spalding Town	2001-2016
33	D6515	Lt Jenny Lewis RN	2011-Present
33	33021	Eastleigh	1999-2003
33	33103	Swordfish	1998-2007
33	33208		1998-2001
37	37025	Inverness TMD	2013-Present
37	37403	Isle of Mull	2016-Present
37	37418		2019-Present
40	D213	Andania	2018-Present
40	D345/40145		2002-Present
45	45112	Royal Army Ordnance Corps	2001-2008
46	D172/46035	Ixion	1994-2003
47	47580	County of Essex	2008-Present
47	47773		2007-Present
47	47828		2019-Present
50	50007	Hercules	2017-Present
50	50017	Royal Oak	1999-2000
50	50031	Hood	1997-2009
50	50044	Exeter	1999-2016
50	50049	Defiance	2000-Present
50	50050	Fearless	1998-1999
52	D1015	Western Champion	2002-Present
55	D9000	Royal Scots Grey	1996-2002
55	55022	Royal Scots Grey	2006-2017
55	D9002/55002	Kings Own Yorkshire Light Infantry	2014-2017
55	D9009/55009	Alycidon	1999-Present
55	D9016	Gordon Highlander	2002-2004
55	55019	Royal Highland Fusilier	1999-2003
56	56301		2012-Present
71	E5001		1992-1996
86	86101	Sir William Stanier FRS	2006-Present
86	86259	Les Ross/Peter Pan	2008-Present
86	86401	Mons Meg	2015-Present
87	87002	Royal Sovereign	2006-Present

Notes

1. 50007 *Hercules* was registered for main line running while owned by Boden Rail Engineering Ltd. The operating period on this table applies to its period under the ownership by the Class 50 Alliance.

2. 50017 *Royal Oak* was registered for main line running during its time as a preserved locomotive between 1999 and 2000. It has subsequently spent time operating on the main line as an asset of Boden Rail Engineering Ltd, but this period is not included in this table as the locomotive could not have been classed as being preserved at the time.

3. 50050 *Fearless* was registered for main line running while a preserved locomotive between 1998 and 1999. It has subsequently spent time operating on the main line as an asset of Boden Rail Engineering Ltd, but this period is not included in this table as the locomotive could not have been classed as being preserved at the time.

4. D9000 *Royal Scots Grey* operated on the main line between 1996 and 2002 when it was owned by Deltic 9000 Locomotives Ltd.

5. 55022 *Royal Scots Grey* operated on the main line between 2006 and 2017 while owned by Martin Walker/Beaver Sports Ltd.

Owned and operated by the Class 50 Alliance, 50007 *Hercules* and 50049 *Defiance* are the current preserved Class 50s operating on the main line, although 50008 and 50050 are also operated over the main line by the commercial owners. On April 14, 2018, 50007 leads 50049 through Black Dyke while working the Birmingham International to Carlisle 'Cumbrian Hoovers' railtour. TERRY EYRES

The most recent preserved diesel locomotive to return to main line action has been D05 Preservation Ltd's 47828, which returned to main line use on hire to the West Coast Railway Company in July 2019. On September 2, 2017, the InterCity-liveried Class 47 stands on display at Old Oak Common open day.
KEVIN DELANEY

87002 *Royal Sovereign* is owned by Electric Traction Ltd, the commercial operating company of the AC Locomotive Group. Since 2015 it has been used for stock movements in connection with the Caledonian Sleeper contract, with the locomotive hired to GB Railfreight along with 86101 *Sir William A Stanier FRS* and 86401 *Mons Meg*. On April 15, 2015, 87002 stands at Carlisle awaiting its next duties resplendent in Caledonian Sleeper teal livery. STEVE KEMP

37025 *Inverness TMD* is another Class 37 that has been returned to the main line under the auspices of the diesel groups at the Bo'ness & Kinneil Railway. The locomotive is now on long-term hire to Colas Rail, but has also seen use on a few passenger charter trains. On July 1, 2017, 37025 hauls a Scottish Railway Preservation Society railtour through Leyland station, with Colas Rail 37219 on the other end of the train. 37219 was formerly preserved on the Pontypool & Blaenavon Railway. TERRY EYRES

On September 15, 2007, Large Logo-liveried 40145 *East Lancashire Railway* hauls 'The Buxton Forester' tour through Combs on the Hope Valley Line. The Class 40s never carried Large Logo colours during their BR operating days, but the colour scheme was carried by a large number of Class 37s and the owning Class 40 Preservation Society decided to repaint and name their main line locomotive to celebrate the 20th anniversary of the East Lancashire Railway opening its heritage line between Bury and Ramsbottom in 1987. TERRY EYRES

Sulzer Type-Two Class 24 locomotive 5081. MARTIN HART

English Electric Type-Three Class 37 locomotive D6948. KEVIN DELANEY

Heritage Diesel & Electric Locomotives - The Directory

CLASS 14

IDENTITY	NAME	PREVIOUS IDENTITIES	OWNER	LOCATION
D9500		D9500	ABL	PKD
D9502	Kerys	D9502	Private	ELR
D9504		D9504	Private	KESR
NCB 38		D9513	Private	EBAR
D9516		D9516	Private	DRC
D9518		D9518	DEPG	WSR
D9520/45		D9520	Private	NVR
9521		D9521	D9521LG	DFR
D9523		D9523	Private	WR
14901		D9524	ABL	PKD
D9525	Ian's	D9525	HST	PKR
D9526		D9526	DEPG	WSR
9529		D9529	Private	NVR
D9531	Ernest	D9531	BHG	ELR
D9537	Eric	D9537	Private	EVR
D9539		D9539	Private	RSR
D9551	Angus	D9551	SVRC14CL	SVR
D9553/54		D9553	Private	Private
D9555		D9555	Private	DFR

CLASS 15

IDENTITY	NAME	PREVIOUS IDENTITIES	OWNER	LOCATION
D8233		D8233, ADB968001	C15PS	ELR

CLASS 17

IDENTITY	NAME	PREVIOUS IDENTITIES	OWNER	LOCATION
D8568		D8568	DTG	CPRR

CLASS 20

IDENTITY	NAME	PREVIOUS IDENTITIES	OWNER	LOCATION
D8000		D8000, 20050	NRM	RMY
8001		D8001, 20001	C20LC	EOR
20020		D8020, 20020	SRPSDG	BKR
20031		D8031, 20031	Private	KWVR
20048		D8048, 20048	MC20A	MRB
D8057		D8057, 20057	Private	CVR
D8059		D8059, 20059, 20302	S&DLC	MRB
2002		D8063, 20063, CFD2002	Private	BFL
D8098		D8098, 20098	T1LC	GCR
D8137		D8137, 20137	Private	GWR
D8154		D8154, 20154	Private	GCRN
D8169		D8169, 20169	Private	WR
D8188		D8188, 20188	S&DLC	MRB
20205		D8305, 20205	C20LC	On Hire

CLASS 20

IDENTITY	NAME	PREVIOUS IDENTITIES	OWNER	LOCATION
20214		D8314, 20214	LHR	LHR
20227	Sherlock Holmes	D8327, 20227	C20LC	On Hire
20228		D8128, 20228, CFD2004	Private	BTR

CLASS 23

IDENTITY	NAME	PREVIOUS IDENTITIES	OWNER	LOCATION
D5910		Built from body donor 37372 BDG		BHR

CLASS 24

IDENTITY	NAME	PREVIOUS IDENTITIES	OWNER	LOCATION
D5032	Helen Turner	D5032, 24032	NYMR	NYMR
D5054	Phil Southern	D5054, 24054, ADB968008	BT2G	ELR
D5061		D5061, 24061, RDB968007, 97201	24061PG	NYMR
5081		D5081, 24081	Private	GWR

CLASS 25

IDENTITY	NAME	PREVIOUS IDENTITIES	OWNER	LOCATION
D5185		D5185, 25035	NT2G	GCR
25057		D5207, 25057	Private	NNR
25059		D5209, 25059	Private	KWVR
D5217		D5217, 25067	Private	Nemesis
25072		D5222, 25072	CRDG	CR
25083		D5233, 25083	CRDG	CR
D7523		D7523, 25173	Private	BFL
D7535		D7535, 25185	SDDT	SDR
D7541		D7541, 25191	SDDT	SDR
25235		D7585, 25235	SRPSDG	BKR
25244		D7594, 25244	Private	KESR
D7612		D7612, 25262, 25901	SDDT	SDR
25265		D7615, 25265	RTG	Nemesis
D7628	Sybilla	D7628, 25278	Private	NYMR
D7629		D7629, 25279	Private	ELR
D7633		D7633, 25283, 25904	Private	Private
D7659		D7659, 25309, 25909	Private	PKR
25313		D7663, 25313	Private	WR
D7671		D7671, 25321	DIM	MRB
25322	Tamworth Castle	D7672, 25322, 25912	NSDG	CVR

CLASS 26

IDENTITY	NAME	PREVIOUS IDENTITIES	OWNER	LOCATION
D5301		D5301, 26001	Private	CR
D5302		D5302, 26002	STR	STR
26007		D5300, 26007	Private	BHR

CLASS 26

IDENTITY	NAME	PREVIOUS IDENTITIES	OWNER	LOCATION
D5310		D5310, 26010	LDG	LR
26011		D5311, 26011	RTG	Nemesis
D5314		D5314, 26014	CRDG	CR
26024		D5324, 26024	6LDAL	BKR
D5325		D5325, 26025	STR	STR
26035		D5335, 26035	CRDG	CR
26038	Tom Clift 1954-2012	D5338, 26038	6LDAL	NYMR
26040		D5340, 26040	Private	WHC
5343		D5343, 26043	CMDG	GWR

CLASS 27

IDENTITY	NAME	PREVIOUS IDENTITIES	OWNER	LOCATION
27001		D5347, 27001	C27LG	BKR
27005		D5351, 27005	SRPSDG	BKR
D5353		D5353, 27007	Private	Private
D5370		D5370, 27024	CRDG	CR
D5394		D5394, 27050, 27106	STR	STR
D5401		D5401, 27056, 27112	NT2G	GCR
27059		D5410, 27059, 27123, 27205	SWC	Leicester
27066		D5386, 27066, 27103, 27212	Private	BHR

CLASS 28

IDENTITY	NAME	PREVIOUS IDENTITIES	OWNER	LOCATION
D5705		D5705, S15705, TDB968006	C-BLG	ELR

CLASS 31

IDENTITY	NAME	PREVIOUS IDENTITIES	OWNER	LOCATION
31018		D5500, 31018	NRM	RMY
31101		D5518, 31101	SP	AVR
31105		D5523, 31105	MRM	MRM
31106	Spalding Town	D5524, 31106	Private	WDR
31108		D5526, 31108	A1A	MRB
31119		D5537, 31119	Private	EBAR
31130		D5548, 31130	SP	AVR
31162		D5580, 31162	A1A	MRB
97205		D5581, 31163	Private	CPRR
D5627	Steve Organ G.M.	D5627, 31203	Private	PBR
31206		D5630, 31206	Private	EVR
D5631		D5631, 31207	Private	NNR
31210		D5634, 31210	Private	DFR
31233		D5660, 31233	MRM	MRM
31270	Athena	D5800, 31270	Private	Nemesis
31271	Stratford 1840-2001	D5801, 31271	A1A	MRB
31289	Phoenix	D5821, 31289	Private	NLR
31327		D5862, 31327	Private	STR
31414		D5814, 31414, 31514	A1A	MRB
31418		D5522, 31418	A1A	MRB
31430	Sister Dora	D5695, 31265, 31430, 31530	Private	SPVR
D5600		D5600, 31179, 31435	Private	EBAR
31438		D5557, 31139, 31438, 31538	Private	EOR
D5830		D5830, 31297, 31463, 31563	T1LC	GCR

CLASS 31

IDENTITY	NAME	PREVIOUS IDENTITIES	OWNER	LOCATION
31466		D5533, 31115, 31466	Private	DFR
31601	Devon Diesel Society	D5609, 31186	Private	EVR

CLASS 33

IDENTITY	NAME	PREVIOUS IDENTITIES	OWNER	LOCATION
D6501	Sea King	D6501, 33002	SDDT	SDR
D6508	Eastleigh	D6508, 33008	Private	BFL
D6515	Lt Jenny Lewis RN	D6515, 33012	71ALG	SR
33018		D6530, 33018	Private	Private
33021	Eastleigh	D6539, 33021	Private	CVR
33035		D6553, 33035	PDG	WR
33046		D6564, 33046	Private	ELR
D6566		D6566, 33048	DEPG	WSR
D6570	Ashford	D6570, 33052	Private	KESR
33053		D6571, 33053	Private	Leicester
D6575		D6575, 33057	DEPG	WSR
33063	R J Mitchell	D6583, 33063	SELG	SPVR
33065		D6585, 33065	SELG	SPVR
33102	Sophie	D6513, 33102	NSDG	CVR
33103	Swordfish	D6514, 33103	Private	EVR
33108		D6521, 33108	C33/1PC	SVR
33109	Captain Bill Smith RNR	D6525, 33109	Private	ELR
33110		D6527, 33110	Private	BWR
33111		D6528, 33111	C33/1PC	SR
D6535		D6535, 33116	NRM	GCR
D6536		D6536, 33117	Private	ELR
33201		D6586, 33201	BRCWG	SPVR
33202	Dennis G Robinson	D6587, 33202	Private	MNR
D6593		D6593, 33208	Private	BFL

CLASS 35

IDENTITY	NAME	PREVIOUS IDENTITIES	OWNER	LOCATION
D7017		D7017	DEPG	WSR
D7018		D7018	DEPG	WSR
D7029		D7029	DTG	SVR
D7076		D7076	BHG	ELR

CLASS 37

IDENTITY	NAME	PREVIOUS IDENTITIES	OWNER	LOCATION
D6700		D6700, 37119, 37350	NRM	RMY
37003		D6703, 37003	C37LG	Leicester
37009		D6709, 37009, 37340	Private	GCRN
37023		D6723, 37023	Private	Studley
37025	Inverness TMD	D6725, 37025	S37G	On Hire
D6729		D6729, 37029	Private	EOR
D6732		D6732, 37032, 37353	Private	NNR
D6737		D6737, 37037, 37321	DDS	SDR
37042		D6742, 37042	Private	EDVR
37075		D6775, 37075	Private	KWVR
37097		D6797, 37097	CRDG	CR

Western Region diesel-hydraulic Class 42 locomotive D832 *Onslaught*. MARTIN HART

Sulzer Class 46 'Peak' locomotive D182. STEVE KEMP

CLASS 37

IDENTITY	NAME	PREVIOUS IDENTITIES	OWNER	LOCATION
37108		D6808, 37108, 37325	Private	CHC
37109		D6809, 37109	Private	ELR
37142		D6842, 37142	BWMLDG	BWR
37310	British Steel Ravenscraig	D6852, 37152, 37310	Private	PKR
37214		D6914, 37214	S37G	BKR
37215		D6915, 37215	GG	GWR
D6916		D6916, 37216	Private	PBR
37227		D6927, 37227	Private	CPRR
D6948		D6948, 37248	GG	GWR
37250		D6950, 37250	Private	WR
37261		D6961, 37261	S37G	BKR
37263		D6963, 37263	Private	TSR
37264		D6964, 37264	Private	NYMR
37275		D6975, 37275	PDSR	PDSR
37294		D6994, 37294	Private	EBAR
37308		D6608, 37308, 37274	Private	DFR
37403	Isle of Mull	D6607, 37307, 37403	SRPSDG	On Hire
37418		D6971, 37271, 37418	Private	On Hire
37674		D6869, 37169, 37674	Private	WR
37688	Great Rocks	D6905, 37205, 37688	D05PL	SVR
37714	Cardiff Canton	D6724, 37024, 37714	HTG	GCR

CLASS 40

IDENTITY	NAME	PREVIOUS IDENTITIES	OWNER	LOCATION
D200		D200, 40122	NRM	RMY
D212	Aureol	D212, 40012, 97407	C40A	MRB
D213	Andania	D212, 40013	Private	BHR
40106	Atlantic Conveyor	D306, 40106	CFPS	SVR
40118		D318, 40118, 97408	16SVTS	TLW
40135		D335, 40135, 97406	CFPS	ELR
40145		D345, 40145	CFPS	BHR

CLASS 41

IDENTITY	NAME	PREVIOUS IDENTITIES	OWNER	LOCATION
41001		41001	NRM	GCRN

CLASS 42

IDENTITY	NAME	PREVIOUS IDENTITIES	OWNER	LOCATION
D821	Greyhound	D821	DTG	SVR
D832	Onslaught	D832	BHG	ELR

CLASS 43

IDENTITY	NAME	PREVIOUS IDENTITIES	OWNER	LOCATION
43002	Sir Kenneth Grange	43002	NRM	RMY

CLASS 44

IDENTITY	NAME	PREVIOUS IDENTITIES	OWNER	LOCATION
D4	Great Gable	D4, 44004	PLC	MRB
D8	Penyghent	D8, 44008	NNLG	PKR

CLASS 45

IDENTITY	NAME	PREVIOUS IDENTITIES	OWNER	LOCATION
45015		D14, 45015	BFL	BFL
45041	Royal Tank Regiment	D53, 45041	PLC	NVR
45060	Sherwood Forester	D100, 45060	PDG	BHR
45105		D86, 45105	PDG	BHR
45108		D120, 45108	PLC	ELR
45112	Royal Army Ordnance Corps	D61, 45112	Private	Nemesis
D123	Leicestershire & Derbyshire Yeomanry	D123, 45125	Private	GCR
45132		D22, 45132	Private	EOR
45133		D40, 45133	C45/1PS	MRB
45135	3rd Carabinier	D99, 45135	PDG	ELR
45149		D135, 45149	CMDG	GWR

CLASS 46

IDENTITY	NAME	PREVIOUS IDENTITIES	OWNER	LOCATION
46010		D147, 46010	D05PL	GCRN
46035	Ixion	D172, 46035, 97304	Private	PKR

CLASS 46

IDENTITY	NAME	PREVIOUS IDENTITIES	OWNER	LOCATION
D182		D182, 46045, 97404	PLC	MRB

CLASS 47

IDENTITY	NAME	PREVIOUS IDENTITIES	OWNER	LOCATION
D1524		D1524, 47004	Private	EBAR
47105		D1693, 47105	BT4F	GWR
1705	Sparrowhawk	D1705, 47117	T1LC	GCR
47192		D1842, 47192	CHCT	CHC
47205		D1855, 47205, 47395	Private	NLR
47292		D1994, 47292	Private	GCRN
47306	The Sapper	D1787, 47306	B&WMLDG	BWR
47367		D1886, 47367	S47G	MNR
47376	Freightliner 1995	D1895, 47376	BT4F	GWR
47401	North Eastern	D1500, 47401	47401P	MRB
D1501		D1501, 47402	Private	ELR
D1516		D1516, 47417	47401P	MRB
1566		D1566, 47449	LDG	LR
47484	Isambard Kingdom Brunel	D1662, 47484	PDG	Private
47524		D1107, 47524	Private	DFR
47579	James Nightall G.C.	D1778, 47183, 47579, 47793	MRM	MHR
47580	County of Essex	D1762, 47167, 47580, 47732	S47G	Carnforth
47596	Aldeburgh Festival	D1933, 47233, 47596	S47G	MNR
47635	Jimmy Milne	D1606, 47029, 47635	Private	EOR
47643		D1970, 47269, 47643	SRPSDG	BKR
47712	Lady Diana Spencer	D1948, 47505, 47712	CDPG	Crewe
47761		D1619, 47038, 47564, 47761	47401P	MRB
47765		D1643, 47059, 47631, 47765	Private	ELR
47771		D1946, 47503, 47771	C47PP	Eastleigh
D1755		D1755, 47541, 47773	Private	TLW
47785		D1909, 47232, 47820, 47785	Private	WR
47798	Prince William	D1656, 47072, 47609, 47834, 47798	NRM	RMY
47799	Prince Henry	D1654, 47070, 47620, 47835, 47799	Private	EDVR
47828		D1966, 47266, 47629, 47828	D05PL	Carnforth
D1661	North Star	D1661, 47077, 47613, 47840	DEPG	WSR

CLASS 50

IDENTITY	NAME	PREVIOUS IDENTITIES	OWNER	LOCATION
D402	Superb	D402, 50002	DDS	SDR
50007	Hercules	D407, 50007	C50A	SVR
50015	Valiant	D415, 50015	BVG	ELR
50017	Royal Oak	D417, 50017	Private	GCR
50019	Ramillies	D419, 50019	C50LA	MNR
50021	Rodney	D421, 50021	Private	Eastleigh
50026	Indomitable	D426, 50026	Private	Eastleigh
50027	Lion	D427, 50027	Private	MHR
50029	Renown	D429, 50029	RRRG	PKR
50030	Repulse	D430, 50030	RRRG	PKR
50031	Hood	D431, 50031	Private/C50A	SVR
50033	Glorious	D433, 50033	TLW/C50A	SVR
50035	Ark Royal	D435, 50035	C50A	SVR
50042	Triumph	D442, 50042	B&WMLDG	BWR
50044	Exeter	D444, 50044	C50A	SVR
50049	Defiance	D449, 50049, 50149	C50A	SVR

CLASS 52

IDENTITY	NAME	PREVIOUS IDENTITIES	OWNER	LOCATION
D1010	Western Campaigner	D1010	DEPG	WSR
D1013	Western Ranger	D1013	WLA	SVR
D1015	Western Champion	D1015	DTG	SVR
D1023	Western Fusilier	D1023	NRM	RMY
D1041	Western Prince	D1041	BHG	ELR
D1048	Western Lady	D1048	Private	MRB
D1062	Western Courier	D1062	WLA	SVR

CLASS 55

IDENTITY	NAME	PREVIOUS IDENTITIES	OWNER	LOCATION
D9009	Alycidon	D9009, 55009	DPS	BHR